THE PIKLERS:

A FAMILY ODYSSEY
ON THREE CONTINENTS

GEORGE M. PIKLER

Plamen
Press
Where Words Ignite

WASHINGTON DC

Plamen Press

9039 Sligo Creek Pkwy, Suite 1114, Silver Spring, Maryland 20901

Copyright © George M. Pikler, 2021

Published by Plamen Press, 2021

Printed in the United States of America

10 9 8 7 6 5 4 3 2 1

PUBLISHER'S CATALOGING-IN-PUBLICATION DATA

Names: Pikler, George M., author
Title: The Piklers: A Family Odyssey on Three Continents/

Description: Silver Spring, MD; Plamen Press, 2019

Identifiers: ISBN 978-0-9960722-7-4 (paperback)

Subjects: LCSH: Holocaust --
Central European-History-- Non Fiction
BISAC: NON FICTION

Cover Design by Roman Kostovski

Cover photo:
Above, from left to right: Edit, Klári, Hansi, Teri, Leika;
Below: Elsa and Móric Pikler

In honor of our parents, with endless love,
gratitude, and admiration

Contents

The David-Leopold-Móric Pikler Family Tree (six out of eight generations)

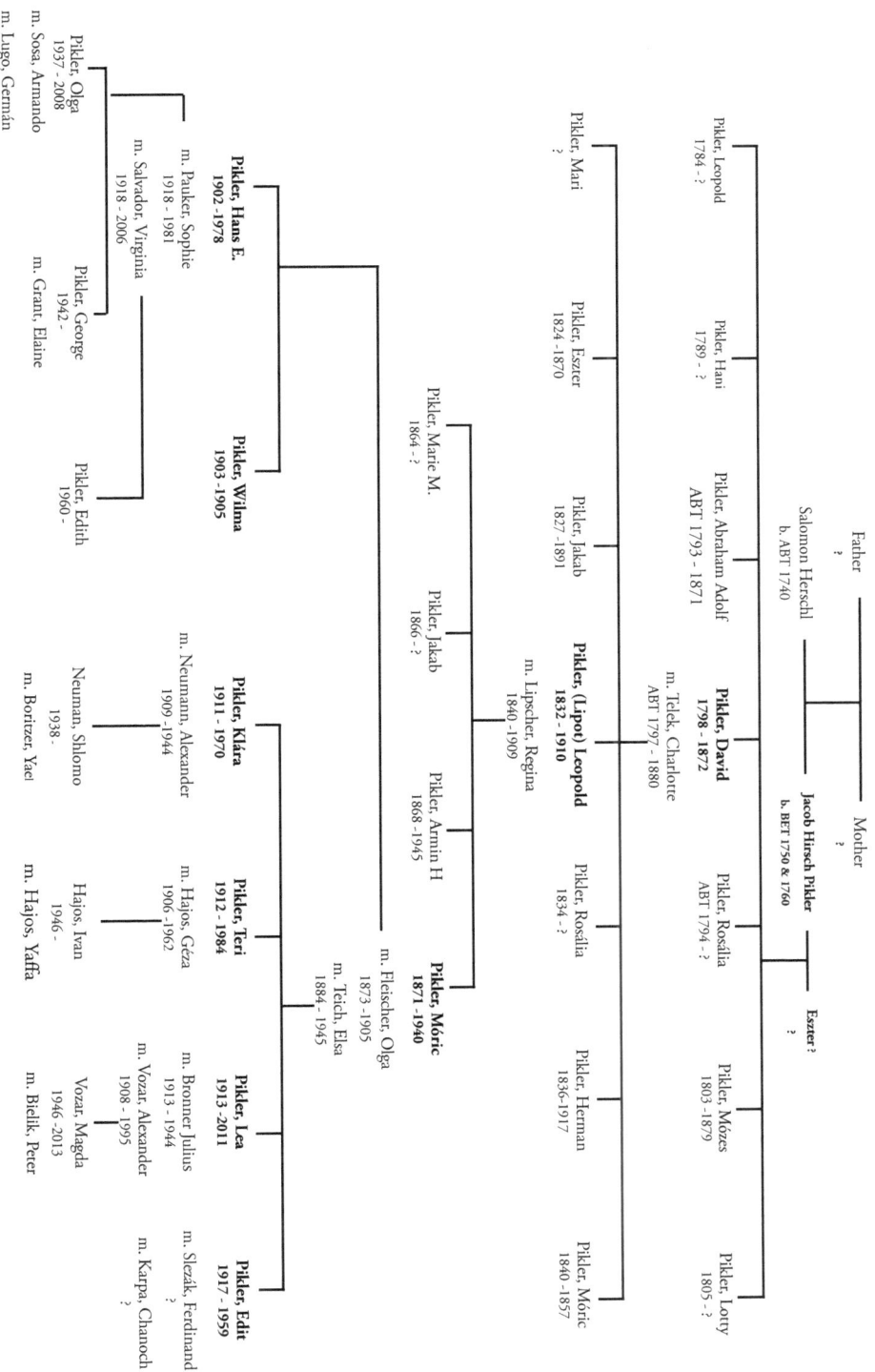

Father — Salomon Herschl b. ABT 1740

Mother — ?

Jacob Hirsch Pikler b. BET 1750 & 1760

Eszter ?

Pikler, Leopold 1784 - ?

Pikler, Hani 1789 - ?

Pikler, Mari ?

Pikler, Abraham Adolf ABT 1793 - 1871

Pikler, David 1798 - 1872
m. Telek, Charlotte ABT 1797 - 1880

Pikler, Rosália ABT 1794 - ?

Pikler, Mózes 1803 - 1879

Pikler, Lotty 1805 - ?

Pikler, Eszter 1824 - 1870

Pikler, Jakab 1827 -1891

Pikler, (Lipot) Leopold 1832 - 1910
m. Lipscher, Regina 1840-1909

Pikler, Rosália 1834 - ?

Pikler, Herman 1836-1917

Pikler, Móric 1840 - 1857

Pikler, Marie M. 1864 - ?

Pikler, Jakab 1866 - ?

Pikler, Armin H 1868-1945

Pikler, Móric 1871 -1940
m. Fleischer, Olga 1873 -1905
m. Teich, Elsa 1884 -1945

Pikler, Hans E. 1902 -1978
m. Pauker, Sophie 1918 - 1981
m. Salvador, Virginia 1918 - 2006

Pikler, Wilma 1903 -1905

Pikler, Klára 1911 - 1970
m. Neumann, Alexander 1909-1944

Pikler, Teri 1912 -1984
m. Hajos, Géza 1906-1962

Pikler, Lea 1913 -2011
m. Bronner Julius 1913 - 1944
m. Vozar, Alexander 1908 - 1995

Pikler, Edit 1917 - 1959
m. Slezak, Ferdinand ?
m. Karpa, Chanoch ?

Pikler, Olga 1937 - 2008
m. Sosa, Armando
m. Lugo, Germán

Pikler, George 1942 -
m. Grant, Elaine

Pikler, Edith 1960 -

Neumann, Shlomo 1938-

Hajos, Ivan 1946 -
m. Hajos, Yaffa

Vozar, Magda 1946-2013
m. Bielik, Peter
m. Boritzer, Yael

Key: ABT= about: b. = born; BET= between; m. = married; ? = unkown (last name/year)

Pikler family tree at https://piklerrribalpages.com Access Code: sokpikler

THE PIKLERS:

A FAMILY ODYSSEY
ON THREE CONTINENTS

Acknowledgements

I wish all the members of the fifth generation of the David Pikler family branch would be alive so that I could personally thank each of them for allowing me to narrate their story. It saddens me that I can only do so posthumously.

I have no words to express my overwhelming gratitude to my father, Hansi, and my aunt, Leika. This book became a reality due to their generosity in sharing their own memories and also those of their sisters, Klári, Teri, and Edit, along with letters, documents, and family photos.

I owe special thanks to my second cousins (of the Abraham branch), Katalin Pikler, for sharing her family research; Támas Pikler for his work on the family tree; and Charles Pikler for making available his father's letters and other documents.

While researching material for this narrative, I came across several historical articles and chapters about the Jews of Slovakia written by Ladislav Lipscher, who, according to Prof. Mestan, the Director of the Jewish Museum in Bratislava, Slovakia, was the most internationally recognized historian of the Slovak Holocaust. Due to this fact, the new Holocaust Museum in Sered, Slovakia (the location of one of the concentration camps during the Slovak state) decided to name its library, archives, and education center after him. He turned out to be a family relative: his paternal grandfather was my great grandmother Regina's brother. His second cousin's son, Ján Lipšer in Žilina, put me in contact with Ladislav's sons who live in Zurich, Switzerland. They had donated their father's archives to the new Sered Museum. One of them, Vladimir—also a historian—provided me with valuable historical information for the first chapter of this book, and his brother, Juraj, shared the Lipscher family tree. I am quite grateful to them. Additional thanks go to other family members with whom I was able to do phone interviews and who made biographical material available to me that is no longer obtainable from other sources.

I traveled three times to Ecuador in search of information from government registries and archives, to interview authors and descendants of European immigrants who were friends of my parents, and to read and make copies of journals and newspaper articles from private libraries. I had the good fortune of lifelong friendships from grade school and high school—Ramiro Ferri Saona, Luis Eguiguren, José Espinosa—to whom I own a tremendous debt for helping me get access to these private libraries. A special thanks to Pablo Better, another childhood friend, who shared with me a historical review of the Jewish community in Quito and gifted me with the newly-released copy of a book detailing the Jewish migration to Ecuador. Additional thanks go to Juan Miguel Salvador, my sister Edulka's cousin through her mother, Virginia, in Guayaquil, Ecuador. Juan tirelessly researched local newspapers notices for the arrival of ships to Ecuador in March 1940 as well as information about my parents' train trip from Guayaquil to Quito.

During a recent trip to Europe, my wife Elaine and I had the great pleasure of meeting Ladislav Židek, formerly mayor of the town of Rajec, Slovakia; Pavel Frankl, chairman of the Jewish community of Žilina in Slovakia; and Ján Lipšer and his wife Viera, also in Žilina. Each welcomed us as if we were longtime friends and provided us with a great deal of historical information. We were glad to be able to thank them personally for their hospitality.

Ladislav Židek put me in contact with Ludmila Pártošova from Bratislava, Slovakia. She is a genealogist and the photographer who took photographs of Rajec and its Jewish cemetery gravestones. I am quite grateful to her for allowing me to include some of those pictures in this narrative. In addition, she made it possible for us to obtain an image of the Hebrew inscription in David Pikler's gravestone which provided the confirmation of the name of his mother, Eszter, the wife of Jacob Hirsh Pikler, among our earliest known ancestors.

I want to recognize Julius Müller of Prague, who did the lion's share of genealogical research about the Pikler family, and whose report informed much of the next section of this book; also performing historical research for me were Ludmila Pártošova of Bratislava, Traude Triebel of Vienna, Madeleine Isenberg of California, Karesz Vandor of Budapest, and Daniel Jurac of Romania.

Librarians, archivists, and scholars at the following institutions I visited went out of their way to help, and provided me with research and reference materials that had a direct and indirect bearing on the Pikler family history: the Leo Beck Institute, YIVO-Jewish Research Institute in NYC; the United States Memorial Holocaust Museum in Washington, DC; the Milton S. Eisenhower Library at Johns Hopkins University, Baltimore, MD; and the Tulsa University Library in Tulsa, OK. I also wish to take this opportunity to express my gratitude to those public librarians in Tulsa, OK, Miami Beach, FL, and Naples, FL who took a very personal interest in my project. In many instances, I was able to locate little-known and hard-to-find materials by correspondence, without the necessity of undertaking expensive and time-consuming trips.

Thanks, too, to all those who contributed translations of original documents from several languages and of Leika's Spielberg interview from Slovak into English.

My sincere thanks are due to my editor, Rachel Miranda Feingold, for the personal interest she took in this project above and beyond her considerable professional skills.

I am most grateful to my wife, Elaine, for tolerating my absorption in researching, organizing, and writing this narrative, and my frustration when I couldn't find a piece of information that I wanted. She spent many hours over so many years listening to me talk about this narrative. She faithfully read evolving drafts, refreshed my memory of many events I had forgotten, and helped me communicate them as clearly as I could.

Prologue

We are the children of many sires, and every drop of blood in us in its turn betrays its ancestor. —Emerson

The best legacy we can pass along to our children and grandchildren is the knowledge of their family history.

Ideally a family narrative ought to start as far back as possible, preferably with the earliest generation. The research should go beyond simply tracing family lines—gathering names, dates and places—to discovering how our ancestors' experiences were affected by the times in which they lived.

The Pikler genealogy tree in the front of this book begins with our earliest known family member: Jacob Hirsh Pikler. His seven descendants constitute the seven branches of the family. Genealogist Julius Müller's archival research findings—whom I hired to help me trace the Pikler roots—indicate that Jacob might have had a brother, Salomon. But as of this writing, we have only the minimal information Müller was able to find about him. So, for the purposes of this family narrative, we will focus on Jacob's descendants.

Gravestones dating back to the late eighteenth century and belonging to some members of those branches are at the Rajec cemetery in Slovakia. There are also late eighteenth and nineteenth century documents (birth, death, marriage, property taxes, etc.) for several of them available on the *JewishGen* website.

This narrative deals with the David Pikler family branch (Jacob Hirsh Pikler and Eszter's son), and more specifically, with the fifth generation of this branch, that is, Móric's children with his first and second wives: Hans, Klára, Lea, Teri, and Edit, each with their spouses. Wilma, who was born after Hans, died before the age of two, and so her brief life plays only a fleeting role in this story. From here on out, I will refer to this branch of the family simply as the "Móric branch."

As for Móric's children, within the family they were called by the diminutives of their names: Hans (the only son) was *Hansi, Hansiko, or Hansinko*, Klára was *Klári or Klárika*, Teri was *Terka*, Lea was *Leika or Lejka*, and Edit was *Edulka* (as is my sister, Edith, who was named after her) *or Editka*. As for their spouses, Klári's first husband, Alexander, was *Sani*, and her second husband, Zoltan, was *Zoli*; Leika's first husband, Julius, was *Julko,* and her second husband, Alexander, was *Sanyi*; Teri's husband, Géza, was *Gézuka*. These nicknames, also including *Oli or Olinka* for my sister Olga, *Petyko or Petko* for Peter (who is now called Shlomo), *Ivko* for Ivan, *Madulka, Magdulka or Mada* for Magda, as well as mine—*Georgi* or *Georgie*—which my aunts used in their correspondence, will appear often in the book in place of their corresponding proper names, as that is how I and my first cousins heard them most often. By using these nicknames, I hope to convey the abiding affection we all felt for one another.

With this narrative, we reclaim their memories and document their lives and struggles, which might otherwise remain hidden, forgotten, or unknown to us and our descendants.

I had wanted to write a family history for most of my life. Starting sometime in grade school, I began to collect names, dates, and demographic data about my paternal family in a shoebox. It might seem strange that a kid would be interested in this type of information, but that was not happenstance. In our home in Ecuador, my father often spoke about his family living in Europe and later in Israel, recounting not only family names and their relationships but anecdotes, travels, happy and sad events. In addition, my two sisters, Oli and Edulka, and I were expected to listen attentively while our father translated letters from his own sisters, which arrived every week or two. As we grew older, we were also encouraged to write short notes to our aunts. We knew our father deeply missed his family and we understood that he wanted us to share his memories and the love he had for them.

At the same time, we grew up with no idea that other Pikler branches existed. So, it was a great surprise to my wife, Elaine, and me when we learned by serendipity in 1971, while living in Rochester, Minnesota, that someone by the name of Charles Pikler lived not far from us in Minneapolis. That was a name we were not familiar with. We had to find out who he was.

Elaine had come home one evening and told me that the manager of her gym had mentioned seeing the name "Charles Pikler" in a playbill of the Minnesota orchestra, and wondered if he was our relative. Elaine asked her to spell his last name; it was identical to ours.

It turned out Charles Pikler was a nineteen-year-old math student at the University of Minnesota and a violinist with the Minnesota orchestra. When Elaine and I learned that they would perform in Rochester on November 16, 1971, we decided to meet this young man. We contacted Charlie through the orchestra and invited him for dinner after the performance.

Charlie was a charming but quiet fellow. At dinner, the interaction was somewhat awkward, and Elaine and I did most of the talking. From a genealogy standpoint, the evening was a disappointment. Charlie was uninterested in talking about the Pikler family. Nothing good about his father had been mentioned as he was growing up and we could tell he did not have a good feeling about the man.

Afterwards I took him back to the Rochester Civic Center where the orchestra waited to transport all the musicians back to Minneapolis. No further contact was scheduled or expected.

In the mid-eighties, I got a phone call in Tulsa, Oklahoma from Charlie Pikler. He had managed to obtain my unlisted phone number from the Mayo Clinic operator claiming that he urgently needed to talk to "his cousin about a family medical issue." Ordinarily Mayo would not provide this information to anyone, but he must have made a convincing argument. Charlie told me that he was married, had two children and was living in Evanston, Illinois; he was the first viola of the Chicago Symphony. His father had died in 1984 and had left for him several boxes with documents about his side of the family.

He told me he had become very interested in his family history and after reading a letter from his father, had become aware that he belonged to the Abraham branch of the Pikler family. When traveling with the symphony to Europe, he had managed to visit, at times with his cousin Katalin Pikler (also from the Abraham branch), cemeteries in Hungary and Slovakia, where they had found and photographed the gravestones of many Piklers dating back to the late eighteenth century. He wanted to know if I was still interested in the family genealogy and offered to share several documents with me, including the letter from his father that had moved him quite a lot.

On December 24, 1951, Endré Pikler (1907-1984), an attorney born in Budapest, Hungary who had emigrated to the US in 1946, typed a 31-page letter to his three-and-a-half-month-old son Charles, whom he affectionately addressed as "Charliepikler." His marriage had ended in divorce before his son's birth and he was unsure as to whether he would be able to see him again. He wanted his son to know about his paternal ancestry. Endré had always been interested in learning about his family roots and had done as much research as he could about it.

Charles Pikler grew up with his mother, who strongly disliked her former husband and imparted her feelings to her son. From that phone call, it was obvious to me that Charlie's feelings about his father now differed significantly from fifteen years earlier.

Elaine and I read Endré Pikler's letter separately, and afterwards, expressed amazement to each other about the contents of the last three paragraphs:

All the Piklers, in all generations, were fighters. They were never reconciled with the petty limitations of their accidental environment, respectively with the limitations imposed on mankind by human destiny. They were fighting for freedom and enlightenment; for art, music and literature; science and mathematics, for social sciences and the social reform; for the better understanding of the human soul and body; for economic progress and social security; for peace, culture and civilization.

They were fighting not only for individual happiness; they were self-sacrificing for their families; for their communities, their nation; for mankind as a whole; for their ideals. All the Piklers were idealists. Many of them enjoyed great successes in their lifetimes while other Piklers were mishandled or were unfortunate. But these things did not alter their final attitude in view of the ultimate issues of human destiny and its objectives.

Already in the past decades, the Piklers were so often scattered in so many continents over the whole world. Often, they lost track of each other. However, a certain unity of the Pikler spirit was and remained overwhelming. [1]

Elaine and I could not believe that two individuals, Hansi and Endré, from two different Pikler family branches who did not know of each other's existence, and had certainly never met, could express themselves about their family using the same words! "That is what I heard my father-in-law say many times," said Elaine. "I heard him make the same remarks, with a sense of pride but never with a tone of superiority toward others."

Endré Pikler's letter was also quite a revelation for me—it included the names and brief comments of several members of the Abraham branch as well as some from other branches, including David's. It took me quite a while to fit all the names from that letter as well as the ones I had collected over the years into a basic family tree.

In 2007, my first cousin Giora, living in Nashua, New Hampshire, found on the internet two second cousins, members of the Abraham Adolf Pikler family: Támas and Katalin Pikler (Charlie Pikler's cousin, mentioned above). Giora related this finding to me, and soon afterward I also contacted them and found out we also shared in addition to our last name, a serious interest in our family genealogy.

Katalin wrote to me in early December 2007, telling me that she was an architect, and had since 1991 been working in regional development for the Hungarian administration. She was a frequent blood donor, and in 1996, during a blood donation, had met Dr. János Simonyi, another cousin of Charles Pikler. Between them, Dr. Simonyi and Charles shared with her all the information they had about the Piklers. Some weeks later, while recovering from an accident, she wrote a summary of that information; to acquire more data, she later visited the Hungarian National Archives and, later still, the Slovak Archives as well.

Támas, a computer programmer living in Massachusetts, Katalin in Budapest, and I in Oklahoma decided then to pool together all the family data we had collected over the years—in my case, the contents of that shoebox. It took Támas only a couple of days to upload all the information to a genealogy website called "TribalPages." My idea of a family history, which had remained an abstract dream until then, began to take shape.

In the summer of 2008, the three of us planned a Pikler family reunion which took place in Budapest in October of that year. Our hosts were Támas's parents, and the event took place at a lovely estate in the outskirts of the city. Forty-four family members, some traveling from as far as Australia and representing three Pikler branches (Abraham, David, and Moses) were present. Leika, with her daughter, Magda, and Oli and I, represented the Móric Pikler branch. My other sister, Edulka, unfortunately was unable to join us.

Despite the language barriers (most spoke only Hungarian or German) we all managed to communicate, and I remember it as a wonderful and loving get-together.

Támas and I had also planned to invite Martin Pikler (from the Moses branch) and his wife, Marianna, (living in Canberra, Australia) to drive with Oli and me to Žilina. Oli was fatigued and struggled to get around. She chose to spend the whole day with Leika. Magda joined us for a visit to Žilina's Jewish cemetery and a tour of Rajec and its Jewish cemetery. The latter had approximately 275 visible graves, and in spite of the overgrown vegetation and total disrepair of the site, it was relatively easy for us to find the inscriptions of several Pikler gravestones.

I had plans to begin writing our family history soon after I returned home, but I postponed them because of Oli's rapidly failing health, and when she died two months later, I had no inclination to even consider it. It was three years later, in 2011, that I decided to resume my research.

Sometime in 2012, I became acquainted with the 2001 research studies by two Emory University psychologists, Marshall Duke and Robin Feivush, showing that "the more children knew about their family's history, the stronger their sense of control over their lives, the higher their self-esteem and the more successfully they believed their family functioned." These researchers observed that the communication of family information across generations, often at informal family gatherings, occurs more frequently in families that have higher levels of cohesiveness, and they contribute to the development of a strong sense of what the authors called "the intergenerational self." They concluded that "children who have the most self-confidence have a strong intergenerational self. They know they belong to something bigger than themselves." [2,3] This research again prompted me to seriously consider writing a family narrative. By then the Móric branch already had nine eighth-generation members. I needed a plan.

When our father died in May 1978, Oli and I, with Virginia's consent, decided to leave all of his documents, which occupied half of a large armoire (my fifteenth birthday gift), in their home in Quito. We had flown in for his funeral. It was a very sad moment for all of us, not the appropriate time to even consider going over any of that material.

The armoire with all of my father's documents in it, moved several times with Virginia after she and Edulka left the house in 1979 and until she found a condo to buy in 1984. After Virginia died in 2006, the documents made their way in an airtight storage bin into our Tulsa climate-control attic.

In early August 2012, after I had read Duke and Feivush's article, I opened the bin for the first time in six years. It was immediately obvious what a daunting and lengthy job it would be to review it all. At the same time, I realized how fortunate I was that all these items I had inherited from my parents, most of them from my father, Hansi, had miraculously not been confiscated or lost during the family's voyage to Latin America before I was born.

I laid out the contents of the bin on tables to facilitate their inventory. There were dozens of legal size folders showing heavy use, most of them labeled and bursting with documents of all sizes. Some of the labels read: Brezoi, Romania, Czechoslovakia, Žilina, ZB (the company my father worked for), Legal, Certificates, Portraits, Personal cards/notes, Newspaper articles/clipings. There were several unlabeled folders and a large number of documents that were not in folders. A beautifully woven basket with a lid and a metal frame was full of photographs. In the bottom of the bin were hundreds of letters, most of them inside envelopes, as well as post cards, photos, and miscellaneous other items including expired driver licenses from Romania and Czechoslovakia, some office supplies and a few tchotchkes.

It took me until 2013 to chronologically file and archive the documents. What became clear as I went along was that two thirds of the documents belonged to the first thirty-eight years of Hansi's life, before he emigrated to Latin America; they were in five different languages: German, Slovak, Czech, Hungarian, and Romanian, none of which I could read. I realized then that getting them translated into English would be a necessary task, albeit a daunting one, as I would want to include any important information they contained in the family narrative. The rest of the documents were those he saved over the next thirty-eight years while he lived in Ecuador, until he died in 1976. They included folders with legal documents, including correspondence with the German attorney handling his petition for the German government's reparation program; a folder with all the immigration visas to Ecuador he had obtained for his family, as well as his Ecuadorian naturalization papers; several folders with business documents in Spanish; and thank you letters as well as notes from clients in the government, military, and diplomatic core, who he and Virginia had invited to dine at their home. Two folders contained Sophie's grammar and high school grades, letters, official papers for her emigration to Latin America and photographs.

When I finished the filing, I had no idea how difficult it was going to be to find reputable translators. I elected to start first with the documents because they were easier to handle. I knew I would have to send clear copies of each. I kept copiers at FedEx busy for weeks. An old friend of ours in Tulsa, a former chemical engineer at Amoco who was of German origin, volunteered to handle the German ones. He had a consulting office in Houston and traveled there frequently. Not wanting to abuse his goodwill, I would bring him no more than a dozen documents at a time. By the time we left Tulsa to move to Baltimore in 2017, one-fifth of the German documents had still not been translated. He was also kind enough to translate many letters. The genealogy consultants in Europe whom I hired to help me in finding information about the family were also helpful with the translations. It just took too long for each of them to reply back! And as I had anticipated, only a fraction of the translated information was useful for my purposes. There were many interesting facts in them, but most were not pertinent for the family narrative.

Handling and filing the extensive collection of letters was the most difficult part of the whole process: many of them were in very bad condition and several fell apart even with careful handling. It would have been impossible to make copies of them. The correspondence, including post cards, was filed chronologically (when dated) and by language over a couple of years. Fortunately, the majority of them were in German. Their translations were completed in late March 2020 and became an important source for Chapter Three.

In 2013, the same Emory University psychologists published a list of twenty questions referred to as the "Do You Know Scale" (DYK) pertaining to people's knowledge about family history. [4] Those questions are listed in the Appendix section for further generations to use.

The basic family tree that I had at the time had no information about the family of my grandfather Móric Pikler's second wife, Elsa Pikler née Teich. I was quite fortunate for the opportunity to have a most pleasant phone interview with Avital Schlanger on January 20, 2014. Avital is the granddaughter of Vali Pfeifer née Teich, one of Elsa's sisters. She worked as an independent researcher at Israel's Ben Gurion University. She was quite generous with her time, and thanks to her, I was able to obtain a lot of information about the Teich family to add to my family "shoebox."

In November 2017, I called Charlie to find out if he knew any more information about Jacob Hirsh Pikler. He did not. I shared my plans to learn to play the violin I had inherited from my father. Charlie did not mince words when he tried to talk me out of it. His reasons: it was the most difficult musical instrument to learn, and I was already too old. He suggested I try the recorder. I decided not to follow his advice. I have been taking violin lessons and enjoying this new adventure in my life.

This narrative includes not only personal anecdotes, written memories, letters, photographs, and official and non-official documents, but also the political, religious, economical, historical, and social contexts in Europe where these family members originated, and the lands they subsequently migrated to. Much of the broader historical picture appears in the notes to each section, so the body of the narrative can focus more on the Pikler family and their experiences.

For eight years, I worked on a way to bring this dream to fruition. Early on, I encountered two significant problems with the task: none of the members of the fifth generation were alive any longer, and, as noted earlier, most of the documents I had inherited from my parents were in languages I did not read or speak. It took considerable time to translate them; some are included in this volume, along with numerous significant photographs.

I used authoritative sources to summarize both the Jewish migration and religious history of the Czech lands and Slovakia, and the chronology of political events in those territories. Many books, journals, websites, and newspaper articles were sources of information about political, economic, social, and religious events in Central Europe, Israel, and Ecuador. They are listed in the bibliography.

In early 2018, I retained the services of Julius Müller to help me find more information about the roots and surname of the family. Müller is a former geneticist and freelance genealogist in Prague, and director of Toledot, the Jewish Family History Center there; he lectures and publishes on Jewish genealogy in journals including *Maskil, Stammbaum,* and *Avoteynu*—where he is also a contributing editor. With full confidence in Müller's expertise, I continued to glean more information about the Pikler family history as I was working on this narrative.

Elaine and I traveled to Žilina and Rajec again in late August 2018. Though volunteers had worked to clear most of the vegetation at the cemetery, many gravestones were broken, and some partially buried, making it impossible to determine which stone belonged to which grave. Several were leaning over and in many, the inscriptions had faded.

After a painstaking search, I was able to find the gravestones of my great-great-grandfather, David Pikler, and his wife, Charlotte Pikler née Telek. I also found my great grandfather Leopold (Lipot) Pikler's gravestone and that of his wife, Regina Pikler née Lipscher. The Hebrew inscriptions on these gravestones were of great interest to me, particularly David's, whose parents I hoped to find out more about.

Our host on that trip, Rajec's former mayor, Ladislav Zidek, told us that at the start of the twentieth century, 50 percent of the houses around the square belonged to Jewish families: one of them was Móric Pikler's. He also pointed to a monument with the bust of Ferdinand Durčansky that now stood, ironically, next to the former Móric Pikler house and in front of the town's museum. Durčansky was a Slovak nationalist leader born in Rajec who was a strong supporter and collaborator of Jozef Tiso, (a Roman Catholic priest and right-wing politician who governed the Slovak republic from 1939 to 1945) and was responsible for several anti-Jewish laws. He was executed in 1947 in Bratislava for war crimes and crimes against humanity.

The former mayor said he considered himself the only "declared" Jew remaining in Rajec, though he believed there might be a few "undeclared" others. His ancestors were Jewish, but he had a brother who was a Catholic priest; there were several Catholic symbols at his son's and parents' graves in a non-denominational cemetery as well as in his farmhouse. But he described himself to be an ecumenical person and recognized his Jewish heritage.

It was an unforgettable visit to the birthplace of the Pikler family, made even more special by the warmth and enthusiasm with which we were treated during our stay.

Over the course of that year, I added more researchers to the genealogical team, people who had access to historical information in other locations, including Bratislava, Vienna, Budapest, and Romania.

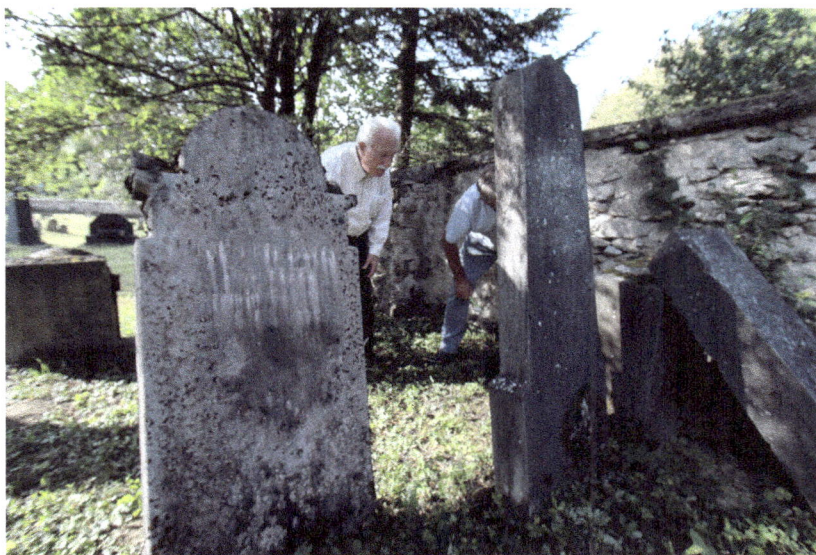

Searching for Pikler family gravestones at Rajec's Jewish cemetery; August 2018

**David Pikler's gravestone (Hebrew and back views) before restoration,
Rajec Jewish cemetery**

Ladislav Židek restoring David Pikler's gravestone (Hebrew inscription)

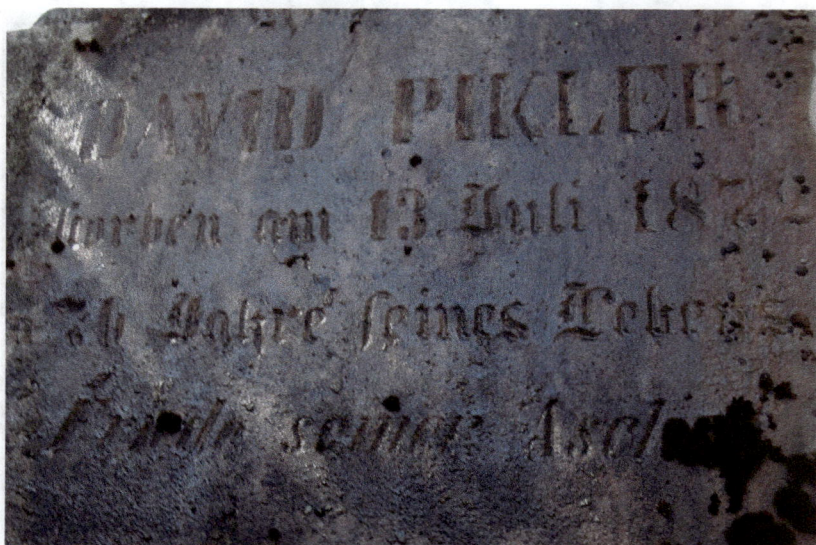

David Pikler's gravestone, front view, after restoration, August 2018

Charlotte Pikler's gravestone, Rajec Jewish cemetery

Regina and Leopold Pikler's gravestones, Rajec Jewish cemetery

Despite best efforts to be as accurate as possible, there will surely be errors in family information because of inaccuracies in the original data, input, and translations, but most importantly, because confirming documentation was not always available. Unfortunately, there were several historical gaps that could not be filled. Family stories are always works-in-progress.

Some events and details described in the narrative I found serendipitously, while others surprised me after translated documents revealed information that was strikingly different from what I had previously thought. There were also disappointments, the most significant of which was my unsuccessful three-year search for my grandmother Olga's cause of death at the too-young age of 32.

Despite the many frustrations and challenges of undertaking this project, the years I have spent working on it have been among the most rewarding periods of my life.

My hope is that by developing a strong family narrative for all of the children and grandchildren, they will understand better where they come from, and will know more about how their forebears were able to overcome and rise above the multiple obstacles they encountered in their lives.

We must also keep in mind that the war took a hefty toll on members of all the Pikler branches and that each of its survivors re-established their lives courageously from the ashes of the Nazi furnaces, the ruins of their homes, and the destruction of their families and former lives. It is due to their perseverance and their great will to rebuild what their enemies had destroyed that we are here today.

It will be up to our children and grandchildren to pick up where this narrative has left off; perhaps one day, they will want to write narratives about subsequent Pikler generations.

Chapter One

Family Historical Background

The curiosity and desire to discover our family roots is probably as old as civilization itself. We want to find the history of our ancestors in the hope that someday our descendants will do the same for us. We are eager to find out where our ancestors came from. If they migrated from one country to another, we want to know from where, when, and why. We want to know how our ancestors lived, how they earned a living, and where they are buried.

Jews search for information that often cannot be found because when our people were chased from country to country, their records were obliterated, their synagogues and cemeteries destroyed by war and revolutions, by economic and natural disasters, by religious and political turmoil. The work of Jewish genealogist Dan Rottenberg sheds light on this process:

> Beneath the fun of stalking one's ancestors and relatives is the humbling and inspiring realization that each of us is merely a link in a chain. We may someday be forgotten, but the contribution we made to the chain, however slight, will always be there, and as long as the chain exists, a piece of us will exist, too. [5]

In this chapter, I sought to list the facts that were known and those that were unknown about the Pikler family roots at the time of this writing: to find the hometown where the Pikler family originated, to find the root of the Pikler surname, and to find information about who were the earliest ancestors of the Pikler family to settle in Rajec, in today's northwestern Slovakia which in those days was part of the kingdom of Hungary.

A brief historical review of the migration of Jews in Central

Europe is necessary at this point, because the family's history is intertwined with the history of this migration, which, per historians Peter and Pavel Frankl [6], began as early as the first century, A.D., following the Roman legions. For those interested in a detailed account, the book by Škvarna, D. (et al.) is highly recommended. [7]

There are records dating back to the early tenth century of Jewish settlements in Bohemia and Moravia (today's Czech Republic), Silesia, Slovakia, and Subcarpathian Ruthenia [8]. Jews from Germany, Austria, and Bohemia, driven to flight by marching crusaders in the eleventh and twelfth centuries, settled in the West as well as in the East (currently Slovakia). Some of them founded the first Jewish community in Bratislava (the capital of today's Slovakia) in the late thirteenth century. [9]

As in most places in Europe, Jews were subject to various discriminatory decrees, pogroms, and expulsions [10]. These persecutions began around the year 1000—the first millennium. They were expelled and then, when a significant economic decline was noted in their absence, they were re-admitted only to be expelled again. Some of them lost their lives after extreme and irrational Christian accusations were leveled against them: the most common one was that Jews kidnapped and murdered Christian children in order to use their blood as part of their religious rituals during Jewish holidays. In some places, such calumny (blood libels) incited people to violence: in 1494 some Jews were burnt at the stake in Trnava and in 1529, thirty Jews were accused of wrongdoing and burnt in Pezinok, Slovakia. Persecution in many forms was rampant.

After the Battle of Mohács[1] (near Mohács, Kingdom of Hungary) in 1526, Jews were expelled from all major towns in Hungary (today's Slovakia) which, along with Austria, was part of the Habsburg Empire.[2] [11] They were accused of collaboration with the Turks (Ottoman Empire).

Jewish settlements in southwestern and central Moravia

absorbed waves of refugees expelled from Moravian royal towns in the fifteenth and sixteenth centuries: from Jihlava, Moravia in 1425-1426 and other royalty-owned towns in 1454,[3] during the Hussite wars [1419-1434] and following the Kurucz riots in 1683[4] when hundreds of Moravian Jews fled to Slovakia seeking refuge from the riots and their living restrictions. Most of these immigrants settled in Western Slovakia, bordering Moravia.

Masses of Jews fleeing the terror of the Khmelnytsky Cossacks during the 1648-1658 uprising in Poland, Latvia, and Belarus fled to Hungary (Subcarpathian Ruthenia was settled by Polish Jews). Many of them wandered farther on, to Moravia. To this day, the Khmelnytsky uprising is considered by Jews to be one of the most traumatic events in their history [12][5] when, according to historian Max Dimont, "perhaps as many as 100,000 Jews perished in the decade of this revolution." [13]

Jews expelled from Vienna and Lower Austria in 1670 settled in Slovakia, and some even moved into rural communities of Bohemia and Moravia. [14]

At the end of the seventeenth century, the Hungarian aristocracy encouraged Jews from neighboring countries to migrate to northern Hungary and to settle near the borders of the states they had come from. Once settled, they maintained religious, communal, and linguistic ties with Jewish communities across the borders [9]. The Esterhazy family[6] [15] allowed the Jews to return and settle in near proximity to their castle in Bratislava. The Hungarian nobility needed money and the Jews needed protection from Emperor Leopold I (1658-1705) and especially from the nobility. To be able to work and practice their religion, the Jews were forced to pay taxes that established a symbiotic relationship, providing the monarchy with their needed funds and the Jews with the protection they needed from the monarchy in order to avoid prosecution or expulsion.

In 1724, the first census of all Jews in the Czech lands was carried out. Approximately 30,000 Jews inhabited 168 towns and 672 villages in Bohemia and approximately 20,000 lived in Moravia, while 2,335 Jewish families (approximately 10,500 Jews) were registered in Prague [10]. A census taken by Hungary in 1735 established that, out of 12,000 Jews living in Slovakia, two thirds hailed from Moravia.

The migrations and settlements of the seventeenth and eighteenth centuries had the most significant impact on the subsequent development of the Jewish community.

Considering the above history of migration, I had to deal first with the question *from where* did our ancestors come? My literature research led me to believe that our ancestors migrated east (to the western part of Upper Hungary) probably from Bohemia or Moravia [9] due to the various discriminatory decrees, pogroms, and expulsions described above. According to Peter and Pavel Frankl, "The first regions they settled were the territories of today's Western Slovakia, along the Moravian-Slovakian border." [6]

Julius Müller's archival research suggests that they most likely migrated from Moravia, more specifically from the town of Kojetín.[7] This is what Müller had to say about where the Piklers come from:

> What became quite clear after the first visit to the Brno regional archives [in the Czech Republic] was the finding that the Jewish migration was not a wild event but rather a controlled process. The records I found at the Brno regional archives indicate that the Moravian authorities tried hard to register everyone en route.
>
> The new emigres had to remain as members of their previous hometown's kehilot (Jewish communities) and they still had to pay religious tax there. Most importantly, the Jewish families in Slovakia and their relatives in the Moravian hometowns stayed in contact for generations—both for business and for family affairs.

Parts of the Jewish Census of places in Upper Hungary in 1725 showed the hometown(s) of new emigres. My research priority was to find all or most of the Census of Rajec in order to learn where the Piklers probably originated from. The main source of important information was the 18 volumes Maygar-Zsidó Oklevéltár[8] published in Budapest. One set of the 18 books is currently stored at the National Library in Prague, Czech Republic.

The Rajec Census published in the Maygar-Zsidó Oklevéltár also showed the population statistics: in 1727 there were 3 Jewish families, in 1736 there were 7 families, in 1746 there were 5 families. The number then grew and in 1767 there were 12 families. The Rajec Census of 1781 and 1788, both found in the Bytca district archives, showed 20 Jewish households and 16 Jewish households, respectively. By 1795 there were 25 Jewish families in Rajec including Jacob Hirsh Pikler's. Their numbers somewhat stabilized, and in 1846 there were 19 Jewish households in Rajec.

Further analysis of the Rajec Census of 1736 and the Register of 1740 were quite instrumental in my efforts to identify the original hometown of the Pikler family:

1. The 1736 Census showed that 3 Jewish families (out of 7 families) came to Rajec from Moravia; one family from the area ruled by Duke Kounitz, one from the area ruled by Duke Rottal and one from Duke Ditrichstein's area.

2. The 1740 register of heads of Jewish households showed both the Moravian hometown which the particular family came from and the name of the town in Upper Hungary where the family settled. The register showed that these 3 Jewish families came to Rajec from Kojetín (The Jewish quarter in Kojetín was

heavily damaged by fire in 1724 and again in 1735 as described in several history books).

It is more than likely that we will never be able to find out exactly *when* the Piklers settled in Rajec. So, we must speculate that it probably occurred sometime during the last quarter of the eighteenth century. Rajec at that time was in territory that comprised the northern region of the Kingdom of Hungary from the eleventh century until the dissolution of the Austro-Hungarian Monarchy after World War I, when it became part of Czechoslovakia [9].

If the Piklers moved to Rajec from Moravia, we do not know with certainty *why* this migration took place. The most likely possibility: the *Familianten* Law (*Familiant Ordnung*) enacted by Habsburg's Emperor Charles VI, ruler over large swathes of current Austria, Slovakia and the Czech Republic, who decided that Jews were multiplying too rapidly and initiated one of the first population controls in history. Henceforth, the number of Jewish families in his country would be limited to whatever it was present and never surpassed. The law not only limited the number of Jewish males permitted to live, marry, and have children but also restricted Jews to living in the ancestral streets and houses they had inhabited until then.[9] [16,17]

The *Familianten* Law was introduced quite fast and efficiently into practice. The rabbis who tried to bypass the Law were severely punished and all the children who were not from the families of *Familianten* were recorded as illegitimate in the birth books. Marriage restrictions served as incentives for the second- and third-born sons to emigrate primarily to Upper Hungary where the *Familianten* Law did not apply. Moreover, the local noblemen welcomed them. Sometimes the same noble clan owned the estate in Moravia and another estate in Upper Hungary. That eased the migration process.

Historian Vladimir Lipscher believes these laws forced many Jewish families to leave and settle in Slovakia [18]. Lipscher's Ph.D.

thesis was about the Jews in the Habsburg Empire from 1620 until the ruling of the Empress Maria Theresa (1717-1780). It also included the introduction of the *Familianten* Law. He was able to trace his own family roots to Lipnik, a small town in Moravia [18], where the Lipscher name is listed in the *Familianten* Books.

Endré Pikler suggests in his 1951 letter to his son, Charlie, [1] that the Piklers probably migrated from Germany and possibly from Bohemia to Hungary at the end of eighteenth century [1]. Julius Müller's findings abrogate that theory. This letter also states that there were three brothers (the letter does not explain where this information originates from). He wrote that one of them chose the name Pikler when the Holy Roman Emperor Joseph II's edict, issued at the end of 1787, compelled the Jews to adopt German family names [1].[10] Again, the letter does not offer a source for this statement.

As to the root of the Pikler surname, Müller reported the following:

> The next step was to study the vital records of those eight potential Moravian hometowns and look for similar surnames and variants of the surname Pikler. The records are stored today at the National Archives in Prague.
>
> In two towns a very specific surname, Büchler—and its variants, Bichler and Püchler—were found (the Uhersky Brod town, formerly from nearby Bzenec, and the town of Kojetín). By doing archival research at the Brno Regional Archives, I found out that this Bichler/Büchler family in Uhersky Brod evolved their surname from Buchbinder. That is a good example of surname dynamics development. From previous research I knew that the surname Püchler/Pichler was also found in the village Schrittens located at the Bohemia/Moravia border. I did not follow that lead since I felt the Moravian connection was more attractive.

I should point out that my research of the *Familianten* Books from Moravia and Bohemia prior to the early 1800s showed that the surnames Bichler, Büchler, and Pichler are variants of the same surname. I saw these variants used for the same person/family quite freely in various books. Minor changes in one or two letters are not uncommon. They occur for several reasons: because the ancestors could not read or write and so the name would be spelled phonetically; or a name might sound differently to different people if they did not speak the same language. In my experience: although the Jews from Bohemia/Moravia spoke German and had German surnames, the clerks spoke Hungarian. There is room for misspelling. Just as some people are tone-deaf to music, so other people are tone-deaf to words, so what the clerks heard is what they wrote down.

In my visit to the district archives in Trencin, Slovakia, I found out that the Trencin Jewish community was established by the Jews from Uhersky Brod in 1689. The presence of the Büchler family members in Trencin records confirmed this.

Since I found evidence of migration between Kojetín and Rajec, I chose Kojetín as the potential hometown of the Piklers as a working hypothesis for further study.

By studying the vital records of Kojetín I found that the naming pattern of Piklers in Rajec resembled the pattern of Bichlers/Büchlers in Kojetín. For example, Jacob Hirsch, son of Abraham Moses Büchler, was born in Kojetín in 1785. Natan Büchler, son of Jacob and Ester Büchler was born in Kojetín and died there in 1796 - recorded as Natan Bichler. The birth book of Kojetín also showed the birth of Moses Büchler, son of Jacob Büchler, on April 11, 1803.

I noticed in the birth records of Kojetín that the children

born before 1787 were recorded without surnames but the same children were listed as Bichlers/Büchlers in the alphabetically ordered index at the very end of the book. The index was obviously compiled later.

I checked the books of Kojetín, and I saw that all the Büchlers were gone by 1820. That indicates that they were not permitted to stay in Kojetín any longer and moved elsewhere. I believe that was the trigger also for the previous generation—it could be that some ended up in Slovakia.

It is also important to note that the Jews around 1800, especially the ones in Moravia, did not want to stop using patronyms (an old biblical Jewish custom) after 1787 (when the decree on surnames was issued); they felt it was an inappropriate pressure from the government to use German surnames. They stubbornly kept using patronyms even after 1787. Hirsh/Hirschl/Herschl (all variations of the same name) are patronyms to identify the child/descendant of someone named Hirsh. Only in some cases when the family agreed to pick Hirsh as an official surname after 1787 did it become so. This was not the case with the Piklers.

The letter from Endré also states that of Jacob Hirsh Pikler's children, only his son Abraham Adolf settled in Hungary's northern region called Subcarpathia, while the others remained in Slovakia. From this it follows, according to him, that the family was known as coming from two regions: Slovakia and Subcarpathia. Finally, Endré states that some Piklers were engaged in the leather tanning trade—one of the best-organized industries in the country— while others devoted their pioneering activities to forestry and the lumber trade, another major industry of Czechoslovakia. State-owned forests comprised about one million hectares of the country's estimated total of 4.6 million hectares under forest cultivation and yielded approximately 25 percent of the country's total production of timber. The lumber industry was centered in the districts of Košice and Žilina (Rajec was part of this district), while in Subcarpathia Ruthenia, Mukačevo was the leading center. [1,19]

The accession to the throne of Austria's Joseph II in 1780 would bring a new era of religious toleration and modernization for the Jews. His goal with the 1782 Edict of Tolerance[11] [20] was to bring about administrative unification in his various domains. The charter abolished Jewish communal autonomy whereby the Jews controlled their internal affairs; it promoted Germanization and the wearing of non-Jewish clothing, the adoption of family names and establishment of secular schools [21]; it lifted restrictions on Jews and opened up communities, trades, and educational opportunities previously barred to them [22]; it imposed upon Jewish merchants the obligation of writing their business books in German instead of Yiddish or Hebrew, and it made Jews subject to military service for the first time. It is quite likely that our ancestors were the beneficiaries of this edict. But many of the restrictions on the Jews remained, and the Josephian emancipation was soon replaced by the conservative and bigoted spirit of Joseph II's long-reigning nephew, Archduke Charles (1792-1835). [23]

The situation changed dramatically in March of 1848. Liberal reforms were enacted between 1849 and 1867 throughout Central Europe. In the Austro-Hungarian Empire, the Jews achieved full legal equality in 1867 when the dual monarchy of Austro-Hungary was established, and Slovakia became part of Northern Hungary. The Hungarian parliament passed the Emancipation Law to promote assimilation among minorities, especially Jews. For more than a millennium, Slovakian and Hungarian Jewry had been closely linked. Now government officials supported Jewish cooperation in industry and finance, and the Jewish population grew exponentially, especially in small, secluded shtetls in Eastern Slovakia.

In 1882 and 1883, anti-Jewish riots occurred in several towns in Slovakia. With the introduction of the "Reception Law" (1896), that placed Jews and Christians on an equal level, the Slovak Clerical People's Party was formed. The Party's main interests were anti-Liberalism and limiting Jewish influence in the country. The main leader was Andreas Hlinka.

Müller learned the following about the Piklers who settled in Rajec:

> The Census/Tax registers research done in the Slovakian archives in Bytca, Trencin and Žilina showed that in 1778 in Rajec both Aron Herschl and Samuel Herschl were there —it could be a misspelled Salomon. (I saw that mismatch Samuel/Salomon quite often.)
>
> In the Rajec Census of 1781 there were 20 Jewish households. There was no Jacob Herschl listed yet. There could be two reasons for this. The Census showed only the heads of a household. He was probably too young to be the head of household, so he was not listed, or he wasn't there yet. His father (quite likely the same name) Herschl was not listed either. So, I am voting for option 2, that Jacob was not there yet. I checked all villages and towns around, and the only Jacob Herschl was listed in Trencinska Zavada in 1781 without any more details. This Jacob was the only Jewish man in Trencinska Zavada.
>
> In the Rajec Tax register/Census of 1788 there were 16 Jewish households. Salomon Pickler and Jacob Pickler were listed; they were written with the c as "Pickler." Next to Salomon's surname, the word arm was noted (in German that word means poor, unable to pay). Jacob owed 4 gulden and 42 krajczár.[12] The amount of tax was listed without any family details.
>
> The 1795 Rajec Census showed 25 Jewish families, but Salomon Pikler was not listed indicating that he had died by then.

11

The Tax register of 1811 of all Rajec men showed only Jacobus (most likely a misspelled Jacob) Pikler as a taxpayer.

In the Rajec Tax register of 1837 Jacob Pikler was not listed; most likely he had died before 1837. Of the 63 Jewish men in the register, I found Moritz Pikler, Abraham Pikler, David Pikler and Leopold Pikler, all listed in the Pikler genealogy tree.

Rajec 1788 Tax Register Census

So, Müller concluded that the Piklers of Rajec came from Kojetín, a small town in the Olomouc region, in central Moravia; that the spelling of their surname changed from the variants Pichler/Bichler/Büchler to Pikler, and that any of these variants was heard as Pikler by someone who wrote it down; he is also fairly certain that two brothers were the family ancestors because they both picked up the same surname Pickler, modified to Pikler soon after the Decree issued in 1787 by Emperor Joseph II, son of Archduchess Maria Theresa of Austria (1717-1780), ordering the use of fixed surnames for the Jews.

Müller's final report included the following specifics:

A. Salomon Herschl (the oldest, b. ABT 1740), already listed in the 1767 Rajec Census, made me think that he was Salomon Pikler and it was he, as head of the household, who invited Jacob to come later; Salomon was a merchant in Rajec at the time.

B. Jacob Hirsh, probably born between 1750-1760, might have been a second- or third-born son of a *Familiant* and left to seek a marriage permit or to set up a family elsewhere. He may be the one who was living in Trencinska Zavada in 1781 and then moved to Rajec.

Müller stated that he attempted to obtain as much information as possible from both the Czech Republic's Moravian and Slovakian archives. His findings are based on a combination of that research and other resources, all listed in the book's Appendix.

Lastly, he described the problems he encountered in his archival research:

Covering two-and-ahalf centuries of genealogical research was obviously not an easy task; the Jewish vital records are fragmentary, not all survived completely; the original Jewish birth records were available starting in 1856, marriage records starting in 1855 and death records starting in 1857.

Earlier records, previous to the dates noted above, were written retroactively: the dates found were not listed chronologically (this created a problem for the accuracy of genealogical tree data for the earliest generation). In fact, George had provided me with a page from his family Tribal Pages genealogy tree showing Jacob Hirsh Pikler's seven descendants with their birth dates. I found a birth book where the birth years were recorded retroactively. The original birth book for his son Leopold for example, listed him as Lobl or Löwi, son of Jacob Hirsh with birth date 1784 (not 1793 as listed in the tree). The German name Leopold was used after 1787. The same book had David Pikler's birth date as 1798 (not 1794).

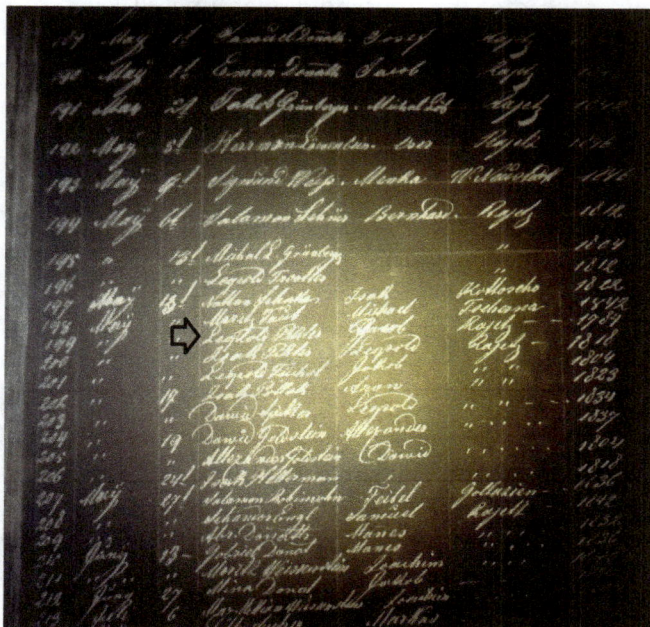

Leopold Pikler's birthdate listed retroactively: 1784

We know then that by 1784, Pikler was already the surname used by the family. Over the years, the surname Pickler has occasionally appeared in several records. This is a common mistake noted even today. The *k* seems to like a *c* in front of it.

A fascinating side note in Müller's report was his finding that the early Piklers were both affluent and influential in Rajec:

> Although it was not the main purpose of my archival research, I was able to document records which seemed to show that in the first half of the nineteenth century the Piklers were a significant part of the Rajec community and that they were quite wealthy. Debt certificates and their negotiations between 1825-1840 showed that Pikler family members quite often lent money to local individuals and Jewish community members.
>
> In the Rajec Chronicle Books there are several entries documenting that some of them were elected members of the town's political administration: Jakub, Leopold, Ede, and Armin Pikler, for example, served as deputies of Rajec's Mayor; also documented is their participation in the economic and cultural expansion of the town: in 1825, David Pikler signed a contract with a local authority to increase and broaden the Jewish cemetery; in 1894, Leopold and Ede Pikler supported the financial investment for the town's train terminal, to name two examples.
>
> Also noteworthy was the finding that in 1840, David and Moses Pikler were able to buy a piece of land – quite an exceptional legal act at the time—as the Jews were not allowed to buy any land until about 1860 when the Jews were granted all civic rights.

Jacob Hirsch Pikler most likely lived during the reign of the Emperor Joseph II [1741-1790]. No further information about him is available. He and Eszter are considered the first known generation. They had seven descendants, all of whom were born in

Rajec.[13] Of these seven family branches, no records are available for Hani (except for her birthdate year 1789) and Lotti Pikler. Rozália married Farkas Ekstein and had two children (Rózsa and Sámuel) but there are no known descendants.

Rajec family register: Hani Pikler, 1789

Móric Pikler and Olga Pikler née
Fleischer; Vienna, March 1901

The family tree at the front of this book includes all the names of Jacob Hirsch and Eszter's descendants and is drawn to depict (in bold) their son David Pikler's branch from which his grandson Móric and his family originates from.

Móric married Olga Fleischer on June 9, 1901 at Innere Stadt, in Vienna, Austria, where Olga was born on December 2, 1873. He was 30 years old and she was 28 when they married. They lived in Kimpulung, Romania and had two children, Hansi and Wilma. Olga died on August 11, 1905 at age 32, from unknown causes.

Jewish record of Móric and Olga's wedding; Vienna, Austria, June 9, 1901

Móric remarried on April 17, 1910 to Alžbeta (Elsa) Teich in Banská Bystrica, Slovakia[14] where she had been born on June 31, 1884. He was 39 and she was 26. After their marriage, Móric and Elsa lived in Rajec where three daughters were born: Klári, Teri, and Leika. In late 1916 or early 1917, they moved to Ružomberok, Slovakia[15] where a fourth daughter, Edit, was born. They owned a large and comfortable home as well as a small dairy or grocery.

In contrast to his forbears, Móric did not continue to prosper. His financial difficulties appear to have started just before the end of World War I but worsened in the early 1920s and collapsed in the late twenties.

Móric and Elsa moved to Žilina, Slovakia[16] in 1928 or 1929. According to my father, Móric lost his business and bank savings as well as their home in Ružomberok. Móric did not want people to know their predicament.

We do not know what Móric did after moving to Žilina. Leika relayed that she had heard he had a business partner named Tiroler whom her parents accused of fraud and theft. It is unknown if this happened before they moved to Žilina or while they were already living there.

Elsa Pikler née Teich and Móric Pikler; Banská Bystrica, Slovakia, 1910

In Žilina, Móric and Elsa first lived in a house that went by the name "Katolicky Dom" (Catholic House). All the children got jobs and contributed most of their earnings toward the family's expenses. By 1923, my father had already moved to Romania to work at a lumber company to earn enough to help his parents. Unfortunately, their financial situation never recovered, and they had to change residences several times, probably because they could not afford to cover the rent.

Móric was known as a strict disciplinarian, especially with Hansi, less with his daughters, and he had a strong-willed character. He was, however, openly affectionate with all of his children. He had a lot of respect for Elsa, and per family accounts, he was keen on Hansi, who was able to intercede with his father on behalf of his sisters. They adored him for that but also because he always spent quality time with each them. Hansi recalled that as they grew older, his sisters would often come or write to him for advice.

Elsa was a very caring and nurturing mother whose steady and calming temperament had a great influence on the family. This was manifested even under the stressful downturn of the family's financial situation in the 20s, during Móric's illness and when she and Leika were at Ravensbrück. She adopted and raised my father as her own and he felt and reciprocated her love.

From all family accounts, the Pikler family was not religious. Elsa used to attend the local synagogue on Yom Kippur out of respect for her parents' memory. According to an anecdote Leika told her nephew Ivan, Teri's son, one time Móric got hungry, so he went to the synagogue to call his wife home: "*Elsa, komm zu haus, du hast schon genug gebeten!*" "Elsa, come home, you have prayed enough already!" Neither Hansi nor his sisters or their future families were religious, though some would visit an orthodox synagogue for Passover, Yom Kippur, and Rosh Hashanah.

Móric spoke mostly German with his family, but Elsa used mainly Hungarian when talking with the children. Both Móric and Elsa spoke Slovak as well. Hansi and his sisters used all three languages among themselves.

In the summer of 1939, my parents and two-year-old sister, Oli, left what was by then fascist Slovakia, with visas to Bolivia, but they wound up in Ecuador in March 1940 after quite an eventful trip (described in detail in Chapter Two). After they left, Leika and Julko moved in with Móric and Elsa, in order to help them.

Móric's health progressively worsened and he died painfully on September 28, 1940, as described in the letters Hansi received afterwards. The home where he died was probably on Hurbanova Ulica (Hurbanova Street) in Žilina. Elsa, as a widow, later lived in Čeklís,[17] a small village near Bratislava.

Soon after my parents and Oli arrived in Ecuador, my father made inquires at the Ecuadorian Department of Immigration as to the process of securing visas for his extended family. The immigration process was set in motion in 1941, but the visas were not issued until December 1946.

In the midst of these prolonged efforts, in early March of 1942, Hansi learned from Teri that all his family members had fled from the Slovak secret police to Hungary. During the following two years, he had only sporadic correspondence with them. He was careful not to include in his letters any information about his efforts on their behalf which could fall "into the wrong hands." In March 1944, as the Nazis were about to overrun Hungary, all of them had to flee back to Czechoslovakia.

Leika and Julko left first and settled in Banská Bystrica. Elsa, as well as Klári and Sani with their son Shlomo, escaped later and lived in Čeklis. Teri and Géza remained in Lučenec, and she wrote to her brother about the unfolding events. Edit did not return to Czechoslovakia with the rest of the family. She stayed in Budapest until 1945.

And then, suddenly, there was no more correspondence from anyone in the family! From June 1944 and for approximately twelve agonizing months, his sisters' whereabouts were unknown to him. The ex-pat European community in Ecuador was aware of what the Jewish population was going through in the territories occupied by the German Army and having no news from his family made him think the worst. He was unaware that three of his sisters—Teri, Klári, Leika, and their mother Elsa—had been captured by the Nazis and sent to different concentration camps as described in Chapter Three.

It was only after the war ended in 1945 that my father learned from their first carefully worded letters, that they had survived their concentration camp imprisonment and were now safe. They obviously did not want him to know any of the unspeakable and painful ordeals each of them had to endure.

Their post war letters always ended with "Do not worry, dear Hansi." There is no evidence that Hansi ever knew of the June 1945 interview of Leika at Ravensbrück, and he had already died by the time she was interviewed for the Shoah Foundation in 1996.

In October 2008, while in Žilina, Oli had a lengthy conversation with Leika and heard for the first time, what Klári and Teri went through during their concentration camp internment. Oli shared with me what she learned. Oli was also told that after their camp liberation the sisters had decided not to share their travails with Hansi. They must have surmised he would not be able to cope with his inability to help them recover from their awful experiences.

By the time my father had achieved approval from the Ecuadorian government for his immigration efforts on behalf of the family, all who had survived were back in Czechoslovakia, and he was happy to share with them the news about their visas to Ecuador. Unfortunately, at the same time, his marriage to Sophie was falling apart. By 1948, the four sisters had written to Hansi that they had decided not to emigrate to Ecuador—a decision that arose out of their own varied circumstances, but that resulted in a more permanent state of separation.

And so, the lives of Móric Pikler's children went off in a multitude of directions. The details of their stories constitute the body of this narrative.

Chapter Two

Hansi

Hansi was born in Pâltinoasa-Bukovina, Romania[18] on Tuesday, March 18, 1902. He was a seven-month premature but healthy newborn. His father, Móric, was 31 years old and his mother, Olga, 29.

His growth and development were uneventful. He was a very active child, rarely ill and quite slender until his mid-twenties.

When Hansi was twenty months old, his sister, Wilma,[19] was born in Bukovina. It appears that she was not a healthy baby. Katalin Pikler recalls being told by Leika that she had "heart trouble." Olga, a very nurturing and loving mother, was greatly affected by Wilma's ill health.

Olga enjoyed playing the piano and had a beautiful singing voice. People used to stop on the sidewalk in front of their house to hear her. Her brother Arthur was a tenor who performed in several major cities in Europe. One of his aunts was also a well-known operatic soprano.

On August 11, 1905, when Hansi was three-and-a-half, his mother died at age 32. There is no information available as to the cause of Olga's death. Her obituary was published in the *Neue Freie Presse* No. 14717, a Vienna newspaper, on August 13, 1905.

In 2013, Yaffa Hajos, my cousin Ivan's wife in Israel, sent me a link to Geni, a genealogy site, with information pertaining to my grandmother. It showed Olga's burial at a town in Romania. I recall filing the information with plans to dig deeper into what I thought at the time was probably an error—if my grandparents lived in Rajec, Slovakia, why would she be buried in Romania?

Olga Pikler's obituary; Vienna, August 13, 1905

Five years later, I searched for the file about my grandparents while writing the Hansi narrative and found the link to the Geni site that Yaffa had sent me. It stated that she was buried at the Câmpolung Moldovenesc Jewish cemetery in Romania. There was no date of burial. I accessed the cemetery data and found her name and burial site number: 785.

Intrigued by this, I reached out to Traude Triebel, a genealogist with GenTeam (*Die genealogische Datenbank*) and asked her to help me find any information that would show any connection between my grandparents and Romania.

She found out that my grandfather, Móric Pikler (a timber dealer), had been in Czernowitz (currently in Ukraine) for business in 1903 and 1907, showing him listed in a local newspaper

(ANNO *Zeitungen Czernowitzer Tagblatt*) as a hotel guest on three occasions: twice in 1903 (one in Hotel Central and the other in Hotel Gottlieb) and on June 18, 1907 at Hotel Central. All of these entries listed him as coming from Kimpulung. Traude's assumption was that grandparents had been living in Kimpulung.

The above information led again to a detailed selection and review of Hansi's cache of documents and photographs looking for any clues that would provide further answers. Translation of several of them proved to be quite revealing: in the Jewish Community of Vienna registry of Móric and Olga's marriage (June 1, 1901) he is listed as living in Pâltinoasa, Bukovina, a town in Romania; a reference letter for Móric dated September 7, 1909 states that he had been employed in timber exploration in Bukovina and then moved to Rajec where he was an independent timber trader; several photographs, including one with his mother, Olga, and his sister, and three of Hansi as a three-year-old were taken in Kimpulung.

It made sense then that Olga was buried closer to home. With Móric and Olga living in Kimpulung after their wedding, I wondered if my father's birthplace, which had been considered all along to be Rajec, was indeed so. Again, translation of several documents revealed the most surprising finding: Hansi's birthplace was Pâltinoasa, Bukovina. The documents I had seen several years earlier have Rajec listed as well. The answer to this puzzle was provided by Mrs. Pártošova. She made me aware of the Domicile Law,[20] which conferred upon him his father's birth domicile—Rajec—and his citizenship—Czechoslovakia.

As far as Wilma was concerned, there had been lingering questions as to when and where she was born and why was she buried at the *Kozma utca* Jewish cemetery in Budapest as I had found out back in 2012. Katalin Pikler, living in Budapest, visited the cemetery at my request in February 2016 and found the place of her gravesite empty. Mr. Vandor's research in the fall of 2018 found her death record in Budapest's district VIII. It showed that Wilma had died at the Stefánia Children's hospital on September

12, 1905 (one day later than the Budapest cemetery recorded date), at the age of 22 months. Her cause of death was listed as "spasms" (perhaps this was meant to indicate epileptic seizures). The hospital reported her death on September 13. The record also indicated that she was born in "(Bukovina), Rajecz (Trencsen county)." It is most likely that the record also reflects the Domicile Law: she was born in Bukovina but her father in Rajec.

Móric lost both his young wife and baby daughter within one month. It is hard to imagine how he could have coped with such tragic events so close together and what kind of support he relied on at the time. He had Hansi, who was only three years old, to take care of. Hansi was too young to understand or mourn his baby sister's death but was old enough to miss his mother's care and affection. For several months, he appeared withdrawn. The family that primarily helped him and his father cope with their losses were Leopold and Regina, his paternal grandparents, as well as his paternal Aunt Marie and Uncle Armin.

It appears that Móric continued to work in Bukovina after Olga died and it also suggests that Hansi grew up in that area until 1909 when Móric moved back to Rajec. I wondered how Hansi's family in Rajec could have been able to console him after his mother died if he lived so far from them?

But in general, Hansi was a very happy child and made friends easily. He had several in his neighborhood and he was well-liked by them, sharing an interest in sports, mainly soccer. But he also enjoyed just being by himself, walking through the forests, climbing fences and trees. He was fascinated by nature, and what he loved most was being around the animals on the farm and the nearby forests. He would bring all sorts of animals to the house and would take care of them. His sister, Klári, later related to her own son, Giora, that "Hansi as a child used to bring home all sorts of wild creatures. He once brought a wolf pup. He raised him until he was too big to be at home and had to release the wolf to the wild."

Hansi was known to have a dry sense of humor just like his

father and grandfather. He also had a mischievous streak—which I inherited as well—and there are a few anecdotes about pranks he played on family and friends. On one occasion, he took a horse upstairs in his house.

In Rajec, he was always surrounded by his paternal family. His maternal family lived in Vienna, and to the best of my knowledge, he did not see them much. In 1906, Philip Fleischer, his maternal grandfather, died in Vienna.

He was seven years old when his paternal grandmother, Regina, died in Plevnik, about twenty miles from Rajec. Ten months later his paternal grandfather, Leopold, died as well. He was quite close to both of them, so—somewhat like his mother's death—this was a painful loss from which it took him a long while to recover. The family, particularly his aunt and uncle, once again helped him cope with his grief.

Hansi remembered Móric as a loving father who was always quite attentive to his son's needs. They shared similar interests: the love of nature and animals. Móric was a strict disciplinarian, just as his father and grandfather had been. From their parents, both Hansi and his sisters learned at an early age the importance of a close family relationship: to love, respect, and support not only each other and their immediate family members but the family at large. They were expected to volunteer and help with the daily chores. Telling the truth was also very important. Punishment for a transgression was always milder if they would tell the truth and acknowledge their mistakes.

Hansi attended grade school and then the *Gymnasium,*[21] receiving the *matura* diploma of graduation at age seventeen.[22] He was a fairly good student: math, drawing, and geometry were his favorite subjects and, as noted in his school report cards (which are in my possession), he excelled in them. In a report card dated May 22, 1915 his singing was graded as "outstanding."

The summer of 1914 was not supposed to be any different from previous summer vacations. But just before Hansi finished his

**Olga Pikler, Wilma, and Hansi;
Kimpulung, Romania**

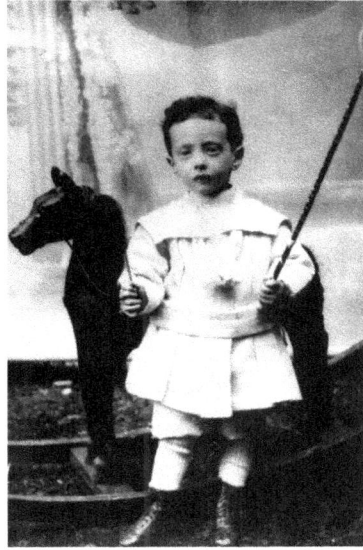

Hansi; Kimpulung, Romania 1905

Hansi; Kimpulung, 1905

Hansi, 3 years old; Kimpulung

last year in grade school, World War I—"The Great War"—began on July 28, 1914. The war came one month after the assassination of Germany's Archduke Franz Ferdinand (the presumptive heir to the Habsburg throne held by his ailing elderly uncle, the Emperor Franz Joseph), in Sarajevo, capital of one of the outlying provinces of the Austro-Hungarian Empire.[23]

Hansi was 12 years old when World War I began, but only reported vague memories of the time. There are no documents or other information to determine what impact the war had on his family.

The Habsburg economy was subject to an almost uninterrupted contraction throughout the war. One of the most noticeable and critical features throughout the Austria-Hungary empire was the rapid fall in foodstuffs supplied to both its civilian population and, sometime later, also to its armed forces. The output of the agricultural sector shrank dramatically as labor, seeds, fertilizers, and transportation were lacking, leading to widespread and progressively serious food shortages. In Vienna, the first food riot broke out as early as spring 1915, and more followed there and in other urban centers over the next years. [29] In Rajec and other small towns in today's Slovakia, the local agriculture sustained, at least for the first couple of years, the demands of the local population.

The disintegration of the railway system was the Achilles' heel of the Habsburg war effort and had a direct impact throughout the Empire's economy. After mid- to late 1916, the carrying capacity of the transportation system declined sharply. By the end of 1917, the railways could only meet half of the demands made upon them. The ability to repair railway cars and engines was reduced as both spare parts and trained personnel were lacking. [29] This must have had a direct impact on the delivery of timber to Móric's customers and it must have affected his bottom line in the last two years of the war. Hansi, his parents, and three sisters—Klári, Teri, and Leika—had been living in Rajec. Sometime between 1916 and 1917, the family moved from Rajec to Ružomberok, a larger town where Edit was born on November 9, 1917. Móric's reason for the move most likely had to do with Ružomberok's wider railroad transportation capabilities.

After receiving his *matura*, Hansi worked with his father in the timber trade for about five years. In order to further help the family—and given his knowledge of forestry and the timber business—he decided to move to western Romania to work for a sawmill company called the *Carpatina Societate Anonimá Romaneasca petru Industria Forestiera* from 11/1/1923 to 12/15/1930.[24] He forwarded most of his monthly income to his parents and would frequently travel back home, a 533-mile trip, to visit them.

He easily made friends both at work and in the community where he lived. He also had a busy social life and was frequently seen in the company of beautiful young ladies. He participated in many of the activities available at the sawmill and was a member of its soccer team. He taught himself to play the violin. He often played at home in Žilina and, many years later, in Ecuador, when Oli and I had the pleasure of listening to him play traditional Hungarian music (czárdás) and Viennese waltzes.

He wrote to me once that he would love for one of his grandchildren to play the instrument—and in late 2017, I had his 87-year old violin, an Amati imitation, restored in Baltimore and began to take lessons. I felt sure my father would be thrilled to watch me play.

The family moved to Žilina in 1928 or 1929, after Móric and Elsa lost their home in Ružomberok. By then, their financial situation had become quite precarious. According to what Hansi later told me, Móric lost all his savings in the economic crisis which culminated with the stock market crash of October 1929 and led to the Great Depression in the United States, Europe, and the rest of the world. Hansi decided then to move to Žilina, to be close to his parents and sisters. He enrolled in a business school, completing his studies in mid-1933. Earlier that year, Hitler was appointed

Chancellor of the Reich,[25] and the events in Germany that followed his election raised significant concerns at home.[26]

Hansi (fifth from left) with company's soccer team; Brezoi, Romania

In late 1931, he began working for *Československá Zbrojovka Brno* or ZB, a manufacturing company for weapons, precision machines, automobiles, typewriters, and ball bearings based in Brno, Czechoslovakia (130 miles southwest of Žilina).[27] In the late twenties, ZB had become one of the largest and most respected rifle and machine gun manufacturers in the world. Hansi was initially assigned to the automobile division but subsequently joined the division of precision machines, and his responsibilities grew with time. He was appointed ZB's sales representative for the southern region of Czechoslovakia and was provided with a chauffeured car for his daily commute from Žilina; his business travels which would take him as far as Vienna. During one of these trips, his car wound up in a ditch after the chauffeur swerved to avoid a collision with an incoming vehicle. Fortunately, neither Hansi nor his driver was hurt. The car was totaled.

AUTOMATISCHE WAGEN SCHINKENAUFSCHNEIDEMASCHINEN DER ČSL. WAFFENWERKE, BRUNN
GENERALVERTRETUNG FÜR DIE SLOVAKEI UND PODKARP. RUS

HANS ERNEST PIKLER ŽILINA
Legionářská 5
Bankkonto: Legiobank, Žilina.
TELEFON 457

Hansi's ZB business card

Hansi at ZB headquarters

31

In 1935, during a trip to Vienna, he was introduced to a beautiful and well- educated Viennese young lady, Sophie Pauker, who was sixteen years his junior.

Sophie was born in Vienna on March 26, 1918. Her parents, who owned a fabrics store, spared no means to provide her with the best education she could receive in Vienna at the time. She excelled in her studies, which included literature, art, and music, in addition to the required curriculum. She had private piano lessons and enjoyed playing music by Chopin, Liszt, and Beethoven.

Sophie; Vienna (date unknown)

She grew up in a strict home where Ruchel, her mother, ruled the roost. While her brother, Max, had few, if any restrictions, she had a fairly sheltered life. She frequently asked her father, Arnold, to intercede for her, often to no avail. She was very well-liked by her peers and many friends who would be allowed to visit her at home. Sophie would often help her parents at their fabrics store and became very knowledgeable about the finest fabrics available. She dreamed of someday making her own clothes. Many years later, when she lived in Miami, she made most of her own dresses, reproducing some she would see in exclusive catalogs. She also made clothes for her daughter, Oli, and later on for her granddaughter, Vivian.

Hansi, the former Don Juan, fell in love with Sophie, whom he saw as a refined, sophisticated, and well-rounded young lady. She, in turn, must have been swept off her feet by this debonair and charming man. The trip log for the ZB sales representative showed a significant rise in trips to Vienna. In the Spring of 1936, Hansi asked Sophie's parents for her hand. A fall wedding was planned.

Hansi and Sophie's wedding; Vienna, October 11, 1936

On October 11, 1936, Hansi at age 34, and Sophie Pauker, 18 years old, were married in Vienna, Austria, at Temple Brigittenauer. Among the witnesses were both his and her parents. Sophie's first cousin, Clara Pauker, was also a guest at their wedding. In a 2014 phone interview, Clara, who was living in Lima, Perú at the time, described the wedding to me as a "most elegant, happy, and lovely occasion."

באחד בשבת חמשה ועשרים יום

שנת המשת אלפים
לחדש תשרי

ושש מאות ותשעים ושבע

לבריאת עולם למנין שאנו מנין כאן עיר וינא.

איך הבחור ירנסט בה משה

הוי לי לאנתו כדת משה

אמר להדא בתולתא סאסיע בת אהרן

וישראל ואנא אפלח ואוקיר ואיזון ואפרנס יתיכי כהלכות גוברין יהודאין דפלחין ומוקרין

וזנין ומפרנסין לנשיהון בקושטא ויהיבנא ליכי מהר בתוליכי כסף זוזי מאתן דחזי ליכי

מדאוריתא ומזוניכי וכסותיכי וסיפוקיכי ומיעל לותיכי כאורח כל ארעא וצביאת מרת
סאסיע

בתולתא דא והות ליה לאנתו ודן נדוניא דהנעלת ליה מבי אבוה

בין

בכסף בין בזהב בין בתכשיטין במאני דלבושא בשימושי דירה ובשימושי דערסא מאה

זקוקים כסף צרוף וצבי הבחור ערנסט

חתן דנן

והוסיף לה מן דיליה עוד מאה זקוקים כסף צרוף אחרים כנגדן סך הכל מאתים זקוקים

כסף צרוף וכך אמר הבחור ערנסט

חתן דנן

אחריות שטר כתובתא דא נדוניא דן ותוספתא דא קבלית עלי ועל ירתי בתראי להתפרע

מכל שפר ארג נכסין וקנינין דאית לי תחות כל שמיא דקנאי ודעתיד אנא למקנא

נכסין דאית להון אחריות ודלית להון אחריות כלהון יהון אחראין וערבאין לפרוע מנהון

שטר כתובתא דא נדוניא דן ותוספתא דא מנאי ואפילו מז גלימא דעל כתפאי בחיי

ובמותי מן יומא דנן ולעלם ואחריות והומר שטר כתובתא דא נדוניא דן ותוספתא דא

קבל עליו הבחור ערנסט

חתן דנן באחריות והומר כל

שטרי כתובות ותוספתות דנהגין בבנת ישראל העשויין כתקון חז"ל כאסמכתא ודלא

כטופסי דשטרי וקנינא מן הבחור ערנסט

חתן דנן בן ל משה

למרת סאסיע

בת ל אהרן

בתולתא דא על כל מה דכתוב ומפורש

לעיל במנא דכשר למקניא ביה הכל שריר וקים.

עד

עד

Hansi and Sophie's *ketubah* (Jewish marriage contract)

The newlyweds moved into a nice Žilina apartment, and their home was a very happy one. They enjoyed listening to classical music, dancing (both loved Viennese waltzes) and meeting other young couples for card games, picnics, and theater. Hansi's family fully embraced Sophie and they would see each other frequently. They made her feel welcome, aware that this was her first time living away from her parents and that she was far from home. On September 29, 1937, their daughter, Olga, was born in Žilina.

Hansi and Sophie with friends in Žilina, Slovakia

She was named for Hansi's biological mother but was often called Oli. Her parents were ecstatic, and Sophie was especially happy that her first child was a girl, as this was what she had wished for during her uneventful pregnancy. . She was a nurturing and caring young mother.

In Žilina, the Pikler family welcomed Oli's birth. Móric and Elsa were particularly thrilled with their first grandchild. She got a lot of attention from them as well as the rest of the family, as they were close-knit and always ready and eager to help each other. They would get together almost every weekend for lively conversations, which invariably included the worrisome political events of the times as well as the struggles of their daily lives. They enjoyed picnics in the forests, listening to music, and trekking the Tatra mountains. Many years later, Hansi would reminisce about these as the "good old days."

Sophie with Oli in Žilina, circa 1938

Hansi recognized years later that his marriage had changed his life completely. He was deeply in love with Sophie and made every effort to make her happy. But he also recounted that the responsibilities of becoming a parent, first with Oli in 1937 and again five years later when I was born, brought him a great deal of anxiety (which clearly intensified again after Edulka was born in 1960). He acknowledged that his nervousness caused him to become quite over-protective.

In 1938, Móric, at age 67, exhibited symptoms of an enlarged prostate and consulted a urologist in Budapest. Hansi would go with him to every appointment and related to me how much his father suffered from this problem. Later, the obstructive symptoms required the insertion of a suprapubic catheter. This was not only bothersome but also quite painful. We do not know if surgery was recommended or not. I suspect (since I am an oncologist) that he had prostate cancer, which most likely contributed to his demise three years later.

When the Nazis came to power in 1933, more than nine million Jews lived in the twenty-one European nations that Germany would come to dominate, either through occupation or alliance. According to the 1930 Census, 356,830 Jews lived in Czechoslovakia at that time, and about 135,000 Jews lived in Slovakia. Within five years, two-thirds of the 9 million were dead [30]. After the Holocaust, it was found that only one out of every four Czechoslovakian Jews had survived.

On March 12, 1938, Hitler's armed forces, without firing a shot, annexed Austria into Nazi Germany, an event known as the *Anschluss,* with full military and political control of the country. Austria ceased to be an independent state.[28] More than 185,000 Jews, including Sophie's parents, Arnold Pauker and Ruchel Schlagid Feferkorn, lived in Vienna at the time.

On that day, in Vienna, the German troops found the streets lined with cheering crowds of jubilant Austrians who greeted them with the Nazi salute, handed them flags decorated with the swastika, showered them with confetti, and threw flowers at their feet.

Sophie's parents owned the *Tuch Haus Brigita,* a fabric store, on the Taborstrasse in Vienna's Second District near the large Schiffmann discount department store, which was plundered for days by storm-troopers with no hindrance by the police. Their store was smeared with anti-Semitic defamations but miraculously was not looted. Business dropped and they felt threatened. Their lives changed radically. The building where they lived was located a few blocks away from their store, and from the windows of their sixth floor corner apartment, they could clearly see along the main avenue groups of looters running up and down carrying items they had "confiscated" after they broke into Jewish apartments and businesses in the course of so-called "wild Aryanizations."

What had the most impact on their daily life, however, were the street attacks on Jews of all ages who were publicly mocked, humiliated, and forced to perform degrading acts. They told Sophie that Grete, the senior sales lady at their store, as well as several of their closest friends (some of whom lived in the same or adjacent buildings) were victims of these attacks. Jewish women, men, and even children were forced to go down on hands and knees and scrub the anti-*Anschluss* political slogans off the cobblestone streets and sidewalks with sharp lye, water, and soap; some were given brushes, others used their bare hands, while uniformed Nazis sneered and non-Jewish citizens jeered and laughed as they watched the humiliating scene. These were called *Reibpartien* or *Reibaktionen* ("scrub parties"), which went on for several days throughout the city. For three days, the Paukers did not leave their apartment, and tried not to be seen, afraid of being dragged and forced into these humiliating acts.

According to historian Leo Spitzer, [31] "For more entertainment, the tormentors often substituted toothbrushes for cleaning brushes. When the "scrub parties" were no longer "necessary" with all traces of painted propaganda brushed away and gone, Jewish men and women of all social ranks and ages, as well as young girls and boys, continued to be rounded up and pressed into degrading labor: forced to wash cars, clean streets, sweep parks and public spaces, and, after the arrival of the SS regiments, to clean and wash barrack latrines as well."

In the aftermath of the Anschluss, the Nazis quickly applied German anti-Jewish legislation with two clear goals in mind: to strip Jews of their citizenship rights and exclude them from the economic, cultural and social life of the former Austria, and to "force Jews by physical and psychological intimidation, to emigrate out of German lands." [31] Months later, in the wake of Kristallnacht, the

Nazis increased the pressure on Jews to leave.

In Austria, Jews lived under constant threat. Many of Vienna's Jews panicked and committed suicide, others left unprepared during pogroms. In Vienna and throughout the country, large-scale raids carried out by the Austrian police led to the arrests of thousands of Jews. Many were later released but those who were not, numbering 1,800 in May/June 1938, were sent by the SS to Dachau near Munich, the first German concentration camp.

These and other events must have scared Sophie's parents and brother enough to seriously consider emigrating and to begin planning for it. The Paukers must have communicated their situation, fears, and concerns to Hansi and Sophie living in Žilina, Slovakia, and it is quite likely that they also began to envision life elsewhere, away from the threat of Nazism.

The March 1938 developments in Austria were followed by the infamous Munich Agreement of September 29-30, 1938;[29] the German annexation of Czechoslovakia's northern and western border regions (Sudetenland) on October 1, 1938;[30] the law invalidating all German passports held by Jews, passed on October 5, 1938;[31] and in Žilina, Slovakia, their hometown, the creation of an autonomous Slovak government by the right-wing People's Party, led by Monsignor Jozef Tiso. These tumultuous and fateful events convinced the family that there was no other alternative but to leave and start a new life elsewhere.[32] [33]

The political situation in the Czechoslovak Republic as far as the Jews were concerned had progressively deteriorated since Hitler was appointed Chancellor of the Reich on January 30, 1933. The attitude of local authorities toward the Jewish population varied. It was harshest in Slovakia where the political upheaval was accompanied by excesses of rhetoric that culminated in physical violence [26]. The influx of refugees fleeing the Sudetenland, including many German-speaking Jews created significant problems in that already-stricken land (about 17,000 Jews from the Sudetenland moved into the interior of Czechoslovakia) [32].

Most refugees found shelter in urban areas, but some landed in smaller, rural places creating shortages of food and housing that resulted in the growth of virulent anti-Semitism fueled by Nazi propaganda. [26,32]

Milena Jesenská,[33] a noted writer and one of the most prestigious Czech political journalists of the interwar period, traveled to the Sudetenland border and wrote a moving report titled, "Beyond Our Strength," published on October 12, 1938 in the respected liberal weekly Prague newspaper, *Prítomnost* [34]. It dealt with the political and human implications of the annexation of the Sudetenland. The Pikler family were familiar with her articles, and this one generated a great deal of discussion among them. Their plans to emigrate accelerated afterwards.

Meanwhile, my parents applied for passports in mid-1938. My mother, as an Austrian citizen, applied to Vienna, while my father and sister Oli, Czechoslovak citizens, applied to Prague. The German law regarding travel documents caused a great deal of uncertainty and fear that it might soon apply to non-German Jews as well.

Hansi's travels from Žilina to Brno, as well as his other business trips, took on a different dimension after the annexation of the Sudetenland. The presence of Czech guards along the main roads and crossing borders was unsettling, but his company, ZB, provided him with the necessary documents proving he was their sales representative to the southern territory of Czechoslovakia.

On November 2, 1938, the First Vienna Arbitration Award, a direct consequence of the Munich Agreement, allocated parts of Slovakia and the Carpathian territory to Hungary [25] and guaranteed the rest of Slovakia autonomy within a federal state of Czechs, Slovaks, and Ruthenes, named Czecho-Slovakia (the hyphen was only removed later).[34]

On November 7, 1938 Ernst vom Rath, an official at the German Embassy in Paris, was assassinated by Herschel Grynszpan, a seventeen-year-old Polish-Jewish refugee born in Germany, whose parents had been deported from Germany to the frontier of Poland a month earlier.[35] This incident triggered, between November 9 and 10, nationwide pogroms organized by the Nazi party in both Germany and Austria, the infamous Kristallnacht. Anti-Jewish demonstrations also took place in Slovakia.[36] [19]

In Slovakia, hostility was generated by the fact that before World War I, Jews had been associated with Hungarian rule. The Slovak Catholic Church tended to favor politicians with nationalist and anti-Semitic programs. Jews were accused of pro-Magyarism and of Bolshevik convictions. The priest Andrej Hlinka (1864–1938) established the main anti-Semitic party, *Slovenska Ludova Strana* (Slovak People's Party), in 1925. Xenophobic nationalism with a strong Catholic component, also espoused by Hlinka's successor, the theologian Jozef Tiso, became a dominant feature of the party. The fascist militia set up by this party in 1938, the Hlinka Guard (*Hlinková Garda*), actively participated in the deportation of Jews to Nazi killing centers. [33, 35]

In Czechoslovakia, 1939 began with an atmosphere of apprehension and confusion among the Jewish population [26]. Hitler had warned Prague that it must withdraw from the League of Nations, reorient its foreign policy toward Berlin, promulgate anti-Jewish laws, and reduce its armed forces [25]. On January 27, 1939, a new decree dismissed all Jews from the civil service. On March 14, 1939, Hitler violated the Munich agreement, and a Slovak parliament officially proclaimed the "independent State of Slovakia," a Nazi puppet and a one-party state. Monsignor Jozef Tiso, an extremely nationalistic, authoritarian leader, and his deputy, Professor Vojtech Tuka, were in power [33]. Following their benefactors' example, they proceeded by means of legislation, propaganda, and terror [conducted by the Hlinka Guard] to assault Jews and lay to waste synagogues and Jewish cemeteries. [36]

German forces occupied Bohemia and Moravia (today's Czech Republic) on March 15, 1939 when Hitler signed a decree incorporating the "Czech Historic Lands" into the "Reich

Protectorate of Bohemia and Moravia." The Hungarian army invaded the remainder of Sub-Carpathian Ruthenia (a sliver of territory in eastern Slovakia) [25], and it is estimated that another 117,000 Jews became victims of Hitlerism during this campaign.

In the interval between September 1938 and the German occupation of Bohemia and Moravia, there was a considerable amount of emigration. Many Jews left for the United States, South America, and other countries, where they had relatives and others to receive them. [37] Within the year following the Munich Agreement and the outbreak of World War II, a total of 35,000 Jews left the Protectorate. But at the time the first shots of the war were fired, more than 90,000 were still in Czechoslovakia. [32, 36, 37]

The very first months of Slovakia's independence saw the implementation of more restrictive measures against the Jews, especially in the economic field: they were expelled from the free professions[37] [38]; their land was confiscated and turned over to Aryan trustees [37,38]; and anti-Semitic discrimination was enacted in the education sector.[38] [38] Hitler and Stalin signed a non-aggression pact on August 23, 1939[39] and World War II began nine days later.[40]

By then, Sophie's parents and brother as well as Hansi, Sophie, and Oli had left Austria and Slovakia, respectively.

The European emigration odyssey had begun in 1933, and between then and 1945, approximately 500,000 Europeans were able to escape the areas of German influence. [39] More than half were Jews. After the Nuremberg Laws[41] were introduced on September 15, 1935, emigration rates increased as departure was considered by many to be "the only salvation." [32]

At a world level, Jews emigrated to 80 countries during that time. After 1937, approximately 130,000 German Jews were admitted to the United States, 75,000 were admitted by Great Britain, 55,000 arrived in Palestine, 13,000 found refuge in Shanghai, and some went to Russia and its satellites. It is estimated that over that ten-year period during the Holocaust era, 100,000 Jews managed to immigrate to Latin America. [39, 40, 41] Hansi, Sophie, and Oli were among them. I was not yet born.

In the first few years, Relief Committees[42] in Germany, Austria and Czechoslovakia had to support the refugees, find lodgings for them, arrange for medical care, clothe them, and help them emigrate to other countries. There were also special projects organized for the children of the refugees. Later on, they also provided financial support which helped some refugees to emigrate to overseas countries, or at least to reach some other temporary asylum. After Hitler's occupation of Austria on March 12, 1938, the Relief Committees in Prague began an intensive search for overseas countries which would accept refugees. Not only the refugees from Germany and Austria, but also many Czechoslovak Jews frantically applied for visas to distant lands. The Democratic Refugee Committee helped a number of them to secure visas to Bolivia. [37] Hansi, Sophie, and Oli were in this group. After the crisis of September 1938, feverish attempts were made to send the refugees to France, England, and Scandinavian countries, while at the same time migration was accelerated for those who possessed visas to overseas countries such as the United States, Canada, South America, and Australia. A Paris-based cluster of three Jewish immigrant aid groups that went by the acronym of "HICEM" (short for the Hebrew Immigrant Aid Society or HIAS, based in New York; the French Jewish Colonization Association; and Berlin's Emigdirect), attempted to send the refugees to Palestine [37].

All these tasks necessitated the raising of substantial funds.[43] Many German Jews, who after 1919 had enjoyed equal status as citizens of the Reich, applied for visas to emigrate. Unfortunately for them, the world had not recovered from the economic crisis which began in 1929, and many European countries exercised a closed-door policy in immigration. Other countries, like the United States, were very slow in granting visas, afraid of prospective immigrants becoming a burden upon the state [32]. In addition, most

European Jews did not have the occupational skills these overseas nations needed—unskilled labor, skilled factory workers, artisans, and farmers. Most were merchants, clerks, traveling salesmen, and commercial employees. The outlook for professional people (lawyers, doctors, dentists) was similarly bleak. German Jewish lawyers had very little chance of exercising their profession abroad, and the medical profession was overcrowded and governed by strict laws and regulations almost everywhere. Other professionals, like chemists, engineers, technicians, and highly skilled workers fared better. [32]

The Relief Committees were quick to realize that it would be necessary to provide Jews with the skills to make them "exportable" (marketable). Prospective Jewish emigrants had to consider whether it was worthwhile to prepare professionally for their stay abroad. The Jewish aid organizations advised it and offered training courses for artisans and farmers so that the emigrants had an alternative profession or knowledge to create a new existence abroad. Those who had practiced a commercial or academic profession or were attending school, could learn a practical trade such as carpentry, shoemaking, locksmithing, mechanics, agriculture, etc. Women, who did not usually work outside their homes, attended intensive courses to acquire basic sewing and beautician skills. It seems, however, that only a minority of them attended these preparatory measures. There was little time left and people had other concerns. On the other hand, there were emigrants who did attend an agricultural school with a view to an exodus to a specific country, for example Argentina, where the Jewish Colonization Association [42] was created by Baron Moritz Hirsh. By failing to obtain the promised visas, they had no other alternative than Ecuador. [39]

The questions they had to consider at that point were common to thousands of other Jews: how and where to go? Because European countries, the main targets for legal emigration between 1933 and 1935, tightened admission and employment requirements for prospective immigrants, they had to consider other potential emigration sites, such as North and South America, South Africa, Australia, and Palestine. Some of these potential sites had, by 1938-1939, began to exclude new immigrants altogether [39, 42, 43], as their situations were more difficult now than that which had confronted the early refugees from Germany. In spite of desperate efforts by the Austrian Jews to overcome immigration difficulties by means of vocational training (in fields such as clothing and metal industries, agriculture, and even domestic service) nearly all countries continued to refuse their admission. Many Austrian Jews had to flee or were illegally dumped by the authorities over the frontiers into adjacent countries, where they lived in constant danger of deportation [44].

In spite of the Nazis' early attempts to force the Jews to emigrate, the emigration process they forced them to undergo was purposely cumbersome, protracted, and often ignominious. Everyone wishing to emigrate had to obtain two types of visas: an exit visa issued by the Germans, and a valid entry visa issued by the consulate of the country of destination. The latter, a passport with the key stamp and official signature, was an absolute requirement to obtain the former. For many potential refugees, this was an insurmountable obstacle as so many countries restricted their admission and issuance of passports to them. [45] Many refugees applied for visas to more than one country at the same time; the visas they did not need, unfortunately, could not be used for some other prospective immigrant. [37]

Beginning in the hot summer days of 1938, my mother's parents and brother, the Paukers, along with hundreds of other Jews wishing to emigrate, stood in long lines, night and day, by the entrance of the Police Commissariat in the Margarethen section of Vienna. When they finally got in, they were provided with a list of exit requirements, documents they had to turn in before they would be considered for an exit visa. They spent months seeking, from several entities, the required certificates: proof that they owed no rent or other fees, tax-clearance certificates that they owed no local, government, utility or sales taxes, proof that they had no previous or current criminal convictions, good conduct certificates from their employers, an affidavit testifying to their "non-objectionable character," a certificate of registration of all of their immovable and most of their movable property, and the payment of two arbitrary special taxes: the "Jewish capital levy" or *Judenvermögensabgabe* and the "Reich flight tax" or *Reichsfluchtsteuer* whose initial intended purpose was to stem capital flight from the Weimar Republic and later on to seize the assets for Jews "fleeing the Reich." [31, 39] Once they had completed this lengthy process, with all these documents in hand, they had to wait in line again outside the Police Commissariat. After this exhausting and humiliating process, my grandparents' ordeal was finally over in late spring 1939. By then they had already lost their store. They had secured entry visas to Ecuador, where they eventually would reunite with Sophie and her family. Their full itinerary in the interim is unknown. From Géza's postcard of January 9, 1940, we learned they were in Budapest for one-and-a-half weeks, but it is not clear in what month.

Nearly half of Austria's entire Jewish population had emigrated by mid-May 1939, leaving only approximately 121,000 Jews in Austria (all but 8,000 in Vienna). Another 28,000 Jews, including the Paukers, were able to leave Austria, between May 1939 and the middle of 1942.

Czechoslovakian Jews had to flee German domination on two separate occasions during this time before the war. The first flight occurred after the occupation of the Sudeten area in October 1938. Thousands of Jews fled, chiefly to the remaining territory of the Republic, others crossed into Poland and were subsequently removed, at the insistence of the Polish Government, to England, Norway and Sweden.

The second wave of immigration followed the occupation and dismemberment of the Republic in March 1939, when the Gestapo took steps to hasten emigration from the Protectorate of Bohemia and Moravia [44]. Approximately 8,000 Czechoslovak Jews were able to emigrate between March 1939 and December 15, 1940 [37], including my parents and sister. To further facilitate the visa application, Jews were advised to obtain Baptism documentation from the Catholic Church. And many did, including the Piklers.

In the puppet state of Slovakia, an anti-Jewish policy was pursued along the same lines as in Germany. 50,000 Jews left Slovakia in the period from October 1938 to July 1939. At the same time the Slovak Government announced that the rest of the Jews would have to leave the country within three years [35, 44]. The Czech people, however, did not support anti-Semitism, even after it had become the official policy.

Slovakian Jews wishing to emigrate (in the late 1930s) were not subjected to the overwhelming bureaucratic procedures to obtain exit visas those in neighboring Austria and Germany had to endure. It is estimated that between September 1938 and May 1939, a total of 7,100 Jews went to Great Britain, either directly from Czechoslovakia or via Poland. A few hundred fugitives left for France or to various Northern European countries, and a considerable number emigrated to the United States, South America, and various Central American countries [37].

A special Czechoslovak refugee agency was established in Prague to help all refugees (regardless of religious creed, political views, or race) who had to emigrate further. A representative of the League of Nations was appointed in Prague with the consent of the Czechoslovak Government. The program adopted by the relief agencies provided for emergency aid to refugees while helping them to emigrate to other countries. Camps were built for Jewish refugees, and local Jewish organizations were granted considerable subsidies for the relief of the destitute among them [35, 44].

Generally speaking, the Jews, whose passports were emblazoned with the letter J, had a difficult time finding refuge in overseas countries. Pressed as they were to escape Germany and other European countries quickly, they became easy prey to all kinds of deceit. A lively black market existed for visas to any corner of the earth. Many consuls or self-appointed consuls, especially from South American countries, considered the granting of visas as a personal source of income, they demanded bribes, and were not above lining their pockets by selling worthless entry visas which they knew their government would disavow [39, 46, 47]. Many of the people who arrived at the shores of those countries were not permitted to enter and were then stripped of all means [36].

The Hamburg-America Line was more than willing to take these refugees. It would charge them everything they possessed for the passage—a round trip passage no less, so that if nobody would receive them, they could be dumped back into Germany at their own expense. This, of course, would mean a concentration camp and death, for although at the time Jews were allowed to leave Germany if they could find a place to go, they were not allowed to return without meeting the worst fate [46]. No Jews could procure transit visas unless they were obviously on their way to a country that had already accepted them.

Entry permits to most Latin American countries stipulated that the Jewish immigrants (*refugiados*) settle in rural areas and engage in agriculture (*agricultores*), industry, artisans' work, or related occupations. The entry visas had to include the "reason for the immigration." (This was the case for Ecuador until the end of the thirties. Later, it was enough for them to state they were planning to establish a residence in Ecuador, indicating a less strict immigration policy.) Other requirements included a work contract or proof they would not become a public burden, and they had to own a sum equal to $400.00 (an "Affidavit" to be deposited in the Central Bank of Ecuador, for example, with a certified receipt issued) which they would have to invest in an industrial project, with the sum returned to them upon arrival in the country [31, 48].

The authorities in these countries soon realized that most of the immigrants had no background knowledge of farming and little experience of rural life (other than as hikers or holiday sojourners)

[32, 49]. Rather, they were actually merchants, industrialists, and businessmen. My father's visa application lists his occupation as "mechanic."

During the calamitous eighteen months from the *Anschluss* of March 1938 to September 1939, the Gestapo offices in Berlin, Vienna, and Prague (where Adolph Eichmann was in charge) controlled emigration with an iron hand: Gestapo agents told Jews when and where to leave for abroad. Upon instructions from the Gestapo, German shipping agents offered false or invalid visas to the stricken Jews; [32] there were mass deportations to "no-man's lands" on the German borders, and other refugees were "dumped" overseas as a result of dishonest conniving among German officials, agents of steamship companies, and some consular official of foreign powers in Germany. The chief promoters of illegal immigration were Gestapo officials, who issued return passports to Jewish refugees even though it was against the law. The Gestapo, as stated before, forced Jews to embark on boats for the Western Hemisphere, though it was obvious that they would not be allowed to land. German shipping agencies abetted the scheme by procuring invalid or illegal visas from various consular officials. When the boats arrived in the New World, they were unable to land their passengers. Then they sailed for other ports, where the experience was repeated, and eventually, the unfortunates were returned to German harbors (e.g., *S.S. Caribia*; *S.S. St. Louis*; *S.S. Koenigstein*). [32]

Thousands of German and Austrian Jews had to pay bribes to leave for Latin America. Swindlers preyed constantly on them and arranged for clandestine departures. In May 1939, 3,000 individuals were reported to have entered Bolivia with illegal documents, while many others, still in Europe, were said to possess similarly fraudulent papers. Permits were sold for the price of $200 to $1,500 each. This prompted the Bolivian foreign minister to dismiss two of his country consuls in Europe. Similar abuses occurred in other consulates, and other officials were ousted;

but at the same time the visas they signed were declared invalid. The Bolivian government, to put an end to this dishonest traffic, requested that HICEM undertake to verify every visa granted on the basis of a permit from the Bolivian government in La Paz, and to affix its seal on subsequent valid permits. Without it, no Bolivian visa was considered valid even if signed by a Bolivian consul. Furthermore, HICEM was asked to limit the number of visas to 400 a month. [32]

My parents, as well as other couples from Žilina, made contacts with the Democratic Relief Committee in Prague. Bartolomeo Stein, a Žilina banker and a close friend of theirs, had relatives in Bolivia, and it appears he was the one who suggested they all go to Cochabamba, Bolivia, a cause they took up with the assistance of the Committee. They felt they should make every effort to secure visas for Bolivia, since by 1938, Bolivia had become one of the few remaining countries in the entire world to accept Jewish refugees, after traditional destinations for European immigration—Argentina, Brazil, Chile, and Mexico—closed their gates or applied severe restrictions to the entrance of newcomers. [31, 49]

In order to obtain these exit visas, potential Czechoslovak emigrants were advised to fulfill all the necessary exit requirements, which were not as stringent as Austria's. In fact, in the beginning, emigration was still encouraged, with Jews who owned no property finding it least difficult to leave the country. After paying taxes (the *Reichsfluchtsteuer* and the "Jewish" tax) the emigrant also had to pay the full value of the household effects he was permitted to take with him. He also had to hand over his apartment and was compelled to give the power of attorney to a bank with regard to the rest of his property, so that he left the country stripped of all his possessions, with the exception of baggage weighing a few kilograms. [37] (My parents were able to take out several trunks of personal belongings, though half of these were confiscated while they were interned in the detention camps in Marseilles, France.)

On November 4, 1938, they traveled 257.5 miles from Žilina

through recently-German-occupied Sudetenland to Prague, which had become a transit center for Jewish refugees awaiting immigration visas for overseas countries. [26] At the Bolivian Consulate, with their exit requirements fully completed, they were issued, on the same day, visas for Bolivia (Cochabamba), though I was never able to find my mother's.

Hansi's visa for Bolivia

51

Hansi's transit visa for Chile

The voyage to Bolivia, a small South American country with no maritime port access, required that refugees disembark at a port in Valparaiso, Chile and travel first by land and then by train to Bolivia. They needed a visa from Chile in order to make this connection.

Hansi and Sophie returned to Prague on March 19, 1939 to obtain transit visas from the Chilean Consulate that would allow

CONSULADO GENERAL DE CHILE EN CHECO-SLOVAKIA, PRAGA

Cédula Consular Visación N.° 401   Fecha 19/III/39

Nombre y apellido paterno y materno Zofia Pikler nac. Pauker

Hijo de Arnold Pauker y de Rosa Pauker nac. Kar er Profesión comerciante

Lugar y fecha de nacimiento Wien.26.III.1918   Nacionalidad checa

Origen   Estado Civil casada   Nombre del Cónyuge Hans Ernst

Nombre y edad de los hijos.

Gertrude Olga,1 1/2 años

Último domicilio Zilina Dlabáčová 4

Religión catolica   Lee y escribe si

Statura 170 cm.   Color cutis blanco

Color cabello castania

Señas particulares.

Impresión digito pulgar derecha

Nombre y domicilio de dos personas: 1.° que acrediten sus antecedentes ante el Consulado.
Eugen Ivanti ,Praha XIII,Ruská 878,Leopold Hexner,Zilina

2.° de su conocimiento en Chile.

Fecha de salida incerta   Lugar de salida La Rochelle   Vapor, Ferrocarril, Avión

Objeto del viaje trnsito a Boliviaa) Viaje en tránsito a Bolivia con estada

máxima de 3 días en Chile. b) Va en visita por / meses a la ciudad de /

con pasaje pagado. c) Lugar donde va a radicarse Bolivia.

Certificado con indicación de precedencias y fecha:

Judicial Todos certificados en orden,con el visa para Bolivia

De moralidad

Político conveniente

De Médico y vacuna

Observaciones

Zofia Pikler nac. Pauker
Firma del interesado

Firma del Cónsul General

Sophie's transit visa for Chile

them a five-day maximum stay before resuming their trip to Bolivia. In Prague, they could already see the swastikas hoisted on a number of buildings—they went up on January 30, 1939, the sixth anniversary of Hitler's coming to power.

When all the required documentation was completed that spring, the last task was to determine what belongings they would want and would be able to take with them. By the time summer arrived, they had already settled on a departure date which would allow them plenty of time to reach the port of Genoa, Italy.

The last three months in Žilina were intensely stressful for the Pikler family. For my father, the thought of leaving his parents behind was devastating. He knew that Móric's health condition would not allow him to travel to Latin America. He hoped, once settled, to try to secure visas for his sisters and their families, but he knew he would not see his parents again. For the rest of his life, the sadness and guilt of leaving them never abated. The entire Pikler/ Žilina family embraced and wept together the evening before their departure.

Back: Sani Neumann, Julko Bronner, Teri, Klári, Sophie, Hansi
Front: Elsa, Oli, Móric; Žilina, 1939

Hansi, Sophie, and Oli began their voyage to Latin America in mid-August 1939 (exact date unknown), traveling first from Žilina to Genoa. Most likely they went from Žilina to Vienna or Bratislava and by train to Genoa, one of the major Italian ports of departure for Jewish and non-Jewish refugees from Western Europe until the end of 1940 when Italy joined the Axis military alliance. [42, 45]

Sophie's brother, Max, did not get an exit visa with his parents. How he was able to leave Vienna is unknown. He sent my parents a letter in Genoa from Paris on August 22, 1939, stating, "I do not have my parents' visa…I have no money and can not get an exit permit during the present political situation." It is believed he immigrated to Ecuador on January 22, 1941. [61]

A letter Leika wrote in 1974 states that she and Julko accompanied Hansi and Sophie and baby Oli to Genoa, and Leika held Oli in her arms up to the time all boarded the ship, probably the *Virgilio* or the *Orazio* [50]. In the letter, she wrote, "A terrible sadness engulfed me as we embraced each other and said good-bye, not knowing whether I would ever see them again."

The *Virgilio*

The Žilina banker Bartolomeo Stein and his wife, friends of Hansi and Sophie, also made the trip to Genoa and boarded the same ship.

When the ship was already in the Mediterranean Sea, it was seized by a French naval patrol and taken to Marseilles, France. The Jewish passengers were split by gender and interned in detention camps. The French Navy, they were told, had frequently been searching Italian ships for possible "enemy agents or saboteurs." [31, 52]

Camp Les Milles, France

Prisoners inspected by Camp Les Milles wardens

My father and other men were sent to Camp Les Milles outside Marseilles. [53] The women and children were placed mainly in Marseille, in the Hotel Terminus des Ports, the Hotel Atlantique, the Hotel Bompard, or the Hotel du Levant in the Rue Fauchier, managed by the CAR (refugee aid committee). My mother and Oli wound up at the Hotel Bompard.

Hotel Bompard where Sophie and Oli were held; Marseilles, France

The internment Camp Les Milles was an abandoned old tile factory south of Aix-en-Provence, on the edge of the small village of Les Milles. It became the largest internment camp in southeast France. The factory, closed two years previously, consisted of one vast main building with three floors, plus various out buildings, spread out over 11.6 acres. It was surrounded by barbed wire and served by the little railway station of Les Milles.

From September 1939 to the end of 1942, the camp served three distinct and successive functions. It was used first, beginning in the early days of September 1939, as an internment camp for those considered "enemy subjects" (mainly Germans, Austrians, Czechs) who had fled the Nazi regime; then, in the autumn of 1940, under the Vichy government, it became an internment and transit camp for "undesirable" foreigners wanting to leave France. In the last and most dramatic phase of the camp's life, from August to September 1942, it was an assembly point for those Jews—men, women and children—who were considered foreigners. The French state handed more than two thousand of them over to the Nazis for deportation to Auschwitz-Birkenau via Dancy and Rivesaltes, thus making itself an accomplice to genocide. [54]

More than ten thousand people were interned at Camp Les Milles from September 1939 until the end of 1942. Until the summer of 1940, the camp population fluctuated constantly. From time to time, new "suspects" were brought in who had been captured onboard ships inspected by the French Navy. The Piklers were in this group.

The internees came from all the social strata and professions: manual workers, farmers, shopkeepers, politicians, doctors, lawyers, sportsmen, architects, teachers, artists, and intellectuals.

The daily life organized by the internees, who were split into groups of 20-24 according to nationality, was consistently precarious. The first floor of the main building was assigned as a dormitory. Each man had to fend for himself and create his own sleeping space using straw spread on the floor and a few bricks. Any tiles that had not been baked disintegrated into red dust that penetrated everywhere. Hygiene was minimal, using homemade equipment installed outside in the open air. At first, a single narrow trench was used as a latrine; it was replaced later by four wooden huts, totally inadequate for the numbers concerned. A single water point with an extension pipe pierced with twelve holes provided nothing more than the possibility of a summary wash. Meals provided by the camp kitchen were taken on wooden tables in the courtyard, or inside in the dormitories when it rained. There was also a canteen where the better-off could buy provisions, and an infirmary.

The days passed in a monotonous routine consisting of a wake-up period from 5 to 6:30AM, roll call at 7:30AM, chores, and meals. Intellectual and artistic activities provided everyone with a moment's respite according to what was on offer: literary and philosophical discussions, painting and sketching, choral and other singing, small orchestras and some concerts, and even some revues and theatrical performances.

Anything was taken into consideration if it warded off boredom, blotted out anguish, and helped create a little more human warmth.

Charity organizations were present on site, including HICEM (for emigration assistance). An official emigration service was actually organized inside the camp, with an on-site post office, too. My parents exchanged letters and received family postcards and a care package during their detention.

The rhythm of departures overseas varied according to French state policy and that of the host states. In order to procure the necessary papers for departure, the internees were allowed to have exit passes. Some of the diplomatic corps were perfectly ready to supply them with passports and visas without hesitation. This was particularly true of the Czech Consul, Vladimir Vochoc, and also the Mexican Consul, Gilberto Bosques, both in Marseilles.

Starting in early July of 1942, the French government, under the aegis of its collaboration policy with the Germans, agreed that the arrangements already functioning in the "occupied zone" should also become applicable in the "free zone." On August 10, the first convoy of internees was herded on board wagons under appalling conditions and taken to Dancy and subsequently to the extermination camps in Eastern Europe, primarily Auschwitz-Birkenau. [54]

The Vichy government demanded that the number of transfers from the non-occupied zone be increased in order to "liberate" the zone of the Jewish population. By October 24, there were still 163 internees. By early December 1942, the Germans had requisitioned the tile factory for their own purposes. No internees were left, and the camp came to an end.

The Vichy French authorities gathered in these camps those Jews whose papers were at least in order and had a good chance of legal emigration; [51] however, many detainees waited there for weeks or months under appalling conditions as they became entangled in one bureaucratic snarl or another. The internees were allowed to receive and send mail and to get in touch with the various consulates in Marseilles. [52]

The stress caused by the unexpected and abrupt changes in their travel plans to Latin America, followed by their separation and living conditions at the detention camps, was bad enough. But the news of Germany's invasion of Poland on September 1, 1939, starting World War II —which led Great Britain and France to declare war on Hitler's Nazi state in retaliation two days later[44]—brought my parents tremendous anxiety, as reflected in the correspondence they exchanged throughout their detention. Added to the uncertainty of if and when they would be released, they now had another worry: Germany had occupied part of Czechoslovakia the year before (Sudetenland), so they wondered what would happen to the family if the Nazis marched through the rest of the country. A few days later, the Soviet army also invaded Poland. Both Germany and the USSR partitioned the country.[45] Two months later, the Soviet Union invaded Finland.[46]

HICEM, the Paris-based Jewish aid organization, was permitted to maintain staff inside the internment camp at Les Milles; they intervened on the internees' behalf and made an arrangement whereby the French Admiralty permitted passage of immigrants on lists submitted by HICEM. These lists were prepared by committees in Italy, which was a neutral country until

Sophie, Oli (on lady's lap), and Hansi on the *Augustus*; February 1940

Hansi and Oli on the *Augustus*

Oli on the *Augustus*

June 1940. [31, 52] In the winter of 1939-40, thanks to HICEM's intervention, about 1,000 refugees were able to sail from French ports on French, British, and neutral ships. [52]

The International Committee of the Red Cross also actively intervened and requested the release of all detainees. A document from this organization dated October 7, 1939 requested the release of the Piklers. It took several weeks for this to happen. After more than five months of separation, they were reunited and allowed to leave the camps in late January 1940.

They traveled back to Genoa, Italy, and boarded the *Augustus,* a 32,650-ton ship first launched in 1926, with capacity for well over two thousand passengers. [50] It had been taken from its North Atlantic service and rescheduled to sail for Central and Latin America beginning in December 1939. There are no records about their voyage on the *Augustus* but there are three photographs of them on its upper deck.

The *Augustus*

The round-trip voyage from Genoa to Valparaiso, Chile would have taken ten weeks and from Genoa to Salinas, Ecuador anywhere from 4 to 5 weeks. Their departure probably took place on February 4, 1940. After its departure from Genoa, the ship's itinerary included: Barcelona (Spain), Las Palmas (Spain),

La Guaira (Venezuela), Cristobal Colón (Panama), Buenaventura (Colombia), Salinas (Ecuador). The last ports were Callao in Peru and Arica, Iquique, Antofagasta, and Valparaiso in Chile.

One of my father's Ecuadorian naturalization documents states that on March 6, 1940, in Colón (the back door of Panama on the other side of the isthmus), he was issued a visa for Ecuador by its Consul (Olmedo Alfaro, son of the former Ecuadorian president, Eloy Alfaro). He carried passport #1/994/1938, issued in Žilina on December 29, 1938.

In my extensive research about their voyage, I came across the name of someone who made a similar stop in Panama on her trip to Latin America: Lilo Linke, whom Hansi and Sophie later knew personally while she lived in Ecuador.

Lilo Linke was a German-born author who wanted to visit the Andean Republics but was hoping before the war broke out to be back in England, where she had been living at the time. Shortly before midnight on a muggy night in June 1939—nine months before the *Augustus*—she arrived in Colón, Panama aboard the *Reina del Pacifico,* a ship crowded with refugees. Linke's travels through several countries—Colombia, Ecuador, Peru and Bolivia— delayed her return for several years. She wrote extensively about her impressions, studies, and interactions with ordinary citizens of those countries. [47, 55]

The several hundred refugees on board the ship with her were mostly Jews from all parts of Germany, Austria, Czechoslovakia, and Poland. They were excited and noisy, feeling at last free of a tremendous weight that had kept them down for years, but also afraid of what might be awaiting them on the other side of the world. Nearly all of them were dragging their pasts with them, in the shape of relatives, furniture, languages, and memories. [47]

Soon after her ship docked, Linke went ashore. She described her first impressions:

> The first contact with the tropics was overwhelming…
> the sultry heat, the rustling of the palm-trees, the waves

running against the shore, the chirring of a million cicadas, and from nearby, almost round the corner, the breath of the jungle...There was also the town with its vicious night-life—prostitutes, sailors, barmen of all races and nations. [47]

That description would not have changed at all nine months later when the *Augustus* docked at the same port, and Hansi, Sophie, and Oli went ashore with their fellow travelers. We do not know if their first impressions were any different from Linke's, nor how long the *Augustus* remained in Colón; perhaps no longer than twelve hours before it pulled out of the harbor to cross the Canal of Panama. Enough time must have been allowed for them and others to meet with several South American Consuls eager to lure the educated Europeans to their countries.

From Panama, the *Augustus* continued its voyage down the Pacific coast of South America and after a brief stop in Buenaventura, Colombia, it entered the territorial waters of Ecuador. It reached the port of Salinas (near the town of La Libertad) early in the afternoon of Saturday, March 9, 1940 on a hot and rainy day, typical for that month, one of the hottest and rainiest in Ecuador's coastal region.

Salinas was a fishing town with small wooden houses, located on the southwest coast of the tip of the Santa Elena peninsula and facing the Pacific Ocean, eighty-five driving miles west of Guayaquil, the country's largest port. Ships the size of the *Augustus* and larger were unable to dock there because the river Guayas which fed the port was not deep enough to handle them. In Salinas, the big ships did not reach the dock either. The passengers had to disembark in the open sea on a rope ladder and travel on boats towed to shore by a motorboat. Immigration and customs, in charge of checking the immigrants' documents and luggage, was located in a small hut. [39]

Of their original traveling group, only Bartolomeo Stein and his wife, after an emotional goodbye to their long-time friends, remained on board and continued their voyage to Bolivia. Bartolomeo would see my father many years later during a brief stopover in Quito, on his way to visit his son in the United States.

The Piklers had arrived in Colorado-sized Ecuador, once the northern bastion of the Inca Empire (*Quito* was the name of the country before and after Christopher Columbus's voyages)[47] the second smallest Spanish speaking country in South America, with its 109,483 square miles exceeding only Uruguay in area. The country lies on both the northern and southern hemispheres as it is divided by the Equator. It lies on the west coast of the continent facing the Pacific ocean, between Colombia on the north and Perú on the south and east. [56,57,58] It also includes the Galápagos Islands in the Pacific, about 620 miles west of the Ecuadorian coast.

Map of Ecuador

By then my mother's parents were already residing in Quito. While writing this narrative, I was unable to find any information as to the date when they arrived, but as a child I recall being told they had been in the country long before their daughter came with her little family.

Ecuador and its neighbors

El autoferro en Salinas, 1930.

Autoferro en la vía a Salinas, 1930.

Desfile escolar en las calles de Salinas a fines de los años 40.

Promoción de niños de la escuela Fiscal No. 143 "Digno R. Núñez, creada en 1933.

Autoferro; Salinas, Ecuador

After a cursory immigration process, the passengers traveled by *autoferro*, a bus-sized vehicle on railroad wheels, to Guayaquil where the official immigration office was located. The railroad distance between Salinas and Guayaquil was seventy-three miles. The *autoferro* took five hours to reach its destination at the amazing speed of fourteen miles per hour!

Guayaquil, the harbor and commerce center of the country and its largest city, had in the early forties a population around 135,000 [59]. It must have been unpleasant for my parents, since they were not accustomed to a tropical and humid climate and arrived in the rainy season that runs from January through April. Average daytime temperatures in March can reach just under 100 degrees and feels even hotter because of the thick fog of humidity.

The Piklers and other passengers with Quito as their final destination checked into a Guayaquil hotel, which had no air conditioning available at the time, and had to wait until Wednesday, March 13, 1940 before they could board the Guayaquil-Quito Railway, *el ferrocarril del Sur,* considered *"the most difficult steam railroad in the world."*[48] [60] The terminal was in Duran, across the river from Guayaquil. There was no bridge over the river, so they had to take a barge to Duran very early in the morning, [39].

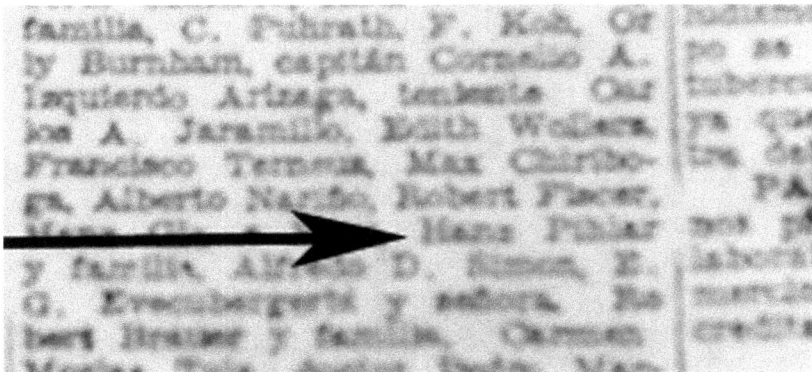

Ecuador train's passenger list, Duran to Quito; March 13, 1940

El Cotopaxi

El Chimborazo

El Cayambe

They traveled in first class. The passenger list shows a misspelled last name: Pihler. Train service was available every two days, and travel time from Duran to Quito, a 288.1-mile-long journey, would take two days, with a night stop in Riobamba. [55] A nonstop trip would take ten to twelve hours. Before railroad service became available in 1908, traveling from Guayaquil to Quito by stagecoach took two weeks.

Quito, the capital, only fifteen miles south of the Equator, is at a lung-stretching 9,350 feet of elevation. But it is overshadowed by the mountain spine of the country with its breathtaking Andean scenery. The German naturalist Alexander von Humboldt, during his visit to South America in 1802, aptly labeled the route south of Quito the "Avenue of the Volcanoes." It includes such extinct or active volcanoes as El Chimborazo; El Cotopaxi, which would erupt again in 2015; El Cayambe; El Iliniza; El Antisana; El Tungurahua,

Otavaleña teenager

which would also erupt in later years; and overlooking the city, El Pichincha. They ranged in elevation from 15,763 feet to 20,703 feet, and as the train approached Quito, the passengers in the six train cars enjoyed the beauty of that Andean scenery [57]. Years later, our parents related that experience to Oli and me.

In 1940, Ecuador had an estimated total population of three million [59, 61]. Quito had a population of around 110,000. It has a fresh, temperate climate, with daily highs in the upper sixties in March and an annual mean of 56 degrees. It is said that Quito passes through the four seasons all in one day, beginning with spring in the morning, summer's cloudy or rainy afternoons, autumn in the evening, and winter at night [56].

Hansi and Sophie took the obligatory tour of colonial Quito and wandered about after dark through its old streets with their silent charm. The colonial center still retains its historic character with magnificent churches and convents, "the cloisters of America," built in the colonial period and covered with gold, that had been expertly restored and contained priceless works of art combining the European Renaissance and Baroque styles with the indigenous and *mestizo* influences.[49] Nearly always, after midnight, groups of minstrels could be seen who, after serenading their own or other men's ladies, seemed at loose ends and continued to play their guitars and flutes, or to sing and dance by themselves in the semi-darkness [47]

In the outskirts of Quito, and in rural areas around it, Hansi and Sophie witnessed how indigenous tribes at communal activities and festivals or after Sunday weddings would walk playing their panpipes in a procession with the stumbling band at its head— flutes and a violin and a queer harp plucked with the fingers and beaten with the palm of the hand like a tambourine or a drum. Some danced along and consumed unlimited quantities of alcohol (*chicha*, a home-brewed liquor made from corn) [47]. They had never had such experiences in Central Europe, and the richness of the native culture left a deep impression.

Several months after settling in, they also visited Otavalo, a town 62 miles north of Quito, in the northern Imbabura province known for the indigenous community of *Otavaleños*, famous for their crafts and colorful textiles. The *Otavaleños*, one of many Andean highland Quichua-speaking tribes, are known for their independent streak. They dress with costumes of silk embroidered or covered with tinsel. Ribbons, tin bells, ornaments of seeds or coins, gold, precious stones, feathers, or beetles' wings are worn around the neck, the arms and wrists, the legs and ankles, or as belts around the waist. Elaborate head-dresses either leave the face free or are part of masks, and often the face itself is painted [47].

My parents walked through the most famous indigenous market in Ecuador, the Otavalo Indian Market, with its impressive variety of Ecuadorian handicrafts. They visited the workshops of these local weavers working on back strap and Spanish treadle looms, as well as other artisans at work making felt hats, knitting sweaters, or weaving straw mats.

The immigration of Jews to Latin America can be divided chronologically into four phases. The first covers most of the nineteenth century. The second period began in 1889 and went through World War I. By 1917, the Jewish population in Latin America had risen to over 115,000 (96% of them resided in Argentina). The third period ran from the conclusion of World War I until the beginning of the 1930s, when large numbers of additional immigrants arrived in Latin America, principally from Eastern Europe. The fourth period, beginning around 1933 and continuing to the early years of the next decade, witnessed the admission into Latin America of large numbers of refugees from Hitler's Europe, especially from Central Europe [62], to which, of course, the Piklers belonged.

While I was researching the history of Jewish immigration to Ecuador, a close friend of mine, a grade and high school classmate who was aware of this research, sent me a book that describes the presence of a Sephardic Jewish community in today's Ecuadorian southern province of Loja dating back to the 16th century![50] [63] But this Jewish population in Loja was unknown to the public, and there was little Jewish immigration to Ecuador in the first three decades of the twentieth century. In 1904, there were only four known Jewish families in the country. [59]

According to historian Gabriel Alexander, [64] two European Jews were officially invited by the Ecuadorian government in the beginning of the twentieth century to improve the living conditions in the country: in 1909, Dr. Robert Levy, a chemist and epidemiologist, was commissioned to come to Guayaquil to redeem it from its yellow fever and malaria epidemics and advise about the construction of a modern sewage system. In 1913, Julius Rosenstock, a Viennese engineer, settled in Quito, and was pivotal in the development, completion, and maintenance of the Guayaquil-Quito railroad, *el ferrocarril del Sur,* as well as other important public construction projects. He later played a crucial role in burgeoning Jewish immigration to Ecuador. By 1917, fourteen Jews were in the country [65]. A handful more arrived after 1924 when the US established its immigration quota system.

The Jewish mass immigration to Ecuador began in the wake of the rise of Nazism and the ensuing Holocaust. [31] Ecuador was the only country in the world without immigration quotas [61] and, in all of Latin America, it maintained the most liberal policy toward Jewish immigrants.[51] In 1939, when several South American countries refused to accept the 165 German Jewish refugees aboard the ship *Koenigstein,* Ecuador granted them entry permits.

The country's charismatic president, José María Velasco Ibarra, first elected in 1934, reiterated several times that Ecuador would permit the entrance of any Jewish immigrant who asked for it. Already in 1945, at the culmination of World War II, Velasco Ibarra favored the creation of the State of Israel and in that same year, stated that "the doors of Ecuador will remain open for every honest foreigner, regardless of race and creed. The Jews who would like to set up industrial companies in Ecuador or till our fields will be gladly welcomed, and also Jews who cross our borders in search of protection against hatred and persecution will receive help, even in cases where they do not have economic support." [48]

During the years 1933-1943 about 2,700 Jews arrived in Ecuador, the bulk between 1937 and 1941. [59] In 1941 the

Jewish population was estimated to be about 3,000, with 1,000 residing in Quito and about 1,250 in Guayaquil (of whom 1,000 were recently arrived refugees). By 1945 there were 3,500-4,000 Jews in Ecuador, 85 percent of whom were refugees from Europe. [65]

For most of them, Ecuador was a second-choice place of exile since they had failed to find asylum in other, preferred countries which had restricted their admission or excluded them altogether. [31, 45, 48] This was also the case of people who had to leave their first country of asylum due to the advance of the war, or whose visas were found to be falsified. [39] Some of them settled in Guayaquil, the biggest city in Ecuador, located near the Pacific coast and with a tropical climate. The vast majority of Jewish immigrants, however, went to the Ecuadorian highlands, *la serranía,* because of its temperate climate, and settled primarily in Quito, Riobamba, Ambato, and Cuenca. [61, 66] A number of families were scattered around in rural settlements, villages, and haciendas. [64, 66]

My parents, like so many other refugees, were not only unfamiliar with the geography of the continent they were traveling to, but also did not speak Spanish. Oli and I learned as we were growing up that these "shortcomings" did not in any way seem to have bothered them. Our parents had arrived in Latin America with almost no preconceived notions, especially about its small countries.

Many refugees chose the larger countries with known European influences (Argentina, Brazil, Chile) and more developed economies. The Caribbean countries (Cuba and the Dominican Republic) were chosen as "waiting areas" for travel to the United States. The Andean nations (Colombia, Ecuador, Bolivia) in large measure also served this function as confirmed by the large emigration of these refugees to the United States and Israel after the war ended.

Most of the refugees came with professional experience as merchants, industrialists, and businessmen, which did not qualify them for the general agricultural work stipulated in their entry visas. Other immigrants were doctors and engineers, painters and musicians, journalists and technicians, industrialists and chemists, university professors, students, actors, artisans, cooks [67]. Most of them spoke German, but some spoke Czech, others Hungarian, Polish, Romanian, Italian. Very few knew Yiddish.

It is true that there were at least a couple of occasions, starting in 1937, when Ecuadorian government officials and even the Chamber of Commerce questioned the fact that many immigrants who had entered the country as farmers became engaged in retail trade. [48, 61, 67] From time to time, a government official demanded an investigation requiring all aliens to produce evidence that they were working in the occupation listed on their immigration papers. After intervention by the World Jewish Congress, these investigations also shelved.[52] [39, 61, 67, 68] None ever materialized.

In his book, *Professions of a Lucky Jew*, [69] Benno Weiser Varon, a journalist, author, and diplomat who emigrated to Ecuador in 1938 and lived there for seven years,[53] points out that "not for all immigrants was Quito love at first sight." Many were too busy finding fault with everything: they complained about the city's high altitude which taxed their breath, the lack of cleanliness, the body odor of the Indios they had to travel with on the buses, and they were "shocked to see an Indian mother, older daughter, and baby, sitting one behind the other, searching for lice in each other's hair and swallowing their finds."

At its peak, in 1954, the Jewish population of Ecuador was estimated at five thousand people (according to the *Asociación de Beneficiencia Israelita de Quito* which included only "affiliated" families, and therefore excluded people like us), the majority living in Quito, several hundred in Guayaquil, and several scores in Ambato, Riobamba, and Cuenca. [61]

I later gathered much information about the Jewish immigration to Ecuador from Gabriel Alexander, a Jewish historian who had been born in Guayaquil in 1951 and had spent the first nine years of his life there. He subsequently moved to Germany and completed his studies, including a doctoral program with a Ph.D. thesis on "Berlin Jewry and Its Community during the Weimar Republic (1919-1933)." Then he returned to Ecuador and lived there for many years, running a bookstore called the *Librería Científica*, where I bought books as a high school and medical student. Ultimately Mr. Alexander sold the bookstore and made *aliyah*; he currently lives in Jerusalem.

Years later, in my efforts to assemble the Pikler family narrative, I remembered the man's interest and vast knowledge about Jewish immigration to Ecuador before, during, and after World War II, and interviewed him by phone. Dr. Alexander told me that he had learned from his own interviews with immigrants to Ecuador that the usual route was from central Europe to France, then onto a freighter that also took some passengers to Cuba, from Cuba to Ecuador on a different freighter, sometimes changing ships again on the shores of Panama before entering the Panama Canal. Other immigrants, like my parents, would leave from an Italian port and make the voyage in the same vessel directly to the Panama Canal and from there to the port of Salinas. Usually, immigrants disembarked in Salinas and transferred by car ferry to Guayaquil, were immigration authorities were located. From Guayaquil most of them "ran away as soon as possible" because of the hot, humid weather and mosquitoes.

Alexander sent me an article [64] about Jewish immigration to Ecuador that he had presented in 2001 at the Jerusalem World Congress of Jewish Studies. In his article, he asks about whether the Jews who immigrated to Ecuador came to "live" or to "settle." He believes that "most of the Jewish immigrants to Ecuador came to live there, not to settle."

In fact, the majority of the immigrants had regarded their stay in Ecuador as a temporary episode, a steppingstone while waiting to obtain visas primarily for the United States and Israel. [64] At the end of the war, many immigrants had their suitcases ready.

They wanted to leave as quickly as they had arrived. In 1946 the Jewish community of Ecuador lost one fourth of its members and by 1948 about half the Jews in Quito had emigrated. Others left after some years of waiting for new visas. Many left because their businesses did not prosper in Ecuador, and due to the country's lack of development and meager cultural environment, but above all, they sought a safer future in other countries. [68]

Hansi's Ecuador naturalization document; June 26, 1950

The emigration trend continued with the new generations, encouraged by the continued support of Ecuador's president. Those who stayed or returned after studying abroad were economically and socially integrated. [39] After the end of the war there was considerable re-emigration with a second wave of Jews, refugees who had spent the war years in Shanghai, many concentration camp survivors from Germany and Austria [48], and relatives who could not come during the war arrived in Ecuador (and other Latin American countries like Bolivia) in the early postwar years. [65] By 1950, the Quito community had about one thousand Jews; in the early seventies, in the course of the oil boom and thanks to easier-to-obtain entry permits, there was also an influx of families from Chile during Salvador Allende's presidency, and towards the end of the twentieth century, many more from Argentina.

My father, on the other hand, applied for Ecuadorian citizenship in the early forties, and in 1950, President Galo Plaza granted his request. I recall how happy and proud he felt at the time: Ecuador, the country which had opened its arms to his family, had made him one of its own. He remained grateful for it for the rest of his life.

As Oli and I were growing up, there were times when our father would reminisce about his family life in Slovakia and his work at ZB; it had been a life of comfort, economic stability, and a pervasive atmosphere of refinement. At times, he could not help making comparisons with words like "over there" or "in Europe." This is what Leo Spitzer describes in his book *Hotel Bolivia* [31] as "nostalgic memory." At the same time, Hansi looked forward to building a new and successful life in Ecuador, whatever hardships and sacrifices were involved.

During the thirties and forties, anti-Semitic propaganda appeared in almost every country in Latin America, aided and abetted by Axis agents and pro-Axis native elements. This menace subsided with the strong action of responsible governments and later with the defeat of the Axis. The presence in Latin America of many ex-Nazis and their sympathizers as well as the unstable economic, social, and political conditions, contributed to fertile soil for such propaganda. Another factor that increased anti-Semitism was envy of these foreigners, some of whom achieved quick success. After World War II, there were smears in print and mail as well as vandalism, bombing of synagogues and other community buildings, defacing of cemeteries, and even attacks on people carried out by neo-Nazis and other anti-Semites.

Before the war broke out, there had been no anti-Semitism in Ecuador, but it surfaced soon afterward. The prejudices against the Jews were encouraged by interested economic and political groups. German economic influence was significant, and Nazi-inspired articles appeared in the press attacking Jews. These attacks took the line that if England defeated Germany, Jews would control the Ecuadorian industry with dire results to the workers. [59] At the time, there was very little organization of any type among the Jews in Ecuador. It was left to individuals like Max Wasserman, a well-known merchant in Guayaquil, who sought to counteract these press attacks with factual statements. [59, 61]

Foreigners, in general, were called *gringos* because of their light skin and their lack of knowledge of the language and local culture. Some locals sought to exploit their shortcomings and deceive them, at times successfully. The label remained even after they had overcome these shortcomings. But they were always treated with respect, no matter what nationality, and addressed as *Mister*. Xenophobia did not exist. An Ecuadorian would rather have rented his house to a *gringo* for three hundred *sucres* (the currency at the time) than to a compatriot for four hundred. To be an *extranjero* was like a guarantee of punctuality, cleanliness, and reliability. German, Austrian, and Czech immigrants found their way made smooth by the outlanders who had preceded them under other circumstances. [68]

Although the Jews were almost unknown in Ecuador until the arrival of these immigrants, there was diffuse anti-Semitism propagated by the Catholic church: the Jews were "Christ killers." In addition, Ecuador was suffering from the war. Imports ceased, and prices rose 500 percent or more. [69]

The establishment of a growing Jewish population in several cities generated some discontent, initiated by merchants who until then had monopolized the prices of mostly imported products. This fear of economic competition along with anti-Semitic and xenophobic prejudices, created social and cultural barriers that impeded a greater rapprochement between Ecuadorians and refugees. [48]

According to the journalist and diplomat Benno Weiser-Varon, "in the late thirties in Quito *judío* didn't mean *Jew*. A *judío* was a man who charged exorbitant interest or who sold merchandise at a very high profit. The term referred to neither a nation nor a race, nor even to a religion." But when the war was underway, "the term *judío* began to mean foreigner. Anyone with blond hair and blue eyes was a judío. The word began to replace the traditional *gringo*." Everyone was a *judío*: Americans, Nazis, Dutchmen, and even Jews. The term "Mister" had fallen out of use. *Judío* sometimes took its place, and even if it was not meant contemptuously, "Mister" had sounded better. [69]

Counter-attacks and educational campaigns carried out by the Jews were mostly effective in neutralizing the anti-Jewish blight. Subsequent Jewish generations starting with the children of former immigrants were better organized, and occupied important positions in public life. They refused to be intimidated and reacted with pride and dignity against any attacks on them. Moreover, they possessed the education to deal properly with the defamations that circulated from time to time. The American Jewish Committee maintained close contact with the national Jewish organizations in the Latin American countries and joined the local groups to combat anti-Semitic propaganda. [67]

My parents did not relate any anti-Semitic experiences to us, nor did I ever witness any, except for stereotypical derogatory jokes in social gatherings. But theirs was not a typical Jewish home.

Up to the beginning of 1942, Jewish community life in Ecuador was harmonious and almost exemplary. Then the effects of the war began to be felt. Overnight, all those distinctions that had hitherto

**Czechoslovak Club: Andean music program with typical costumes
(George standing in the back); December 1949**

**Czechoslovak Club: Andean music program with typical costumes (Oli standing,
far right back, and George sitting, fourth from left); December 1949**

been insignificant—nationality, mother-tongue, and so on—
assumed paramount importance. Following the lead of the United
States, South America began to distinguish between friendly and
unfriendly aliens. Suddenly the Czech Jews belonged to the Allies
and the German Jews to the Axis. A Polish Jew was an ally of the
United States, an Austrian Jew occupied an intermediate position
and tried to shake off the German nationality imposed on him by
his passport. New organizations mushroomed: the Czechs opened
a club with its own restaurant, the Poles had their own club, the
Germans a *Heim,* the Austrians a *café*. Everyone talked politics,
they boycotted each other's social events. The Jewish organizations
were no longer social nuclei. [68]

The problems of acculturation not only referred to adaptation
to the new environment, but to mutual adaptation in the given
conditions. Apart from differences of national origin, immigrants
formed a very complex social group. Some had no connection
with the Jewish religion and its traditions, while others defined
themselves as strictly religious and Jewish nationalists. In this way,
the behavior of the immigrants was quite contradictory: on the one
hand they created enterprises and developed a strong bond beyond
all linguistic, social, cultural, religious, and political differences. On
the other hand, the conflicts inherent in every community exploded
disproportionately. People who, under other circumstances, would
never have banded together, now lived in a limited space and shared
daily life and free time in a foreign environment. [39]

Culture shock, uprooting, loss of psychological balance, and
conflicts between competing ideas are some of the factors that
explain the aggressive overreactions among fellow immigrants.
They manifested themselves in internal struggles and disputes
between groups and organizations, and in hostility and contempt
among individual people. The discussions around political goals
(for example, the correct attitudes toward Germany or Zionism)
were also part of an identity crisis caused by their exile. [39]

Early on, my father decided to remain as an unaffiliated member of the Jewish community in Quito, avoiding any participation in political organizations and discussions. That is one of the reasons why he was welcomed by the immigrant community and was able to cultivate friendships with members from diverse political ideologies.

My parents frequented the Czechoslovak Club. Many refugees like them would meet there to socialize, play board games, cards, chess, etc., and play musical instruments (Hansi played the violin; Sophie, the piano). Children were welcomed and often invited to participate in organized stage plays.

Ecuador in the first decades of the twentieth century was an undeveloped country, with very little infrastructure. [64, 66] It had a predominantly agricultural-based economy, dominated by one product at a time, which subjected the country to periods of boom followed by dramatic downturns. From 1885 to 1922, the exportation of cacao accounted for 65 to 70 percent of the value of all exports. World War I interfered with Ecuador's export of cacao to Europe, and by the 1920s increased competition and a blight on Ecuadorian plantations ended Ecuador's advantage. Although it continued to export cacao, its revenues were much less important to the economy. In 1940 the principal products grown in the Sierra were: maize, barley, wheat, rye, potatoes, and lentils. On the coast: rice, sugar, coffee, cocoa, castor beans and bananas. [55]

From 1947 to 1960, Ecuador's economy centered on the export of bananas. In fact, by 1950 Ecuador was the world's leading banana producer. However, by 1955 Ecuador faced increased competition from other banana-producing countries and its dominant share of world production started to decline.

According to the 1950s census, 50 percent of the population worked on the land. At the time, the country had 3,202,757 inhabitants with 212,000 living in Quito and 266,000 in Guayaquil. [55] According to Lilo Linke's research, income per capita up until the early 1950s was about $40 per year. [55]

Within a very short time after the immigrant Jews arrived,

Jewish community life sprang up in Quito. Of the four thousand Jews who constituted the Jewish contingent in Ecuador between 1940 and 1945, over 95 percent were refugees from Hitler's Europe. They came from Germany, Austria, Czechoslovakia, Italy, Poland, the Baltic countries, the Soviet Union and Romania. [39] They were mostly Ashkenazi and German Jews. Sephardic Jews were extremely rare. Almost everyone understood German, so that became the common language. Spanish was used only in contacts with the Ecuadorians [68].

Jews found no bar for practicing their religion or founding Jewish associations.[54] My parents felt no threat or need to conceal the fact that we were Jewish (within the European immigrant community), but they did not practice Judaism at home. I recall only one time during those years going with my father to the synagogue for Móric's *yahrzeit*. From time to time, they would buy some kosher products from the *shohet,* the kosher butcher in town who was also a shoemaker.

Hansi taught Oli and me the first of four stanzas of Luise Hensel's classic children's prayer, *Müde bin Ich*[55] ("I Am Tired"), which we would recite every night before going to sleep:

Müde bin ich, geh' zur Ruh',	*Weary now, I go to rest,*
Schliesse meine Augen zu.	*Close my eyes in slumber blessed.*
Vater, lass die Augen dein	*Father, may Thy watchful eye*
Über meinem Bette sein.	*Guard the bed on which I lie.*

What did the Jews find upon their arrival? They found themselves within a society of unfamiliar structure and mindset. However, they were received with curiosity and kindness by the Ecuadorian population. They witnessed the absolute lack of development in the country, the widespread poverty, the subordination of the indigenous population, the ever-present dirt on people, houses, lodgings, and inns, and the custom of relieving oneself in public.

[66]

A few decided to live in Guayaquil, but eventually left because of its hot and humid climate, cockroaches, and crickets. Most preferred the temperate weather of the Andean provinces and settled in Quito.

The visas they received from the Ecuadorian government were granted for the express purpose of working in the agricultural industry. Except for a very few, all abandoned this work because of the undeveloped nature of the rural areas, the isolation which did not allow them to educate their children, and the lack of comforts to which they were accustomed. [64]

Jewish immigrants were generally people with technical training, professional experience, business knowledge, and cultural background; some had higher education degrees. In some cases, they had important businesses in their home countries and had been part of the European intellectual elite. But above all, they were imbued with values that had accompanied Jews during their long history: unblemished industriousness, diligence with savings, a sense of organization, a willingness to do manual work, perseverance, initiative and innovation, dedication to fulfilling commitments, both personal and corporate austerity, and a practical sense of life—quite a different mentality than what reigned in Ecuador at the time. [64]

Initially, the newly-arrived Jews worked in any activity that allowed them to feed and clothe themselves. Teenage girls who emigrated from Germany would earn a living in domestic service. As "the wife could cook and the husband wash," some immigrants began to make consumer products in their homes (butter, bread, chocolates, cookies, cakes, noodles, cheese, cream, sausages and ham), which had been unknown in the country or manufactured with "unsatisfactory quality for the European taste." [66] They sold them from house to house, in bakeries or on demand, until they opened their own stores. Their culinary skills were also used to install the first restaurants and comfortable hotels in Quito, whose first clients were members of the large Jewish community.

All of this allowed them to introduce innovations previously unknown in the area, and to remain competitive and inventive. For example, they introduced sales by installment plans, door-to-door sales, and the use of display cases in the small and dark shops typical of the times. Paper bags produced in a local factory replaced the sheets of used newspapers and containers that were used to pack or carry groceries purchased by locals. They started dry cleaning services and offered their clients the option of having their garments picked up from their homes. Many of the bridges built in mid-century Ecuador were made from steel produced by companies created by Jewish immigrants, who started dozens of companies and many industries. By 1948, fifteen exporting firms and some 140 industries, including fifteen hotels and boarding houses, had been developed and were employing about two thousand workers. Later, the first computers were brought to the country by Italian Jews who founded the pharmaceutical company, LIFE. [39, 48]

Many had arrived penniless and suffered hunger, which spurred them to work tirelessly, from sunrise to sunset, regardless of the lack of resources, lack of instruments, tools, or materials, poor public services, the informality of Ecuadorians, and the lagging development of the country. [64]

But thanks to the asylum they received that had saved their lives, the difficulties seemed to them a trifle, and Ecuador, a "paradise." Women as well as men contributed to the initiatives they took and the businesses they established: in addition to housework that they did without the help of servants (to which many of them had been accustomed), they helped their husbands in everything from office paperwork, preparing invoices and making collections, to preparing homemade products and selling them door-to-door for extra income. Their knowledge, experience, and connections with their countries of origin, were used to establish import and export houses. Ultimately, the fact of living in a country where they had to do everything themselves allowed them to easily identify business niches. [64]

Those who managed to acquire machines to make knitted products changed the Sierra fashion by introducing warm sweaters that replaced the shawls and scarves women wore to ward off the cold weather. A large number went into business, in stores or as peddlers of all possible products. Some started accounting offices or commercial and technical consulting firms or dedicated themselves to the sale of foreign currency exchange, insurance, and transportation. Those who managed to bring certain resources in money and jewels or were able to acquire them with profits from their initial business, ventured into a variety of industries: metal and mechanical, hotel, food products, pharmaceutical, chemical, ceramics, paper, liquor, textile, cleaning, tannery, folklore, construction and manufacture of furniture, clothing, shoes, jewelry, paintings, and other products. [66] Many of these activities were successful and eventually led to large and prosperous companies; some of them are still among the most important in the country.

Finally, among the Jewish immigrants were also a variety of professionals (chemists, doctors, psychologists, musicians), intellectuals and artists, teachers, writers, archaeologists, anthropologists, and those who by their experience in Europe contributed to the diffusion of reading or opened bookstores. Others helped to awaken the love for classical music among Ecuadorians.

They were not interested in, nor did they participate in local politics (with the exception of a childhood friend of mine[56] who also belonged to the second generation of Jews).

As noted earlier, the Piklers spoke no Spanish when they arrived in Ecuador, though they both knew several languages (seven for Hansi, four for Sophie). My father related that, soon after arriving to Ecuador, he immersed himself in learning Spanish by reading the local evening newspaper, listening to the radio, and befriending as many Quiteños as he could (at the time, no Rosetta Stone, Berlitz, or television were available).

He also moved quickly to meet influential local businessmen and share ideas for potential business enterprises. During that first train trip from Guayaquil to Quito, he noticed the train had no dining car. He had traveled extensively in Europe and was used to that luxury. So, he suggested to people connected with the railroad system that they start this service and he helped them get it started.

Though I never learned my parents' first place of residence in Quito, by the mid-1940s they felt relatively comfortable in a small apartment near a residential area in the town. The political news from Europe of the capitulation of various countries to the German army and its progressive territorial gains, caused significant sadness and anxiety in their home.[57]

The mood in the country was also quite gloomy. World War II had by then wiped out a number of nations both big and small, and the people in Ecuador were frightened, wondering what might be in store for America and for themselves, a poor, defenseless country. [47] And, in September, the local newspapers were beginning to report an increasing number of frontier soldier incidents in the territory adjoining Perú.

Within a week, in early October 1940, letters from home arrived with dreaded news: Hansi's beloved father had died on September 28.[58] Though Klári's letter was not found, below are excerpts from the other letters:

My beloved Hansi, Sophie,   October 4, 1940

With heavy heart, I sit down to write to you, my dear brother, to tell you of our precious father's passing. Dear Hansi, we joined our precious one on his last journey on Monday, September 30 at 3 pm. My dear brother, we missed your presence with a heavy heart, but we were with you in our thoughts during these difficult hours and days, and we share this burden with you, my dear brother, even while the oceans separate us.

Do not cry and grieve too much about our precious one and let him gain the rest for which he fought so hard. These were difficult hours that we spent at his bedside, because he suffered inhuman pain, and we had to just stand there and watch him suffer while unable to do anything to help. All we could do is to ask dear God to relieve his inhuman suffering.

Don't despair, my dear brother, but thank God that he has been relieved of unbearable pain. Give him both peace and rest. Your letter, dear Hansi, reached us precisely on Monday. It arrived as the last greetings from you for our loved one. How much did the poor one wish to get this letter from you, yet he was not meant to live for this joy, and these last greetings we could only pass on as the cold earth was covering him. Had he only been able to read your letter, he would surely have passed on in greater peace, because he would have known that you, my dear Hansi, do not forget us and remain faithful to us. The knowledge that he had to leave us behind under such difficult circumstances must have made his last hours even more difficult.

Only during these hard days did I learn to value the true personalities of Julko and Sani, who stood by and cared for him with love and respect during these bitter hours with exemplary dedication. But to show you the love and the respect given to our poor father in even greater detail, my dear brother, I want to tell you something else. The boys, who did not say Kaddish for their own fathers because this would have violated their beliefs, took turns in the Temple morning and evening to perform this task, one they freely took on with love and respect for our father, until such time that you can take this duty from their shoulders.

And something else, my dear brother, I'd like to tell

you. Never forget that you still have a good and faithful mother and sisters who love you with all their heart, and that you may rely on us, come what may, we are ready to receive you with open arms, and that you will find love and a home. And never forget that our mother, whose body and soul are wracked by misfortune, thinks lovingly and tenderly of you, and that she is a faithful and loving mother, just like she is for the rest of us. With dedication, love and patience she stood by our father until his last breath. But why am I telling you this? You know this yourself, and I know of your concern and love for her, just as ours.

Write to me, my dear Hansi, really soon, and in great detail. Olinka is surely a sweet kid just as our Petyko, who is a strong lad, and our only joy.

Don't despair, my beloved Hansi. With warmest kisses, I embrace you all with love,

Your loving, *Edit*

October 5, 1940

My dear little children, my dearest Hansinko!

Today it is eight days since dear Papa closed his eyes forever. I still can't comprehend and believe that his bed is empty, that he no longer calls for me, no longer needs my help. I search and call in vain, and he no longer answers! My Hansinko, what we've lost in him. Nothing and no one in this world can replace him. I can vividly imagine that you, my dear child, must feel deep pain, the hard blow of fate twice.

How I would like to stand by your side now and comfort you, my boy. It's hard, very hard! Believe me, my dear child, I cannot find any words, my heart is bleeding, and I am trying to numb myself. One thing that may reassure you is, we did everything that was humanly possible to give him healing and relief. Every single child has sacrificed and readily expressed their love. Julko and Sani both behaved well and decently, they couldn't have cared for their own father more lovingly. I will be eternally grateful to them for that.

My Sofinka, do me one favor, assist Hansi in these difficult hours, be good to him. Life is so short. How can we know what's ahead for us? Therefore, stick together, love each other, and never forget that we form a family together, for better or for worse, we are always there for you. God should protect you, my dear child, Olinka, your dear parents, and also feel embraced by your eternally loving, *Mama*

My dear ones, my Hansinko!   October 6, 1940

It is very, very hard for me to write and look for words that could express all of our feelings to you. I want you to feel our closeness, our love, in spite of the distance, and this will help you to endure the terrible pain that hit us all more easily. My Hansinko, our dear father has left, nothing more hurts him. He does not struggle any more. He needed the rest, this should and must serve to all of us as a consolation; we must not disturb his hard-won peace with our moaning. It would hurt him infinitely if we did not bravely endure this terrible blow of fate for us.

When we were in Budapest the last time, the professor told me openly, that there was no longer any help for our dear father. He got a diathermy treatment, which should have at least relieved him of the terrible pain and agony, but unfortunately the effect did not materialize. With a heavy heart, I accompanied my parents home after a 3-month stay with me and have not had any rest since that minute. The professor and also the doctor in Losonc prepared me for an impending urine poisoning (kidney failure). Unfortunately, this also happened.

He mentioned you every day and almost every hour "Hansi, my Hansi" and it still pained him that he couldn't have you with him, it was a great comfort for him to know that you were safe and it was his wish that we too soon would come to you. I know how terrible you feel that you will no longer see him.

You must not forget how deeply sad you would make Papa if he saw you desperate, discouraged, powerless. I trust your energy and your love for us, which will help you overcome our serious misfortune. Do not forget that Mama and your siblings are trembling and fearful to send you these lines. Do not forget that our suffering would be even more terrible if we did not know you were strong and courageous.

Hansinko mine, we stay together always and over everything, our love and attachment to one another should be our common consolation. Be strong and we will take the hard blow more easily. I kiss the little girl and you both in sisterly love, *Teri*

My very dear ones!   October 7, 1940

I believe that never in my life have I had to write something as hard as today. I have this terribly difficult task of telling you that on Monday afternoon at 3 p.m., the 30th of September, we carried our dear good father to eternal rest after inhuman torments and sufferings. It is terribly difficult for us and the thought of you makes this irreplaceable loss even more difficult.

Perhaps it was not right for us to keep hidden for so long that our dear father was lying in bed for a full year and suffered unspeakably. After his last trip to Budapest, the prostate problem got worse from day to day, the pain was stronger and then the catheter was not taken out for months. Prof. Unterberg told us that unfortunately there was no hope of recovery, not even of an improvement, and so it was, unfortunately. The poor man lived only on morphine and only got out of bed temporarily. But mentally, he was alert the whole time, everything interested him and if he had a better day here and there, he even hoped that an improvement would come soon. The coup de grace came from urine poisoning that suddenly occurred three weeks ago. Papa began to lose his appetite, he ate less and less, felt weak, and the doctor diagnosed this as poisoning. He immediately told us that there was unfortunately no help, nonetheless everything that was possible was tried, unfortunately in vain. He had hallucinations that manifested themselves especially during the night. He saw things before him that were never there. He woke up asking Mama: "What does this man want from me?" When Mama said that there was no one there, he said: "But now, now, Rudi was here with me too and gave me a cigarette," and when he turned on the light and saw that no one was there, and Mama told him that it was night, he said, "Nobody is here." At that time, Mama still believed that he was dreaming, but when these hallucinations were happening more and more often, we saw that this was not the case and, as the doctor said, this also came with the disease, it was also a symptom of this poisoning. The matter got worse from day to day, he did not eat any food for 13 days, only water, lost consciousness, which he temporarily regained for a very short time.

These moments were the most terrible, because he knew exactly how things were with him, as he had known for a long time that there was nothing to help him. As I said, he only gained consciousness for a very short time; then he fell asleep again. He was getting out of bed until one day before his death. Of course, we had to lift and support him because he didn't have that much strength. When he was conscious here and there, all his thoughts focused only on his illness, he became very apathetic, he was not interested in anything, and when Teri came home ten days before his death, he didn't speak to her, he then recognized her for a few minutes, maybe on the second day, when he became conscious, and then he lapsed again. His last two weeks were not life anymore.

The pain became more and more violent; instead of urine only pus and blood came out, and not even the strong morphine injections eased his pain. Two days before he left us, he said nothing more, but was still suffering, and on Saturday, the 28th of September, he fell asleep around 11 a.m., at that time without pain, and then at 6:45 p.m. after three deep breaths, he closed his eyes forever.

I know, my dear Hansinko, that it is twice as difficult for you because you could not be with us and next to our dear ones, but the thought should really comfort you that he no longer suffers, that he is no longer forced to endure his inhuman pain, to end the suffering himself he wanted to several times. Our good mother would not leave his side during this year. What can I tell you that she did not go to the front door, to the alley, the courtyard, or know what the kitchen looked like, so to speak. She was tireless in her care, love, kindness, and patience; and poor Papa could appreciate it fully. She has lost more than all of us, and we should all take her example of how much inner strength she has.

Poor Papa mentioned you very, very much and once, even as he was already doing poorly, when he woke up and regained consciousness, he cried and said: "What will Hansi say about this, when he finds out?" and wept bitterly. Of course, Mama tried to deny everything, but unfortunately he knew his own condition too well. In general, his thoughts lingered with you a lot. My children, we do not stop thinking of you, and it should also reassure you that we reminded him to think of you."

Immediately, one-and-a-half hours after his death, he was taken to the cemetery (because now there is such a rule in place here) and we accompanied him also on your behalf and thought of you. On Monday at 3 o'clock the poor man was put to eternal rest. Many were present, Finy, Stefi, Rudi, etc, all relatives from [Banská] Bystrica, Rajec and also very, very many from Žilina. Countless telegrams have arrived. The Rabbi gave a beautiful speech, emphasized his character and beautiful family life, and said goodbye to our Papa also on your behalf. This fact should also serve as a consolation for you. Until you get this letter, Sani and Julko take turns saying Kaddish.

My Sophinko, I have also a few words to you, I want to ask you to be very, very good to Hansi, because you know best what has been snatched from him and all of us! Have patience with him.

My children, farewell, let's pray that God will give our dear, unforgettable good father his well-deserved rest.

In our thoughts we are always with you and we greet and kiss you with an incredible amount of love.

Your, *Lea*

We wish a merry and Happy New Year to all of you.

Móric was buried in Žilina's Jewish cemetery on September 30. The feelings of guilt my father had carried since August of the previous year, having left his family behind, not being at his father's bedside, and then learning how his beloved Papa suffered for so long before he died, greatly intensified this guilt, and for several months he was quite depressed. For weeks he was literally unable to write back to them. This was a traumatic psychological event in his life, from which he never recovered.

In late November, a letter from Elsa arrived:

My dearest Hansi!

A few days ago, your long-awaited letter of November 18th finally arrived. We couldn't explain your silence at all. We thought that you were sick, God forbid. I was prepared for it knowing that the news of your dear Papa's death would hit you so hard. I know, my dear child, that you must feel it twice as hard because you are so far away and could not be near him for a whole, full year.

He unfortunately knew that he could no longer be helped. He often complained that he will no longer see all of you! What did we say about this, Hansi!? Of course, I always said that we would someday see you all again. If you had seen how badly our dear one suffered, you would grant him his rest. Unfortunately, Dr. Jassninger was right when he told us "he will perish miserably". And so it was. You can't even write that down. When we get together once again, I'll tell you a lot about him. Now, my dear child, calm down, you have duties to your wife and child now. The mere thought that our dear one is no longer here is terrible in itself for us, and further, more incomprehensible, more incredible! I often think to myself again that God was good that he called him away, now he will be spared a lot of grief and worry.

We have at least one reassurance that, praise God, you are doing well and that you don't know anything about any of these things. You don't write anything about Olinka. How happy poor Papa would have been to see his grandchildren. Unfortunately, it was not granted to him! How are Sophinka and her parents?

So, Hansinko mine, keep your head up, and don't be stingy with your reports. You know how longingly we always wait for news from you, and that we are interested in everything that concerns you. We also want to write to you more often if possible. Farewell, my dear child, I hug you all deeply. Your loving *Mama*

Dear Hansi! Next time I will try to write more. Just write diligently.

Greetings and kisses from *Julko*

It took him a while, but Hansi understood the reality of his situation—he was now far from "home" and he had to put all his strength and efforts into building a new home in the country that had provided them the opportunity to start over.

As soon as he settled in Ecuador, he began the immigration process to bring over his sisters and their families. He was unsure whether his parents would be able to make the long journey and at the time, was unaware of Móric's declining health. In spite of all the political turmoil, the thought of uprooting them to unknown lands must have been quite stressful and sad.

The war in Europe rapidly progressed, with the Germans taking Yugoslavia and Greece[59] and, despite the non-aggression pact they had signed ten months earlier, Germany began its assault on the USSR.[60]

In January 1940, two months before my parents arrived in Ecuador, President Mosquera Narváez died suddenly. General elections were held that month and Dr. Carlos Arroyo del Rio, a university professor and wealthy company lawyer from Guayaquil, was elected president. He took office on September 1, 1940. Lilo Linke arrived in Quito just in time to watch the solemn ceremony. [47] The United States had a sizable delegation.

To the misfortune of Dr. Arroyo and the country, from May 5 to 31 of the following year, the Peruvian armed forces invaded the southern coastal provinces, on the pretext of the century-old border dispute. The Piklers, by then fairly fluent in Spanish, followed the news in the press and on radio. Hansi recalled how the Ecuadorian Armed Forces—largely made up of poorly trained and equipped volunteers—were speedily defeated. On July 31, a ceasefire agreement went into effect. After the Japanese attacked Pearl Harbor on December 7, 1941, the United States declared war on Japan and four days later on Germany and Italy.[61] Two months later, Dr. Carlos Arroyo del Rio signed the infamous *Protocolo de Rio de Janeiro*.[62]

From Lučenec, Teri wrote to Hansi in May 1942 that a month earlier, the Slovak secret police had made a threatening visit to Julko at home, and the family had left Žilina for Budapest. They were afraid that they were in immediate danger of being deported to a concentration camp, aware that a few days earlier, a transport with entire Jewish families had left Slovakia for such camps. These transports continued until October 20, 1942 and then suddenly stopped until September 30, 1944.

The Slovak Catholic hierarchy protested these deportations and even issued a pastoral letter protesting against them. The Vatican also expressed its unhappiness with the Slovak government policy of deporting Jews.

In Ecuador, the Pikler family grew by one when I was born on June 4, 1942. My mother's obstetrician was Dr. Isidro Ayora (1879-1978), a distinguished physician and obstetrics professor with a remarkable and extraordinary professional, academic, and political history.[63]

Unbeknownst to me, my birth had been in some doubt, as my parents' marriage had been strained since shortly after they settled in Quito. Sophie's mother, Ruchel ("Rosa"), who had a great influence on her daughter, had been interfering in my parents' marriage from the beginning. She was a frequent figure in their home, and Sophie would also spend time at her parents' home while Hansi was at work. When Rosa found out in 1941 that Sophie was pregnant, she strongly suggested Sophie should not go through with it. Fortunately for me, in this instance my mother did not listen to her. When I was a teenager and learned of these conflicts, I was very unhappy imagining what must have been happening at that time in my parents' lives, both at home and in the world.

Oli, on the other hand, remembered some happy times at home during this time, a social life where friends, mostly European expats, would come to play cards, discuss topics of the day, or listen to classical music.

On July 11, 1943, the Sunday edition of *El Comercio*, the leading newspaper in Quito, brought news of the Allied invasion of Sicily which began the day before. Two months later, Italy surrendered.

El Comercio; July 11, 1943

Also in 1943, Leika and Julko, who were living in Budapest, were found to be illegally in the country and were imprisoned for a year. They managed to escape and fled back to Czechoslovakia, settling in Banská Bystrica where they lived under the assumed Slovak name of Bučan.

El Comercio, "Gemany Surrenders"; May 7, 1945

The German army continued to advance in Central Europe and by March 1944 it was threatening Hungary. Afraid to be arrested in Budapest, the rest of the family, except for Edit who remained in Budapest, fled back to Czechoslovakia. They settled in Čeklis, a small town near the capital Bratislava, under the name Modos.

Teri kept Hansi informed of the family's ordeals and the fact that they were living under different names. Correspondence had to be curtailed somewhat and he was alerted to use the aliases and avoid any information that the authorities could use against them if the letters were to fall into the wrong hands.

I can't recall my father ever sharing with Oli and me any information about these travails during the war, including the internment of three of his sisters in Hitler's concentration camps. The only thing my father mentioned was that for several months, beginning in June 1944, he received no replies to the letters he wrote to his sisters. The same was true of their Czechoslovakian friends: none of them heard anything from the family members they had left back home.

The weekend of June 10-11, 1944 was quite a festive one at the Czechoslovak Club in Quito. The news of the Allied forces' Normandy invasion on June 6 brought joy and hope that the war would end soon. There was a music program that both my father (violin) and my mother (piano) participated in, along with others. Oli attended but I stayed home with Dolores, my nanny.

As detailed in Chapter Three, which includes Leika's Shoah interview, in late August 1944 the Slovak state became the scene of an armed uprising against both Nazi Germany and the Slovak fascist regime led by President Tiso. This was the Slovak National Uprising. [24, 81] Julko fought in several battles and in one of them, he lost his life. Leika, who had always traveled with him, joined the family in Čeklis a few days later. The insurgency was defeated and ended on October 27, when Banská Bystrica was occupied by the Germans without a fight. The security police arrested about 13,000 people, many starting on September 30, of whom almost 10,000 were Jews, and most of whom were transferred to concentration camps, while the rest were given "special treatment," that is, they were murdered without trial. [24]

The news on May 7-8, 1945, of Germany's surrender, called V-E Day,[64] was all over the radio and local newspapers, bringing a great deal of jubilation to the Jewish immigrant community. It was learned later on that close to seven million displaced people were staying in the Western zones of liberated Germany.

El Comercio; May 8, 1945

By 1945 the Piklers had rented the first floor of a two-story house in La Mariscal neighborhood, a very nice residential area. It had four bedrooms but only one large bath with a water tank attached to the bathtub and heated by burning wood. It had a dining room but no living room, a kitchen with a wood stove, and an outside pantry (cold enough to keep items fresh) next to the kitchen. Clothes were washed by hand with cold water and elbow grease at an outdoor laundry area. To help pay expenses, one room was always rented to boarders. In an adjacent building there were two rooms for the housekeeper and the nanny. There was also an outside bathroom and a large backyard.

Sophie, Oli, George, and Hansi; Quito, 1946

We had a German Shepherd guard dog, the first of several over the years. Some of them were poisoned by robbers who regularly broke in to steal the chickens, turkeys, ducks, and geese kept in an enclosure on the side of the house. Such robberies were commonplace, and still are; as a result, it has become quite typical to see homes in residential neighborhoods surrounded by tall brick walls embedded with glass shards on top. These measures are meant to deter robbers, but they probably only work for the amateurs. The professionals now break in and steal household items and vehicles

Sophie with Oli and George at their grandparents' home; Quito, 1947

Sophie with George; Quito, 1947

George with Arnold, his maternal grandfather; Quito, 1947

from locked garages, so well-to-do citizens have taken to hiring full-time guards for their homes.

Friends of my parents, also Czechoslovak immigrants, would frequently socialize at both homes, while I played with their children.

Sophie, Hansi, Oli, and George with his fourth birthday party guests; June 1946

As noted earlier, between 1945 and 1946, my father was able to secure visas for his sisters and their families to come to Ecuador, but in the end, they decided to stay in Czechoslovakia, and ultimately dispersed.

On October 24, 1946, my mother moved out of our home and in with her parents. Oli remembered coming home one day and finding our mother's closets empty. She was gone. This was a very traumatic experience for Oli, who was nine at the time—old enough to understand its implications.

Two months later, on December 24, 1946, I was "abducted" by Sophie just outside our family home. I remember very clearly being told to lie down in the back of the car (which belonged to my grandparents). After that, I lived with my mother and maternal grandparents for about one year. They owned a soap factory—the American Soap Works or *Fábrica de Jabones Finos*. I was only four-and-a-half years old and have several memories of the time I lived with them. However, I do not have any recollections of how I felt being away from my father and sister. I was eventually returned to my father's care since the Ecuadorian laws regarding custody favored him, considering that my mother had "abandoned" the home and the children, and had filed for divorce with no evidence of infidelity or maltreatment, claiming only "irreconcilable differences." Hansi was assigned custody of both Oli and me.

To the best of my recollection, no one ever discussed these events again. Certainly not with Oli or me.

In later years, Oli related to me "the cloud of sadness" that hung over our home after Sophie left. She recalled her sense of desperation when first our mother was gone and then when I was taken away. As if that wasn't bad enough, in the middle of our parents' divorce proceedings news arrived that Hansi's extended family would most likely never be together again. Oli recalled this time as "two awful years of unbearable sadness."

Hansi and Sophie divorced in August 1948. He was forty-six, she was thirty, Oli and I were eleven and six, respectively. My personal belief is that a divorce is about more than just the dynamics between spouses. I have always felt that my maternal grandmother played a pivotal role in the dissolution of my parents' marriage. This thought has remained with me and shaded my relationship with her. Even so, I was always polite and treated her respectfully.

In spite of the emotional trauma of having his son taken away and the acrimonious divorce proceedings fueled by Sophie's family, I never heard my father utter a bad word about my mother. Hansi was certainly bitter about the interference of his mother-in-law in their marriage, but he never dwelled much on this unfortunate situation and kept his feelings to himself. He never hesitated to contact Sophie to discuss any issues related to the welfare of their children, and years later when they would meet their interaction was always cordial and respectful.[65]

Sophie and Sam; Quito, 1950

In November 1950, Sophie remarried to Sam Luftig in Quito.[66] I first met Sam at a synagogue in 1947. Sophie recalled that I twice tipped Sam's hat as he sat in front of us during services. Afterwards, she apologized to Sam. From then on, they were friends. Sam was a smart, steady, and very pleasant person with a quirky sense of humor.

Sophie and Sam emigrated to the US in 1951 and settled in Miami despite the fact that Sam had a very good job offer in Chicago as a trained furrier. Sophie had several family members there but told Sam she wanted to be as close as possible to her children.

My mother became an American citizen on April 25, 1958.

She was a master dressmaker and worked at an exclusive bridal shop in Coral Gables, Florida. Sam became a well-respected salesman for a handbag company. He had a showroom in the Miami Merchandise Mart, and traveled the southern states extensively, with Sophie joining him on some of his trips. They gradually became members of a group of friends whose company they enjoyed. Those who knew the Luftigs felt they made a charming couple. They always seemed to get along very well, except when Sophie felt one of Sam's quirky jokes was not funny.

Sophie and Sam; Miami (date unknown)

My mother was a very attractive woman with a flair of distinction and sophistication. She loved music, particularly classical music (violin and piano concertos were her favorites). She was a happy, caring person, who enjoyed a good laugh. She was not opinionated; in fact, she avoided any type of controversy or conflict. I don't recall ever having had an argument with her. She was affectionate with Oli and me, and years later, with Elaine, and our children.

Hansi remarried to Virginia Salvador Moreira on April 21, 1951, in Quito.[67] She was also a caring person and made sincere efforts to welcome Oli and me into her life. It was certainly more difficult for Oli, at age 14, to accept Virginia occupying Sophie's place. I believe that Oli clung for many years to the hope that our parents would someday reunite. There were times of friction and disagreement between Oli and Virginia, but they managed to get along as best as they could until Oli went to live with Sophie.

Virginia and Hansi's wedding; Quito, April 21, 1951

My experience was somewhat different. I did not have much time to bond with my mother before she left, so I was able to accept a stepmother's presence much more easily. Still, Virginia left all discipline to Hansi, and I learned early on not to confide any secrets to her because they would soon be passed along to my father. But overall, any conflicts we had would be considered normal between a stepparent and a child.

What I do recall is that when I was around six years old, I began to ask my father for details about our family background and

Countryside picnic; 1955

**George and Hansi at Alangasí pool;
August 1955**

**Hansi and George after hiking in the
country; August 1955**

life in Europe. This happened often when he would translate the letters he had received from his sisters and their families. I began collecting scraps of the family history in a shoebox that—decades later—provided the seeds for this narrative.

Hansi and Virginia's social life included his previous European immigrant friends, who welcomed her, as well as Virginia's Ecuadorian friends and others they both met at work, who were frequent guests in their home. Virginia's mother would come from Guayaquil and stay with us for a few days and other relatives of hers would visit and frequently stay for dinner. By then, the Czechoslovak Club was no longer.

As a family we enjoyed going to nearby thermal water spa located about 45 to 60 minutes southwest of Quito, at a lower altitude with a warmer climate (about 2-5 degrees fahrenheit higher, on average). In those days, the trip took longer because there were only two-lane stone roads; today the same trip would take twenty minutes. San Pedro del Tingo, or *El Tingo*, was located at the foot of the Ilaló volcano in Los Chillos Valley. It had a large public pool with surrounding cabanas. There were also a few small indoor pools (for 6 to 10 people), with water temperatures ranging from 98.6F to 104F degrees that were advertised as having "medicinal" properties for individuals with a variety of health disorders. Hansi greatly enjoyed visiting El Tingo. It reminded him of the days when he would travel to Karlovy Vary (Karlsbad), the most frequented spa in Czechoslovakia, where patients from many countries went seeking relief for stomach and other ailments. At El Tingo there were several local restaurants and a couple of inns run by European immigrants where our family, along with friends, would stay for a few days.

On other occasions, we would go with other families to another spa, Alangasí, and afterwards we would have a picnic nearby.[68]

In the early fifties, Hansi and a business partner started a delicatessen called Sabrosano in midtown. It was a successful restaurant, frequented by immigrants, and a novelty for the local population. The business and partnership, however, fell apart after one year because his partner was found to have absconded with business funds.

In February 1952, Hansi joined Casa Ortega, a diversified import firm in Quito. He became the sales manager of Westinghouse equipment and home appliances. Virginia had started working at the firm two years earlier—the firm's owner was a distant cousin of hers—and she oversaw the Helena Rubinstein cosmetics department.

Hansi did very well for the company. He was known as an honest salesman and every year he surpassed all sales and profit expectations. His business interactions with government, embassies, and institutional clients brought him another circle of friends, many of whom would invite him to formal official events.[69] He and Virginia, in turn, would have "official" dinners at their home with dishes they prepared.[70]

My mother traveled to Ecuador twice in the early fifties to visit Oli and me. In 1954, she asked Hansi to allow Oli, at seventeen, to live with her in Miami. He agreed to it. At the time, I was very unhappy to see my sister leave, but later on, I understood her decision came from a need to be closer to our mother. Sophie was not a disciplinarian which also appealed to Oli's teenage desire for self-control.

In 1954, Oli attended college in Miami, and then worked for a year as a medical secretary. For six months from October through April 1956, Sophie and Oli lived in Lima, Peru with Sophie's parents. The reasons for this are unknown. Oli subsequently decided to attend beauty school, and after her graduation, she worked in an exclusive beauty salon in Miami.

In 1955, Hansi entered the South American Westinghouse Salesman's contest and won the top salesman award. On March 23, 1956, Westinghouse congratulated him and asked if he would consider joining its sales force in the US. He and Virginia seriously considered the proposal, but despite the generous offer he received, he turned it down. Ecuador, he often said, was the country that had opened its arms to welcome him: "No money offer or job position could ever equal the wonderful life this country allowed me to have."

That year, they rented a house located across a large park (El Parque del Ejido). In those days, it was considered "the Central Park of Quito," offering entertainment activities for children and adults. I walked across the park every day on my way home from school. It was the best place in "midtown" to go for a picnic, play on the swings, or ride a bike. While in high school and later as a university student, it was my favorite place to go to study.

My father's daily routine began at the crack of dawn, and he was always the first one up. After freshening up he would go to the kitchen for a lifelong ritual of brewing coffee. He used a three-piece porcelain coffeemaker he brought from Europe, now prominently displayed in a curio cabinet in our Florida home.

He was quite choosy as to which Ecuadorian coffee beans to buy. After grinding them by hand (also with a grinder from Europe), he placed the coffee in the upper half of the coffeemaker and slowly added hot water to the grounds. He then transferred the coffee essence to a tall, dark glass bottle and corked it. The essence was never reused the next day no matter how much or how little was left. It had to be brewed every day. In Ecuador, whether at home or at a restaurant, a cup of coffee began with a cup of warm whole milk (there was no skim or two percent), to which the coffee essence was added at whatever strength was desired by the drinker. If just the essence was served in a smaller cup, it was called a *tinto*, or if served in a small cup with just a little milk, it was called a *cortadito* in the Cuban tradition.

Our father would prepare breakfast for both Oli and me: a slice or two of dark bread spread with butter and honey. I was never hungry for breakfast, so when my father was not around, I would hide some of the bread slices in the back of the table drawer where he or the housekeeper would find them days later. After I was found out two or three times, my father was alerted to check the drawer and I had to finish all my breakfast.

Oli and I went through similar experiences at lunch and dinner. If there was a dish we did not like (I hated spinach soufflé and Oli did not like polenta) and we would ask for "a little bit less," we could expect two or more spoons of it on our plates with the admonition: "This is not a restaurant, we must be grateful that we have food to eat." If we refused to eat what was served, the plate would be removed. We quietly rejoiced for what we thought was a victory, only to have the same reheated food served at our next meal. Needless to say, after two or three such events, neither one of us said a peep at mealtime. We learned to eat everything, and as we grew older, it was not unusual for us to ask for an extra serving of the foods we previously disliked.

Once a year, for our birthdays, we were asked what dishes we would like to have. My favorites were *Wiener schnitzel mit Kartoffelbrei* (mashed potatoes) *und Sauerkraut;* years later I added fried plantains to give the dish an Ecuadorian flavor, and Hungarian goulash *mit nockerl* (with dumplings). I don't recall Oli or Edulka's favorites.

Hansi and Virginia were at work by 8:15 every morning. We all had lunch and dinner together. Mealtimes were always respected and were a chance to discuss the events of the day. The radio Hansi had brought from Europe sat on a desk in the dining room and we often enjoyed listening to classical or easy listening music during meals. After lunch, Hansi would lie down for a short siesta and would get up quite refreshed and ready to be back at work at 2:15PM. Evening meals were served around 7PM. When we were very young, we would eat much earlier, but we would still join our parents when they dined. They never owned a car.

My father's hobbies included cooking, collecting Ecuadorian stamps, and listening to music on the radio. He would readily admit that he did not know much about cooking before he got to Ecuador. He asked his sisters to send him cookbooks, and every weekend, he would spend hours reading them and "experimenting" in the kitchen. Virginia also enjoyed cooking. In the late 1950s they bought a mixer similar to a large Kitchen Aid with many attachments. Over the years my father became a gourmet cook, preparing delicious European dishes as well as diverse cakes and pastries, two of which could be found most weeks in the dining room. Among the favorites were: *mohnstrudel* (poppy seed strudel), either the Austrian or Hungarian style (*mákos retes*); the Esterhazy Hungarian torte; and an *oblatne wafer torte* with marmalade in between the wafers and covered with chocolate. A *kugelhopf* (Bundt cake) was definitely a staple as well. Oli, Edulka, and I had the best of both worlds: both typical Czechoslovak cuisine and Ecuadorian dishes. They would also bake cakes as gifts for friends or for officials in government offices. They would even bring a cake to the US when they came to visit us. Those were the good old days with no TSA regulations.

Hansi would go to the market once a week, usually on Saturdays, an open large market with vendors sitting on the ground with their fresh products in front of them. The place was scented with mingled fragrances of fresh fruits, vegetables, flowers, etc. The housekeeper would carry two large baskets of strong woven straw (canastas). From time to time, he would take Oli or me along. That was when we learned the art of bartering. We watched how he would choose the best products and barter for the best price.

He did not like alcoholic beverages. However, he would serve them to friends and dignitaries who he invited to dine at our home.

Hansi had a sweet tooth. He would bring home bars of Toblerone chocolate, bonbons, and a variety of candy. He had hard candy in his pockets and a bag of candy would sit on his night table. Every night, if he was not listening to the radio, he would read the evening newspaper and enjoy his candy.

His stamp collection consisted only of Ecuadorian stamps. He would spend hours reading catalogs and adding new stamps to his album. He was a member of the local philatelist society and would attend its monthly meetings.

He very much enjoyed listening to music and other entertainment on the radio. He brought one from Europe (now in our Florida home), and years later, bought a large Zenith radio which allowed him to tune into European stations and listen to their news and classical music. When the Ecuadorian congress was in session he would listen to the speeches and comment on those he found hilarious.

He frequently bought lottery tickets and several times won small amounts. On February 2, 1960, the day my sister Edulka was born, he bought a ticket that combined the numbers of the day, month, year of her birth with the number of the maternity room where she had just been born. It was a lucky number: as I recall, his winnings paid for all the medical expenses.

Throughout his life in Ecuador, my father maintained a close correspondence with his sisters and their families, both in Europe and Israel, and spared no effort to support them in any way they needed. He made sure that everyone in the family received a monetary gift for their birthday. For several years, Hansi and Virginia would also send his sisters a pound of coffee in a bag that would have a gift hidden inside. The sac was meticulously sewn; a plastic surgeon would have been proud of the quality of the stitching. If a friend or one of Virginia's relatives were traveling to Europe, they would ask them to take a small package and mail it to Leika.

He would dictate letters to the family which were typed by Mr. Levy, a polite, kind, observant Jew, an elderly gentleman who made a living as a typist. For several years he came to the house at least twice a month, usually late on Saturday afternoons. He was always invited to stay for dinner.

After Mr. Levy died in February 1970, Hansi struggled to find someone to replace him. This was not easy. It was unusual to have someone to make 'house calls' for this purpose, more so a typist who would patiently listen to a dictation in German. He found someone in the European community but this replacement lasted only a few months. This took a toll on the frequency of his correspondence. At the time, his sisters wondered if the lack of news from Ecuador was due to illness. Despite it all, he did manage to reply to them. For several years, with the help of contacts in the telephone company switchboard, he and Virginia were also able to make short calls to Leika, Sanyi, and Klári.

Years later, when my aunts would write to me in German, they would mail the letters to Hansi who would translate them into Spanish and Virginia would type them and send them to me.

In the mid-fifties, during the summer, Hansi, Virginia, and I spent ten days at a European hotel in Playas, a seaside resort town not far from the port city of Guayaquil. We traveled by bus, and with window seats, enjoyed the view of the Avenue of the Volcanos from Quito to Ambato. It took at least three harrowing hours on cliff-hanging roads to reach the town of Santo Domingo de los Colorados, named after the Colorado Indians with their distinctive looking orange-dyed hair and bodies (using achiote) and their bright clothing. One summer, we also went to Manta, a city on the Pacific coast where Virginia was born and still had family at the time. We enjoyed eating freshly caught fish cooked on the beach.

In August 1956, while we were vacationing in Playas, my father suffered a massive heart attack. He was 54 years old. He had been quite athletic in his youth, and played for the company soccer team in Romania, but since his late twenties he had acquired a portly figure which was fashionable in Europe and a sign of "good living." He had no time for any physical exercise and was a heavy smoker. He was hospitalized in Guayaquil and was critically ill in an oxygen tent for several days. He was released three weeks later, returned to Quito, and went back to work. He stopped smoking for a few months, but afterwards he slowly resumed the habit.

In the summer of 1959, I was welcomed by Sophie and Sam for my first US visit with the warmth of a Miami summer. I very much enjoyed my 2½-month stay. The weather was hot and humid—

something I was not used to, coming from the temperate climate of the Ecuadorian *serranía*.

I had not seen Sophie and Oli since 1954 (although we kept in touch through sporadic correspondence and occasional phone calls). My mother took off from her work for the entire length of my stay, and on weekends, when Sam was not on the road selling handbags, the three of us visited many tourist attractions, and took a week-long trip along the East coast to Cypress Gardens. Later that summer, Sophie and I decided on a sightseeing trip to New York City, traveling by train to Washington, DC and by bus the rest of the way. We had a lot of fun together and plenty of time to bond and catch up.

My beloved Papi and Mami (Hansi and Sophie)

My mother and I learned a lot about each other that summer. We had long conversations and recalled events going all the way back to our childhoods. My parents' marriage difficulties and subsequent divorce was never discussed. Neither one of us would have brought up the topic. We took turns relating our experiences. Sophie had a strict but loving upbringing; her favorite school subjects were literature and art; she had read and enjoyed Stefan Zweig's writings; piano lessons started at age eleven and she had a wonderful teacher whose studio was near her house. She was not one to brag but admitted that her love of music came naturally, and she practiced piano every day. Over the years she relished playing her favorite composers' music but she also liked "lighter music," mainly operettas and the waltzes of Johann Strauss. She related how happy she was when Oli was born in Žilina a year after her marriage, and also spoke of the happiness that Oli's birth brought to Hansi's family. She confided that she had wished her second child would be a boy (no sonograms were available at the time) and how thrilled she was when the obstetrician gave her the news in the delivery room. Hansi and five-year-old Olga wanted to hold me all the time, but the clinic rules allowed only limited visits. She also reminded me of all the mischievous things I had done during my year-long stay with her and we laughed a lot reminiscing.

In New York, I met Sam's two brothers and their families and we spent a lovely evening with them. Sophie and I then visited most of the important New York tourist sites including its museums, including the Soviet National Exhibition where the replica of the first Sputnik was on display.

Sophie and Sam lived on the first floor of a typical Florida two-story home with two bedrooms, one bath, a living room, and a kitchen. The house owner, a lovely elderly lady, lived upstairs. She was a historian and a professor at the University of Miami. Several years later, she sold the house to Sophie and Sam, and after Sophie died in 1981, Oli bought the house from Sam.

Sophie introduced me to many friends who had kids my age, and in this way, I met several nice young people as well. When it was time to say goodbye, I felt as if I had never been away from my mother and looked forward to visiting her again.

Oli was still living at home with Sophie and Sam that summer. She had one of the bedrooms, and there were two double beds in the other one. During my visit I slept in one bed, and my parents in the other one. Oli and I got along very well but did not spend too much time together. After work (she was working as a secretary for an OB/GYN) and on weekends she spent time with her friends and her future husband, Armando Sosa.

Hansi and Virginia also came to the US for the first time that summer. They spent a restful two-week vacation in Miami Beach. Oli, who had not seen her father for five years, made every effort to spend as much time as possible in their company. She also introduced them to Armando, a handsome, Cuban-born man. Hansi related later that he was taken aback when Armando addressed him by his first name, definitely not in the European manner Hansi was accustomed to.

Sam, Sophie, Oli, Hansi, and Virginia; Miami, 1959

Oli married Armando the following year and they moved into a rental apartment. They welcomed a daughter, Vivian, on November 1, 1961. Both sets of grandparents, in Ecuador and Florida, were ecstatic with their first grandchild.

The year before, Hansi and Virginia had also welcomed a new

daughter: Edith (Edulka) Wilma. At the time, he was 58 years old and she was 42. Virginia had had a miscarriage a couple of years earlier, and for both parents, as well as Oli and me, her birth was quite a joyful event. But for Virginia, who had wanted a child of her own, Edulka was a true blessing. A year earlier, my father had purchased a reel-to-reel Phillips audio tape recorder. He taped many Hungarian, Austrian, and Eastern European music programs and occasionally, speeches from Ecuadorian congressional sessions. But after Edulka was born, he and Virginia mostly enjoyed taping their interactions with her from the time she was a couple of months old, as well as conversations with Virginia's relatives. In 2016, I had all of the tapes digitalized and sent Edulka a copy of the recordings from her childhood. It was quite an emotional day when I heard my father's voice for the first time in 38 years.

Virginia with Edulka; Quito, 1960

In March 1962, we moved to the only house Hansi and Virginia ever owned. It was a beautiful two-story house with four bedrooms and two-and-a-half baths, as well as unattached quarters for live-in staff and a laundry room. The property was surrounded by a garden with tall trees, some of them fruit-bearing (figs, oranges, and lemons). A gardener took pride in keeping it in good shape, in spite of the guard dog who would chase those walking outside the fence and run over the landscape.

The Piklers' house in Quito (three views: from the garden, from the street, live-in and laundry); 1962

Edulka was raised Catholic by Virginia and went to Catholic schools. They regularly attended church services, but religion was not overtly observed at home until years later in the seventies. This did not sit well with Hansi, who did not object to sending Edulka to those excellent schools but was uncomfortable with the religious emphasis at home.

They did, however, have a Christmas tree every year, and exchanged gifts for the holiday. Years later Virginia would, from time to time, invite the priest from the nearby church she attended to come for dinner. Hansi would always welcome him in the same polite manner that he treated members of other religions (the Church of Latter-day Saints, Jehovah's Witnesses) who would ring the house bell. He would invite them in, offer them a beverage, and after they finished their proselytizing pitch, he would politely tell them that he was Jewish.

In the Spring of 1967, Hansi retired at the age of 65. I felt at the time and continue to feel that this was not a good decision on his part. Although he was in fairly good health, I feared retirement would dramatically change him. He had always been a workaholic and suddenly could not find a meaning to his daily life. He seemed to lose interest even in his hobbies. Although Hansi denied it, I believe he became progressively depressed.

Elaine and I married in October 1962, after my second year of medical school, and our daughter, Vanessa was born in October 1967. When she was eight months old, in June 1968, I graduated medical school in Quito, and we left Ecuador for my post-graduate training in the US. My father had always encouraged me to pursue my dreams, even if it meant traveling abroad. His dream, which he would at times mention in his letters, was for me to return some day to Quito and build a clinic in the beautiful garden next to his house. I vividly recall that early morning goodbye, when I could hardly control my tears. My father was still in bed. I knew I had his blessings, but I didn't know when I would be back or when I would see him again. Hansi assured me he would be fine, we hugged and said "I love you" to each other before I left.

My parents and I kept up a regular correspondence, sometimes exchanging letters as often as every seven to ten days. We also spoke on a few occasions. These were short calls, as long-distance rates were quite expensive. In addition, they would send the bi-monthly issue of the popular *Vistazo* magazine I enjoyed reading. I made four short trips to visit them in Quito between 1969 and 1974.

Oli, Klári, Hansi, Virginia, Vivian, and Edulka; Quito, August 1968

A month after my departure, Hansi underwent emergency surgery to repair an inguinal hernia. He had had a similar procedure on the opposite side in 1963 which, due to his frequent coughing spells, recurred years later and became a significant problem for him, eventually reaching a point where it was no longer safe for him to undergo surgery.

Oli and Armando's marriage faltered after a couple of years and they divorced. It was overall an amicable process. Oli continued to work as a beautician and Vivian's care fell mostly to her grandmother, Sophie.

Hansi, Virginia, and Edulka; Miami, August 1969

Elaine, Vanessa, Hansi, Oli, Virginia, Edulka, and Vivian; Rochester, MN, 1969

My father's spirits were briefly restored by Klári's visit to Quito in August 1968. They had not seen each other in 29 years. He met her as she stepped down from the ramp stairs (in those days the Quito airport did not have jetways available like today; he also had security clearance so he often would meet family members, friends and dignitaries at the bottom of the stairs leading from the airplane to the Tarmac). Oli and Vivian also came to Quito to meet Klári. Their encounter was quite emotional! Hansi, who dearly loved his sisters, related that event to all of us countless times in ensuing years, each time with tears in his eyes as he must have known they would not have another opportunity to meet. Before his sister left, he made recordings of her, Oli, Vivian, and Edulka. Klári's message, in German, is also an emotional one, and it is obvious that she also shared the same feeling that this would be the last time they would see each other.

From Quito, Klári made a one-day trip to Baltimore, where Elaine, Vanessa and I had arrived in late June for my medical internship. We met her at the airport and had no problem spotting her as she looked just like my father. Her stay was short but a very pleasant and happy one. We had no language barrier. She was excited to share details off her visit to Quito. We very much enjoyed listening to them all and were moved that she would come to meet us.

Two months later, Sam, Sophie and Elaine's mother Lillian came to Baltimore for Vanessa's first birthday party on October 20. In August 1969, Hansi, Virginia, and Edulka came to the US for a month's visit. They first spent a few days in Florida and visited Oli and her family as well as Sophie and Sam. They then came to Rochester, Minnesota, where I had started a medical residency at the Mayo Clinic. They stayed in our apartment. My father was not feeling well after they arrived. I insisted that he be_evaluated at the Mayo Clinic, and he was found to be in early heart failure. After a brief hospitalization, he was discharged to be followed as an outpatient. He fully recovered. We took Hansi and Virginia on several sightseeing tours, including a lovely day boating down the Mississippi on a pontoon boat.

Sophie's parents, Arnold and Rosa Pauker, also split up, sometime in the sixties. Arnold stayed in Lima, Peru where he had a soap factory. His son, Max, took over the factory, and with Rosa's help, he forced Sophie to relinquish her inheritance to him. He even tried to have Sam and Sophie's bank accounts transferred to his name! Arnold died in Lima, date unknown. Rosa emigrated to the United States on January 13, 1964. She lived in Sophie and Sam's upstairs apartment. Sophie took care of her mother who had renal failure and required dialysis. Rosa died in 1971 and was buried at Mt. Nebo Cemetery in Miami, Florida, where Sophie and Oli would later join her.

In January 1970, I visited Quito for six days while Elaine—who was three months pregnant at the time—and Vanessa stayed in Miami with Elaine's parents. During my visit, Hansi and Virginia mentioned for the first time the possibility of emigrating to the US, to live closer to Oli and me, if they could sell their house. They were considering asking Oli to sponsor them for immigration purposes.

A couple of weeks before our son, Jason, was born on July 28, 1970, both of his grandmothers came to Rochester to help Elaine. His birth brought happiness to us and the entire family. We had had no clue that he would be a boy, but my father and I were especially overjoyed that the Pikler name would carry on.

Letters from Israel brought worrisome news: Klári had been ill for two months with annoying abdominal pains and had also difficulty climbing stairs. She had not responded to treatment. She was hospitalized in Haifa that summer, and at the same time, Teri was in the hospital in Nahariya. A letter from Teri's son, Ivan, in October reported that Klári had been diagnosed with lung cancer with liver metastases and appeared jaundiced. His mother's health had not improved, either. Klári died in November. I was asked by the family to break the news to my father, knowing how he felt about his sisters. They were afraid of his reaction and whether his health was strong enough to handle it. I recall that, as expected, he was terribly saddened, but also relieved that Klári was not suffering any longer. In a letter a month later, he wrote: "Klári was a fair adviser and a guide for all of us. I always appreciated the wise advice she offered me in her letters."

Oli remarried Germán (pronounced "Herman" with the accent on the á) Lugo on June 28, 1971. When they announced their engagement in 1970, Hansi spoke with Sophie about his future son-in-law. The fact that she vouched for him seemed to relieve any paternal concerns he had, but all that changed after he learned that they were considering moving to Venezuela to live. Letters from home revealed his desperation, not knowing what kind of life Oli would have living so far away from her mother. Uncertain about Oli and Germán's plans to move to Venezuela, Hansi and Virginia decided then not to pursue any further plans to emigrate to the US.

George, Elaine, Jason (2 years old), Vanessa (5 years old)
with Hansi, Virginia, and Edulka; Quito, 1972

Vivian, Elaine, Sophie, George, Vanessa, and Jason; De Ridder, LA 1973

Although I would have been thrilled to have them closer, where we would have been able to visit each other often, I agreed with their decision.

Elaine and I decided to visit Quito in early 1972. My parents wanted to spend time with us and our children. Jason met his grandparents for the first time; my father wanted to hold and hug him and Vanessa all the time. Virginia prepared the dishes we liked, and we did a lot of sightseeing. It was a short but wonderful trip.

Hansi, Virginia and Edulka came to Miami that summer for a month's vacation. They stayed at a hotel in Miami Beach. I had joined the army that month and was at Fort Sam Houston for basic training prior to a two-year deployment to Fort Polk, Louisiana. I called them several times. My father expressed his disappointment that he would not see me that summer. As usual, he claimed to be doing well, but Virginia and Edulka shared that back at home he

Jason, Hansi, Edulka, Elaine, and Vanessa; Florida, 1972

smoked a lot and was always very anxious. They got to see Elaine, our children and Oli's family several times. Oli and Germán also kept them busy with trips to tourist attractions and window shopping at various malls, which they loved.

In 1973, Sophie, Vivian, and Sam, along with another couple, drove around the US in a Winnebago. They made a brief stopover to visit us in De Ridder, Louisiana where we had bought a house.

In mid-1974, after my military commitment was over, we returned to Rochester, Minnesota to continue my doctoral research program at the Mayo Clinic. A couple of months later, my parents and Edulka came to visit and stayed with us. I noticed some worsening of my father's depression. I strongly suggested he undergo a general checkup at the Mayo Clinic, but he declined.

In December of that year, while crossing a street on their way home, Hansi and Virginia were hit by a car which was attempting to pass another vehicle. Virginia suffered trauma to several ribs with multiple bruises but without any fractures. Hansi was fortunately unharmed.

Oli, German, and their son Kenny moved to Maracaibo, Venezuela in 1975. Vivian, Oli's daughter (from her first marriage)

Hansi with Vanessa and Jason; Rochester, 1974

moved in with Sophie and Sam until she finished her school year. They all returned to Miami in the Spring of 1978. During those three years, Oli was largely out of contact with the family; the lack of news from her increased Hansi's anxiety and was a constant complaint in his letters.

In a December 1976 letter, Hansi wrote: "I feel very old and tired of my past life. I have no enjoyment of anything." Six years earlier, he had stopped working on his stamp collection. His interest in cooking had waned as well.

1977 was not a good year for Hansi's chronic health problems. He smoked a lot, which worsened his emphysema and chest congestion. The coughing spells increased the size of his inguinal hernia, and the surgeons felt that his overall condition would not allow another surgical repair. Varicose veins in his legs had grown larger and caused constant leg pain, which limited his physical activity. In September of that year, Virginia added a note to a letter stating that "his nerves are getting worse." He declined to follow his doctors' advice or take the medications they had prescribed. In January of 1978 Virginia wrote "your father has no desire to get better." Edulka's letters often described him as very nervous, irritable and worried "all the time."

His refusal to follow his doctors' advice for evaluations and medical treatment were strong indicators of depression. He had repeatedly asked Virginia not to share any details of his health condition with Oli and I. In a brief, undated letter Virginia

Hansi, Virginia, and Edulka on Hansi's last birthday. March 18, 1978.

mentioned that his health was deteriorating and how frustrating it was for her and his medical team to be unable to help him. He did not want his children to worry about him. But it was his failure to take care of himself that made it impossible for the family not to worry.

In May 1978, he wrote a congratulatory letter for my upcoming birthday, and closed with "I say goodbye now my dear son and on June 4 at ten and one minute, when God brought you to life,

I will be, as every year for the past 36, thinking a lot about you. It is amazing that after so long, a few days ago I dreamed of your grandfather, my dad, sleeping next to me in my bed, how wonderful those days were." I kept this letter in my pocket for weeks and read it over and over again with an uncontrollable sadness being so far away and unable to be with him at a time when it appeared obvious that he was preparing to die.

The right time never came for me to return and build the clinic of my father's dreams. I completed my specialty medical training at the end of June of 1978—six weeks after Hansi died.

On May 17, the day before he died, one of Hansi's family physicians, Dr. Rosenthal, had been asked to see him at home. He left a prescription for a medication to treat cardiac and vascular problems. It is not known why Dr. Rosenthal was called or whether the prescription was filled.

Every evening, Hansi would set his alarm clock so that, in the morning, he could wake up Edulka as soon as he had woken up and gone to the bathroom. On the morning of May 18, Edulka heard the alarm clock go off but Hansi did not walk into her room. She thought that was strange and Virginia also felt it was unusual; when she went to look for him, she found him on the bathroom floor. She called to Edulka who thought he was not breathing. She tried mouth-to-mouth resuscitation and he began to breathe and was lucid. They helped him to stand up and he walked to the bedroom and lay down. Years later, after Edulka finished medical school, she said that this episode was most likely a respiratory arrest rather than a cardiac arrest.

Virginia immediately contacted Dr. Luis Granja, a surgeon who was also the family physician and a dear friend. It was 6:30 AM. He was not able to come to the house and asked one of his colleagues, an internist, to see Hansi right away.

The doctor promptly arrived and, after examining him, drew a blood sample and took an EKG. The doctor felt that Hansi's condition was serious and strongly recommended immediate hospitalization. Hansi refused. Dr. Granja, after speaking with Virginia, requested an ambulance to go to the house and it arrived at 7:30 AM. He refused to be hospitalized and the ambulance left after waiting for forty minutes. He claimed he needed to sleep some more and would feel better afterwards. Edulka asked the physician if he would force him to go but he said it would not be ethical to do so, because the patient was conscious and able to choose what he wanted to do.

The physician took the blood sample to the lab to check for blood gases and returned soon after with the diagnosis of metabolic acidosis, a serious situation requiring immediate hospitalization and intravenous treatment. Hansi refused again. He said, "no one is taking me out of my house." To Edulka, who kept insisting, he said, "I am not going, let me to sleep in peace—*déjame en paz.*" He turned to his side and seemed to go back to sleep. Edulka thought he was breathing well.

In light of Hansi's decision, the physician recommended that an oxygen tank and the appropriate equipment and medications be brought to their house, to which Virginia agreed. By then it was around 9:00 AM. Edulka went downstairs to have breakfast. A few minutes later, however, Virginia desperately called her to run upstairs because Hansi again had stopped breathing. It seemed that he had vomited and had undigested food in his mouth. Edulka began CPR, this time with no success. She called for the ambulance to return but was told that they could not do so because the patient had previously refused its services.

Virginia told Edulka then that she had spoken with Hansi but had been unsuccessful in convincing him to follow his physician's orders. Hansi said to Virginia, "Look, as you know I'm not good at taking medications or being bedbound. If I'm going to be that way, I would prefer that God take me once and for all." It was then that he stopped breathing.

Virginia called a friend of hers, Marta Escudero, who earlier that morning had spoken with Virginia and was already aware of the situation. She had offered to take Hansi to the hospital in her car, but he had declined the offer. Now, Edulka continued CPR for the several minutes it took Mrs. Escudero to park her car and arrive at the house. Then Virginia, Edulka, and Mrs. Escudero placed Hansi in a large blanket, covered him and carried him down the stairs and all the way to the car. At the time, Edulka did not know that she had to continue external chest compressions, so she held him in her lap. They went to the Santa Cecilia Clinic with the escort of a motorcycle policeman who happened to be passing by at the time. At the clinic, an emergency physician opened the car door and told them that Hansi was dead. The clinic would not allow them to bring him in. Virginia called Dr. Granja while Edulka waited outside with Mrs. Escudero and her father's body. Dr. Granja ordered the staff to take Hansi in on a stretcher until he was able to get to the clinic.

Hansi died on Thursday, May 18, 1978. His death certificate listed cardiopulmonary insufficiency as the cause of death. The clinic would not allow Edulka to stay with Hansi. Virginia and Mrs. Escudero left to make funeral and burial arrangements. Edulka went to the house to look for a suit for him. She found a fairly new black suit he wore on special occasions. Dr. Granja and Edulka decided to proceed with a formaldehyde embalming because Oli and I were abroad, and they had no idea when we would be able to come for the funeral.

Edulka then tried to contact Oli and me, but as she reminded me recently, in those days there were no cell phones and the clinic would not allow her to make even local calls, much less long-distance ones. She tried later to place a call through the telephone operator. Apparently, she was unable to find either one of us. She reached Sophie, who called to notify me of my father's death.

Elaine and our children were in Rochester, Minnesota at the time, where they had remained while I completed an oncology fellowship at the MD Anderson Hospital in Houston, TX. Leaving the children with friends, Elaine traveled to Miami where we met with Oli at the airport. The three of us flew to Quito on May 19.

In the few photographs taken in the last four years of Hansi's life, mostly on his birthdays, it was obvious that he had lost weight; he appeared shriveled and his eyes had lost their spark.

But when I walked into the living room where the coffin had been placed, I was impressed by my father's appearance; his face had a peaceful, tranquil look in distinct contrast to the photographs I had received of his last birthday two months earlier. I imagined he was telling me, as he had written the year before, that he was now "lying next to his own father" and was therefore at peace and did not want anyone to worry about him anymore.

I was unable to give my father a last kiss because the coffin had a glass covering. I suddenly remembered that in my wallet I carried a beautiful photograph of both Vanessa and Jason. I took the photograph and carefully slipped it down the edge of the glass and it miraculously fell next to Hansi's face, near his cheek. I felt

Hansi and Virginia's gravestone at Parque de los Recuerdos cemetery, Quito

that the children would give their grandfather the last kiss for me.

I stood by the coffin for what seemed like an eternity, and a lifetime of memories of my beloved father came to my mind at lightning speed and then I whispered to him, "Someday, I will also lie next to you."

By midafternoon, Virginia had arranged for a Catholic service, to be led by her favorite priests. The service was attended by several friends of the family, their physicians, and relatives of Virginia who came from Guayaquil. Oli, Elaine and I did not know about these arrangements. We and several of Hansi's Jewish friends who came to express condolences were surprised and unhappy about the lack of a Jewish service. Afterward, Hansi was buried at El Parque de los Recuerdos, a general cemetery. Edulka recalls Virginia telling her that Hansi had left the funeral arrangements to her.

After the burial, Elaine and I went to the synagogue to say *Kaddish* for him. A day later, the two of us met with Dr. Rosenthal. He had also been our physician and we liked and trusted him. He confirmed what I had learned from Virginia at the time: sedatives and other similar medications had been administered and mixed with Hansi's daily food, supposedly to keep him "calm." With his medical history, the potential side effects of this type of medication were unpredictable.

A letter from Leika expressed the family's profound shock at Hansi's death that seemed so sudden to them.

May 21, 1978

My dear Virginia, Edulka, Georgie, Olinka, and children,

It is with heavy heart that I write you, but I feel the need to talk to you. Like a bolt from the blue came the awful news that my much-loved brother was no longer among the living. Any words of consolation for you all would be too banal, for I know too well

136

what you have lost—husband, father, lovingness and goodness! For although Hansi had a temper—like our poor father—his heart was in the right place and he lived only for his family. The loss to all of us is just too great, and the pain. I believe that, next to our poor Edulka, I was his favorite sibling—of course, he loved all of us and he transferred that love to all of you as well. Your affection and the heartfelt words in your writings were so welcome, and I can only wish that our contact, and the feelings between us, will not only continue now that Hansi is no longer with us, but will deepen if at all possible. That would surely be his wish as well.

Since the terrible news reached me, my thoughts are always with you, and they often go far back into the past, conjuring up images of everything linked to him. Naturally I know that we cannot live on that alone, we must go on with normal life and leave Hansi to his rest. Unfortunately, I don't know when you will be accompanying our Hansi to his final resting place, and it pains me that I won't be with you, but I'll be with you in my thoughts always and I'll at least accompany him that way.

I'm not one to go visiting graves, which don't give me any comfort, but this time I feel the need to visit the grave of our poor father and at least lay down some flowers for our poor Hansi; perhaps it will bring some comfort, as though I was really accompanying him. Perhaps today is the day you're carrying our Hansi to his final resting place and saying goodbye in all our names. When the telephone rang at 11:30 at night, I immediately thought it was you. A few days earlier your sweet letter arrived with photographs, dear Edulka, in which you wrote that Hansi would give us a detailed report in a few days, so I thought he'd be calling instead of writing. I don't understand English very well, but unfortunately what you told me I understood all too well. It was the first time I'd heard your fine-sounding voice so clearly, and now I hear it constantly and I thank you for thinking of us even in your great pain and being able to carry on so bravely. You, dearest Virginia, certainly couldn't find the strength to come to the phone.

Naturally I want to hear every last detail. What could have happened?

On May 8, dear Edulka, you wrote without mentioning the possibility of any illness. Then you, dear Georgie, wrote that Hansi was suffering from a hernia but wouldn't see a doctor. We haven't answered that letter yet—if I could write to you in German it would be easier, but now I hope that someone will translate my words for you. Sanyi understands your letters in English fairly well but can't handle the translation. But feel free to write completely in English—though it doesn't alter the sad fact of what happened.

Georgie, we assume you are in Quito. But now that you are not with Elaine and the children, it seems doubtful that they could come along to the funeral, with Olinka and family. I also don't know if Hansi could be cremated, though I don't think that's in accord with your religion, Virginia. And in what cemetery is Hansi buried?

Virginia dear, is your and Edulka's future secure? Do you receive a pension now that Hansi is gone, and is it enough to live on? I worry about you a lot, and the distance is so frightful! I also think that Pepe [Virginia's brother in Guayaquil] and his family are with you now—your relationship is so close.

I intend to write to Madulka [Magda], and it will be entirely up to her if she says anything about all this to Terka just now. I fear for her, since her condition is not good. I feel very sorry for Ivko [Ivan] too, who has too many worries on his back.

My dears, I can't bring myself to write any more today. Take care of yourselves, and know that we're always there for you, as we've always been. I hope that one day we'll finally get to know one another personally. It is painful to realize that we never had the chance to get to know Hansi after all those years, though we so greatly longed to. Alas, I was unable to bury either Editka, Klarika, or Hansi.

Be strong, my dear ones. I kiss and embrace you all with much, much love. Your loving, *Lea*

P.S. 5/22 I'm just sending this off today. In the meantime, a telegram from Madulka to my girlfriend in which she asks her to tell us about Hansi—not knowing that I already knew. She wrote that it was a heart infarct—a consolation for us telling us that our Hansi didn't suffer much. Have you telegraphed Madulka? She has no telephone right now; they're still not in their own apartment.

Edulka—many thanks for your letter and good wishes; we enjoyed the photos, though Hansi looked like he'd lost a lot of weight. Now I'm double glad to have the photos.

A copy of the letter is going to Georgie, since I want to congratulate him on his birthday. I don't know how long he can stay with you or if these lines will reach him.

Dear Georgie—a sad birthday for you. But life must go on. I know how attached you were to your father, and how proud he always was of you. You have your family and a happy home for consolation. Today I kiss and embrace you, my Georgie, and wish you all things good for your birthday, good health to you and the others. I hope that we shall be able to meet while we are still alive and well. Write us about all of you, and how Edulka is getting along. I'd also like to know how your mother is, whom I always think of with love. When you see her, please tell her so. I'd be very happy if she'd write some time again. Kiss the children and Elaine for us. And kisses for you, Georgie, on your birthday. When will Olinka move, and is she happy in her new marriage?

Love, *Lea*

A year later, at Virginia's request, a *Yahrzeit* light in Hansi's name was added to the memorial board at the *Asociación de Beneficiencia Israelita* in Quito (the Jewish Community Center). The house they had bought seventeen years earlier was rented to a family, and Virginia and Edulka moved in March 1979 into a rented two-bedroom apartment not far from their house.

In 1956, the German Government decided to expand the original Reparations Agreement signed in 1952 to compensate Israel and Jews who left Europe because of the war. Over the years, Germany paid billions of dollars to the victims of the Holocaust. Hansi was one of the recipients of the reparation payments, starting in the late sixties. After he died, Virginia tried unsuccessfully for more than a year, with the help of an attorney in Quito and his colleague in Germany, to have these payments continued. Unfortunately, the German government denied her appeals. She also had to go through a lengthy process to have his Social Security payments transferred to her, and in this endeavor, she was successful.

I always remember Hansi as a loving and affectionate father, who did not hide his emotions, but showed his feelings with hugs and kisses and his true love with deeds, not just words. My earliest recollections: the scrape of his whiskers on my cheeks when he kissed me (a habit he never stopped, even when I was a married man); Hansi's daily interest in finding out what my school day was like and what I had learned (which I often did not want to talk about); his encouragement to excel in my studies and his questions about why a certain grade on my report card was *only* "very good" and *not* "excellent" (which I perceived at the time to be an unfair remark). When I got older, I realized he meant well, and I worked harder to meet his expectations.

But Hansi was also a strict disciplinarian, just like his father, grandfather, and great grandfather. He insisted that the children always, no matter the consequences, tell the truth. He continued to be over-protective with me and my sisters until the end. For example, he did not allow Oli or Edulka to go on school trips, though I, in high school, was able to convince him to let me go on those trips; if medicines had been prescribed for me that I could easily have taken at home, he would bring them to my high school and that would embarrass me; it took years for me to convince him to buy me a bicycle, which I had to wait for until I was in ninth or tenth grade.

When my father and I had occasional disagreements and did not see issues eye to eye, we both retreated to our own corners and avoided talking for a while, to control our quick tempers, and so we always remained respectful of each other.

Those who knew Hansi well would agree that he was "street smart." But in his interactions with the public, friends, and relatives, he never acted superior to anyone; he was always very generous and selfless, always ready to help those in need. He was a decent and honorable man, respectful of others and their opinions, honest not only in business but in all his interactions with family members, friends, clients, and the public in general.

Although he was not trained as a mediator, on occasion he was asked to mediate in a dispute, either at work or between acquaintances, because he was considered to be a fair-minded person. Family members, friends, and colleagues often asked for his advice, and everyone admired his wit and dry sense of humor.

After Hansi's death, Virginia and Edulka spent every Christmas and New Year in Guayaquil with Virginia's family. Correspondence with Europe and Israel continued, although less frequently. A friend of Virginia's was kind to translate the letters for her, for the most part written in German.

In October 1978, my family moved to Tulsa, OK. I was asked to chair the oncology department for a teaching hospital and I opened a private practice in Oncology-Hematology. In 1979, Virginia and Edulka came to the US and after visiting with Oli and her family, they came to Tulsa and stayed with us in the house we had bought earlier that year. Klári's son, Giora, then on his first US trip, was also invited. At the time, I was struck by how much Giora looked like Hansi at the same age.

For about four years after his death, Virginia maintained a very frequent correspondence with me, and Edulka would occasionally add some lines or write a short note. I replied in kind, and we also exchanged cassette-taped conversations at least once or twice a month. After 1984, there was a gradual decrease in the frequency of Edulka's correspondence, and after she moved to Brazil in 2003, her letters stopped coming, though she and I continued to speak over the phone from time to time.

Sometime in late 1978, Sophie described a feeling of facial fullness but did not notice any change in her appearance. She had an occasional cough but no shortness of breath. Laboratory tests and a chest X-ray were normal. When I first learned about this, I recommended she ask her physician to order a chest CT scan. Her complaint worried him because of her previous history of breast cancer.[71] I had had patients with a previous history of cancer who later noticed similar symptoms and were found to have a recurrence of their cancer diagnosed as "superior vena cava syndrome."[72] The CT scan confirmed the presence of a large mediastinal mass, and I referred her to the Mayo Clinic in Rochester, Minnesota where she underwent a biopsy which showed a recurrence of her previous breast cancer. She underwent radiation therapy to the mediastinum (the central compartment between the two lungs). Sophie and Sam came for a short visit to Tulsa after these treatments. She was obviously tired but in good spirits. Her evaluation at the Mayo Clinic had shown no other evidence of disease.

In 1980, a follow-up evaluation determined that the cancer

had metastasized to her bones, as a consequence of which she had sustained a fracture of her left arm. She was started on a chemotherapy clinical trial which included a high dose of a drug known for potential pulmonary toxicity. That year, while still undergoing her treatments, she attended Vanessa's bat mitzvah, along with Elaine's mother and aunt. Although it was obvious that Sophie was not feeling well from the side effects, she never complained.

During Sophie's illness, Leika and Virginia would often ask about her condition and sent best wishes for her recovery. In their letters, the aunts often asked about Sophie and said how much they had loved her.

Late in the spring of 1981, Sophie's health began to deteriorate, and in May she was admitted to the hospital. I went to Miami to be with her. I recall that when I walked into her hospital room, she seemed to light up a bit, and said, "my son the doctor has come to see me." On the evening of June 2, 1981, expecting her to die any time, I asked Sam, who was staying in her room, if I could also stay.

Strangely, that night I recalled an event that took place in August 1949. My mother and I were supposed to spend a few days in Baños, a town with thermal spas in the province of Tungurahua, in eastern Ecuador. We were to leave Quito around 3:00 pm for a four-hour bus ride, but just as we were leaving for the bus station, sustained land tremors were felt in Quito and adjacent provinces. Sophie immediately cancelled the trip. That afternoon at 2:00 pm, a serious earthquake in that province claimed the lives of four thousand people and laid waste to the entire province, one of the richest agricultural provinces in Ecuador.

At the hospital, no one slept much that night. Sophie asked for water (*wasser*) several times during the night, and early in the morning of June 3, she quietly died. Oli and I had witnessed our mother's progressive decline and agonizing last days. Her oncologist, a colleague of mine, had warned us of her dismal prognosis and impending death. He also apologized then and later

Sophie's gravestone at Mt. Nebo Jewish Cemetery in Miami

when we would meet at professional meetings, for including her in a clinical trial with such high potential pulmonary toxicity. Her death was traumatic for all of us. Sam, who had witnessed so much pain, suffering, and death in concentration camps, tried to put it in perspective saying we needed to be grateful that Sophie was no longer suffering.

In the spring of 1983, Oli and Germán traveled to Ecuador for a short vacation. During that trip, he complained of back pain. Upon their return to Miami, he was diagnosed with metastatic lung cancer and extensive bone involvement to the spine, the source of his pain. He received palliative radiation therapy with partial control of his symptoms, but died in July, shortly afterward.

Calls between Oli and me became more frequent after our parents died, and she was a regular dinner guest when we wintered in Florida. She never came empty handed. We would sit on the balcony and enjoy each others company.

In August 1984, Edulka graduated from medical school. I traveled to Quito for a reception party Elaine and I hosted for her. It was held at the home of Dr. Luis Granja Mena, one of Hansi's

Virginia and Edulka at her medical school graduation party. Quito, 1984

**Magda, Edulka, Elaine, and Sanyi (back), Oli, Leika, and Virginia (front)
at our Tulsa home; September 1988**

145

physicians and a former surgery professor of Edulka and I. He and his wife graciously volunteered their home for this event.

That same year, Virginia found a buyer for the house and bought a comfortable small condo located not far from the same residential neighborhood where she and my father had lived, which was close to several of her friends' homes. At street level, the condo building had a small grocery store, a post office, and a boutique.

Magda, with her husband, Peter Bielik and their two boys, moved to Detroit, MI in September 1987. Leika and Sanyi came to the US to visit them the following summer, and they happily accepted our invitation to come to Tulsa. Magda and her parents as well as Oli, Virginia, and Edulka were our guests in September 1988. We thoroughly enjoyed their visit, with fun moments at the pool and visiting nearby tourist attractions. Oli and I also had the opportunity to listen to Leika's stories about her early family life.

Sanyi, Leika, and Magda in Tulsa; September 1988

In the fall of 1999, Virginia lost consciousness in her apartment in Quito. Her housekeeper, who was also feeling ill, was able to yell for help. Neighbors managed to open the apartment door and

Virginia was subsequently hospitalized. Her housekeeper promptly recovered once the apartment was aired. According to Edulka, very fine ashes from a recent volcano eruption near Quito had affected many people's breathing, and when they were advised to close their windows and doors to avoid the ashes getting into their homes, apparently Virginia had hermetically sealed all windows and ventilation ducts. She probably suffered mild carbon monoxide poisoning and lost consciousness. She was fortunate to have been rescued promptly. Once she recovered, she spent several days with her brother's family at the coast. Dr. Granja wrote to me after he saw Virginia. He noted that she appeared very nervous and had some signs of senility. In July 2002, I went to Quito for a week of lectures and didn't notice any signs of senility.

Edulka wanted Virginia to move to Brazil so that she could look after her mother and keep her company. At the time, I questioned whether this would be a good decision. After all, Virginia had family in Guayaquil who she would visit and communicate with very frequently. She also had a circle of friends in Quito she would see from time to time. She did not speak Portuguese. Edulka was very busy and often on call at the hospital.

Virginia went to Brazil in 2003 to visit Edulka, not planning to stay. But for unknown reasons, she never made it back to Ecuador. In our phone conversations, I had the feeling she was unhappy. She told me that she spent most of the time watching TV in a language she did not understand, she could hardly communicate with Edulka's housekeeper, and Edulka was on-call most of the time.

Virginia died on May 22, 2006 in Niteroi, Brazil of a cerebral hemorrhage. She was on numerous medications including an anticoagulant. Apparently, she fell in Edulka's apartment and suffered head trauma. She was admitted to a hospital where the severity of the intracranial bleeding was found to be quite extensive. Efforts to keep her alive failed. She was cremated in Brazil, and in June, Edulka brought her ashes to Quito for burial. Oli, Elaine, and I traveled to Quito for the religious services and her funeral. The urn was placed above the cement slab that covered Hansi's coffin.

Sam died on October 22, 2014 at age 95. Until his death, Oli's children, Kenny and Vivian, living in Miami, always watched after their grandfather and took excellent care of him. When Elaine and I wintered in Florida, we saw that they frequently visited with him. In spite of multiple health issues, his mental acuity remained intact until the end. When the end came, Kenny, Vivian and I were present. He was buried at Mt. Sinai Memorial Park in Miami.

I kept all 803 letters I received from my parents after I left Ecuador in 1968 along with those from Oli, Edulka, Virginia, my aunts, and their families in Europe and Israel. Oli had also kept letters that Hansi, Virginia, and Edulka had written to her, and after she died, her children gave them to me.

I read each of these letters again as part of my research for this narrative, and in many of them, I found information I had forgotten or had overlooked before. It was quite an emotional endeavor. The true meaning of love was palpable in each of those letters, and I spilled more than a few tears.

I always felt the richness of my father's love and truly believe he was a wealthy man, with a wealth not measured in stocks or bank accounts. Its currency was his love, which he spread to his entire family every day. I am grateful to have been the recipient of such unqualified love and feel privileged to be his son. No day goes by I don't think of him. His memory has been and will always be a blessing.

Chapter Three

Klári, Teri, Leika, Edit

The narrative I have compiled in this chapter about the lives of my father's four sisters has arisen from a wide a variety of sources: I have first-hand oral and written information from the conversations Oli and I had with Leika; Leika's interviews, one from just after the liberation of the Ravensbrück camp in June 1945, and the second from her participation in the 1996 Survivors of the Shoah Foundation; and the extensive correspondence my father received from his parents, his sisters, and their families.

I have also made use of second- and third-hand accounts of my aunts' experiences, much of which I learned from my sister, Oli. In October 2008, after the Pikler family reunion in Budapest, Oli spent a whole day in Žilina talking with Leika, who recounted for much of that day what she, in turn, had learned from Teri and Klári about their concentration camp experiences.

Soon afterward, Oli and I traveled back to the US together, and Oli spent the whole trip recounting as many details as she could recall about her day-long conversation with Leika. Since we lost Oli only two months later, I was very glad to have taken careful notes on everything she told me. Keeping in mind that my goal in writing this family narrative was to paint as complete a picture as I could of that generation of Piklers, I have faithfully reproduced the contents of that crucial conversation with Oli wherever I thought it was needed to round out the picture, despite the imperfect process of conveying information that was told from sister to sister, then from aunt to niece, and then from sister to brother before being written down here.

Oli and I were fortunate to have had the opportunity to spend time with Leika in 1988 (Tulsa), 1997 (Tucson), 2003 (Miami Beach), and 2008 (Žilina). Oli spoke German and was able to elicit from Leika, at different times during those family meetings, some prewar reminiscences of the Pikler's family life in Slovakia; her own recollections of concentration camp internment and those of Klári and Shlomo's at Terezín; and excerpts from a 1976 meeting in Israel, at which Leika and Sanyi were present when Teri related the traumatic events she experienced at Auschwitz through an interview with Peter Dansky (a former kindergarten pupil of hers in Lučenec).

Leika's interviews of 1945 and 1996 also describe in painful detail both hers and Elsa's internment at Ravensbrück, the political situation of the Jews in Czechoslovakia after the Germans took over the Sudetenland, and several other travails of the Móric branch and their families during the war years.

Invaluable resources in my research were my father's extensive collection of documents, the letters and postcards to Hansi from Klári, Teri, Géza, Leika, Sanyi, and Edit as pre- and postwar events unfolded in Slovakia, and those my father received after Klári, Zoli, Shlomo and Giora, Edit, and later Teri with Ivan, migrated to Israel. I have also added some photographs and excerpts from correspondence I received from these family members.

The vast majority of these letters (translated from German, Slovak, and Hungarian) were handwritten, and the rest were typed, single-spaced, on thin onion paper. It was quite unfortunate that several of them did not survive the passage of time and fell apart even with careful handling. In several instances, the translators were unable to read them in their entirety because the ink had faded or was smudged; a few were undated, so no timeline could be determined, and the postage stamp with the shipping date on the envelopes had faded as well. The translation process was laborious and lengthy. Finally, I don't know if my father kept all the correspondence he received. We will never know.

When reading those translated documents, it warms my heart to see how all of the Pikler children—Hansi, Klári, Teri, Leika, and Edit, along with their husbands, Sani, Zoli, Géza, and Sanyi—were closely bonded together throughout their lives, no matter how much distance separated them. The letters reflect the interaction of a close-knit family: they shared details of their daily lives and work, news from other relatives, music they enjoyed and books they read, trips they took, and interactions with new and old friends. They always included birthday wishes and offered words of comfort if one of them was distressed or not well, or if someone had died. In each letter, they asked about Oli, Edulka, and me (and often sent greetings to Sophie). Lastly, they wondered if and hoped that they would see each other again. With the exception of Klári, who visited Hansi in 1968, my father never saw his other sisters after he left Slovakia in 1939 with Sophie and Oli.

1909-1929

As noted in Chapter Two, Móric and Hansi remained in Kimpulung, Romania for four years after Móric's wife, Olga, and baby daughter, Wilma, died in 1905. They then moved to Rajec, Slovakia in 1909. Móric bought a two-story small home which faced the square in the center of town. It had three bedrooms and a small bath upstairs, a kitchen and dining/living room downstairs. There was also a small backyard. After he married Elsa in 1910, they had four daughters: Klári on February 5, 1911, Teri on July 31, 1912, Leika on October 22, 1913, and Edit on November 9, 1917. The first three were born in Rajec. Edit was born in Ružomberok, Slovakia.

My father, would reminisce from time to time about his younger years, going all the way back to Kimpulung. Although he was only three-and-a-half when his mother (Olga) died, he claimed to remember not only how affectionate and caring she was, but also that she played the piano and sang for him. He also spoke of Elsa, and said, "I was so lucky that Elsa came into my life, she was every bit as nurturing and caring. I felt her love every day. Papa was quite strict and affectionate as well, and Elsa always wisely knew how to smooth everything at the right time." He also related how fortunate and joyful he felt when his sisters were born. After school, in addition to his chores, he helped Elsa to look after them.

Hansi, Leika, Elsa, Móric, Klári (top), and Teri (bottom); Rajec, circa 1915

During World War 1, Móric's timber dealership business in Rajec began to feel the impact of the war when the breakdown of the railway system impeded his ability to deliver timber to his customers. Sometime between late 1916 and early 1917, with the war still ongoing, he moved his family to Ružomberok, where he felt that the wider railroad system would allow him to keep his business afloat.

Teri, at age 10 or 11, went to live with Margit (Manyi) Krausz, one of Elsa's sisters, and her husband Elemer, who lived in Poltár, a small town near Lučenec.[73] This event will be described later in this narrative in more detail. Although Leika could not remember the year Teri left, she stated that "perhaps it was around 1923." She thought it occurred "sometime before" Hansi left Ružomberok in 1923 to work at a lumber company in western Romania. She recalled how everyone at home "was very sad" when Teri was no longer at home, "but I think I missed her the most." When Teri would come to visit, "all of us had such wonderful time together." Leika also was very happy, as was the rest of the family, to know that Margit and Elemer "were raising her as their own daughter." Later on, when Teri worked as a secretary at their brick factory in Lučenec, Leika remembered, "she told me she liked the responsibility she had."

Leika recounted that of the four daughters, only Klári had the opportunity to get both a grade school and high school education and obtain a *matura*. Unfortunately, their parents' financial situation prevented Klári from pursuing university studies. Sometime in 1926, however, they did allow her to travel to Nancy, France, where she studied accounting, office management, and French literature at the Alliance Française school. She graduated on March 31, 1927, and upon her return home, took a job as an apprentice bookkeeper.

According to my father, by the time the market crashed in the late twenties, Móric's financial situation had already become severely strained and the family had moved again, this time to Žilina, an industrial town in northwest Slovakia, sometime in 1928 or 1929. By 1923, Hansi had already moved to Brezoi, Romania so he could earn enough to help his parents. All the children got jobs and contributed most of their earnings to the family.

Leika finished middle school by 1928 and a year later took two part-time jobs as a secretary and also went to a vocational business school. She quit the part-time jobs to take a full-time one as an administrator for a local builder in Žilina.

Klári (date unknown)

Edit (date unknown)

There are, unfortunately, no records or information about Edit's formative years. She was, according to Leika, the one who always had a positive and comforting attitude. Hansi felt she was the most affectionate of the siblings and made every effort to make her parents and siblings happy no matter what the circumstances.

I found twelve letters that Hansi's sisters wrote to him between 1923 and 1930, while he worked in Romania. Unfortunately, eight of them had not survived the test of time and were not in good enough condition to read. Of the remaining four, one was from Edit, one from Leika, and two from Teri that could only be partly translated, one of them undated and all without envelopes. All were short, handwritten, half-page letters in Hungarian. Edit, seven years old at the time, sent this message (in her beautiful handwriting):

Dearest Hansi!

Don't think you can stay away so easily, oh no, I won't allow it, because I was already incredibly happy looking forward to your coming. So Hansi, you didn't mean it seriously that you weren't coming, right? It was just a joke, right? Prove to Mom and Dad and kids that it was all just a joke, and please write only this much: I will come on the 15th. It'll be great, won't it? I hope that you will write right away and the letter will only say that you will definitely come.

See you soon. Your loving sister kisses you many times, *Edit*

I already miss you very much. You will see our little dog if you come home for sure!

On August 17, 1924, Teri, age twelve, wrote:

I was so happy to receive your card for my birthday... We went for a car ride. I have two nice friends, they came to the house and we had cake and ice cream...I have [illegible] happy here but miss everyone at home. We are going to visit them next week. When are you going home? Write often and good things. We all miss you so much! Please write often. A thousand kisses.

In the undated note, Teri wrote:

Your letter brought me so much joy...I liked your soccer team picture... Editka wrote that you came home two weeks ago. Can you come to us, too? The house is bigger than in Póltar. Lots of hugs and kisses.

We can assume that the family had moved to Lučenec before this letter was written.

On December 14, 1924, Leika—then age eleven–wrote:

Yesterday we played theater and it turned out very well. Klárika and Papa came to see it, too. Imagine, if Papa came, that means it must have been beautiful. Regi, Teri, and I danced ballet. They applauded so much that we had to do it over again. Did you get the photo, the one I sent you? We got yours, but you don't look very good (it is too shiny). Are you well now?

Thank God, we're all healthy. One more week of school
and after that we have vacation. We're probably going
to Rajec. I will be happy to go. But my school grades
are not too good. I kiss you lots, your loving sister.
Write!!!!!

There were also nine letters, all in German, that Móric and Elsa
wrote to Hansi during those years. Five were from Elsa, each
palpably showing her maternal love and preoccupation for his well-
being. She asked for details about his work and daily life and offered
sound advice. She also brought him up-to-date about his sisters
and family life in Ružomberok. Móric's letters did not mention
the difficult financial situation, though he did go over details about
the business (with which Hansi was familiar, having worked with
his father for five years) and wanted to know about Hansi's work
at the sawmill in Brezoi, Romania. He answered Hansi's questions
and gave him a great deal of advice. All the letters were addressed
to "our dearest Hansiko" and signed individually, "Mama" and
"Papa."

1930-1939

By 1930, my father and his sisters lived with Móric and Elsa in
Žilina—with the exception of Teri, who lived in Lučenec. When
Hansi returned home, he attended business school and soon after
was hired by the ZB company, as noted in Chapter Two. Klári
worked as a bookkeeper, Teri as a secretary at her uncle Elemer's
brick factory, Leika as an administrator for a local builder. It is not
known what Edit did.

In the early 30's, Klári became interested in a political group
known as *HaShomer HaTzair*,[74] a fact that Oli learned from Leika
decades later, in 2003, when the family were in Miami Beach for
the wedding of Oli's son Kenny. Klári had come home one evening
after attending one of their political rallies and, in Leika's words,

"could not stop talking about it." She had met one of the speakers—Alexander "Sani" Neumann. He was two years older than Klári and owned a quite reputable photography studio in Žilina. Leika recalled him visiting their house several times, and believed it was in the mid 30s when Klári and Sani became engaged. Leika was unsure when they had gotten married, but she thought it was before Hansi and Sophie got married in Vienna in October 1936.

Leika and Oli; Miami Beach, October 2003

Hansi met Sophie in Vienna in 1935. After a one year courtship they were married on October 11, 1936 in Vienna. None of Hansi's sisters were able to attend his wedding, but Teri wrote a lovely note to Hansi before he left Žilina for his wedding:

> Most beloved Hansi, words cannot express how much happiness [illegible] your life I wish for you and Sophie...For all of us in the family, this will always be a very joyful day...Lots of kisses and hugs to you both, *Teri*

Klári and Sani (date unknown)

Oli with her daddy; Žilina, 1938

In the mid 1930s, Leika met Julius "Julko" Bronner, a Žilina attorney. They married in Žilina on December 23, 1936, with her parents present, as well as Edit, Klári and Sani, Hansi and Sophie.

On September 29, 1937, in Žilina, Oli was born to Hansi and Sophie. The entire family had a joyful celebration at the Pikler home the following weekend. Móric at the time was already suffering from an enlarged prostate but according to my father, he was in the best of spirits to celebrate the birth of his first grandchild.

Sometime in the 1930s, Teri spent time in Vienna, undergoing training in kindergarten education. It is unknown how long she was there, but once she was back in Lučenec she met Géza Hajos, an attorney six years her senior, who had been born and now practiced law in that town. He became her husband on September 18, 1938, and as with Hansi and Sophie's wedding, none of the other sisters were present. Twelve days later, the Munich agreement was signed and as a consequence, southern Slovakia—including the town of Lučenec—was cut off from Czechoslovakia and fell into the region occupied by fascist Hungary.

Leika remembered another family celebration in Žilina when Klári and Sani's son, Peter, was born on October 28, 1938. He changed his name in 1949 to the Hebrew *Shlomo*, for his paternal grandfather, Salomon.

Klári with Shlomo; Žilina, 1938

159

According to my father, the family continued to get together most weekends, and always looked forward to Teri and Géza's visits. They were there just before Hansi, Sophie, and Oli left for Latin America in August 1939. Hansi never forgot how sad and tearful that family gathering was, and how guilty he felt for leaving his parents behind. By then, Móric's health had weakened, he had diffuse discomfort and abdominal pain, and his breathing was labored at times.

Teri, Klári, Shlomo, and Leika; Žilina, circa 1938-39

1939-1949

Leika and Julko accompanied my parents and Oli to the port of Genoa where they were to board the ship to Latin America. Decades later, in 1986, during the trip Elaine, Jason, and I took to Žilina where we met Leika and Sanyi for the first time, Leika related to us how unhappy Hansi had been after he said good-bye to his family. She told us:

For several days before their departure, Hansi was uncommonly rattled and anxious. During the entire trip to Genoa, he had a somber expression. He struggled to contain his tears as he worried that he would not be there to take care of Papa. I promised him that Julko and I would move in to help take care of our parents. I told him, "Please, don't worry, Hansi, you have your own family to take care of now."

Soon after Leika and Julko returned home from Genoa, they did move in with Móric and Elsa. A letter from Teri, dated August 25, 1939, reached my parents in Genoa a day before their boarding. She was clearly trying to console them when she wrote:

My loved ones, whatever may come, stand tightly side by side...I can only repeat once again how important it is for you to understand and be patient with each other...I know from my own experience that the greatest worries, the greatest sufferings are much easier to bear when you are with each other and not against each other...Hansi, don't give up, we will all see each other again in good health... I am doing everything I can to get Papa here soon [to Losonc] and you know that we will do everything in Papa's interest.

Hansi, Sophie, and two-year old Oli had left Slovakia in August 1939 with visas to Bolivia, but they wound up in Ecuador in March of 1940, after quite an eventful journey. They spent over five months of that time separated and interned at two detention camps in southern France after their ship was boarded by the French navy in the Mediterranean Sea and diverted to the port of Marseilles.

Klári, Leika, Géza and Teri exchanged correspondence with my parents during their detention camp internment. From Losonc on October 15, 1939, Géza wrote:

Our father [Papa] is doing well and I am making it possible to obtain transportation for him to see his doctor in Budapest...Julko is already back home and it is possible that he may remain a lawyer...Let us know if you need something so we can send it without delay.

We know my parents received at least one parcel of clothes from Teri and Géza. But it was this December 8, 1939 postcard from them that brought hope that they, too, would eventually be allowed to leave. It read:

Today I received your letter with news from November 27. You can imagine what joy we have from every sign of life that we get from you. We want to assure you that we will do everything possible to help you. We immediately contacted HICEM in London and Paris, and we got news from the London HICEM that they turned over the matter to the Parisian directors and International Red Cross [IRC]. We trust you have already received the package of clothes. Should you need anything at all, please just write to us. Oh, how much we would like to help you!! Just don't lose courage, children.

What is Olinka up to, what is she babbling about?... Sophie dearest, you are a strong woman whose courage deserves only amazement.

My Hansulke, you are equal to your wife in that regard...And don't hang your head...Thank God, Papa is doing better, everything is in order here at home... So, don't worry. All of us are healthy and working.

Write as soon as you can. A big kiss to you both and Olinka.

Yours, *Teri, Géza*

On January 9, 1940, Géza and Teri wrote:

The HICEM in Paris has informed us that everyone will be free to continue the journey...As you may

hope that we will all be together in a happy reunion someday. The loss of the things you had must not be a reason to feel defeated. You are young, your whole life is still ahead of you. You will find everything that was lost again, through your diligence and seriousness. For the time being, the greatest wish we all have is to receive a message from you that you have reached your destination and landed happily. Hardly a day goes by when we don't think of you. I am glad that you also spoke with our dear parents. It must have been a great comfort for Papa, even if he was perhaps very upset at the moment, which was understandable. When news comes from you that you are happy in your destination, I am sure that he will be calmed.

Petyko is developing nicely—he reminds me a lot of Olinka. He calls me "Aunt Eja," and when he hears me coming, he screams for me and calls, "ah, ah," which means so much to me, that he is expecting something good.

Julko might keep his job as a lawyer but he is only allowed to represent non-Aryan clients...We are getting along modestly... Sani is also working and sometimes has little to do, sometimes more. I still have my old job and in the afternoons, I help Julko.

Once again, I wish you a good trip. I will be with you a lot in my thoughts. I send kisses and very, very much love, and a big kiss separately to dear little Olinka, from your *Lea*.

Edit added a few words:

I am sorry I was not home and couldn't say goodbye to you. I just hope everything will go smoothly for you now and that you will finally reach your destination happily. Lea has already written what there is to report. I kiss you all very deeply.

Yours, *Edit*

As Hansi, Sophie, and Olga were settling in Quito, a letter from Teri in 1940 (date illegible), brought news that Géza had been detained in Lučenec as a consequence of the Hungarian anti-Jewish laws,[75] and had been sent to a forced-labor battalion, composed mostly of Jews, attached to the Hungarian army near the town of Vac. "We had not anticipated this happening," she wrote, and added, "I am keeping busy and can only hope Géza will stay healthy."

As recounted in the previous chapter, Móric died in Žilina on September 29, 1940. During the months of October, November, and December 1940, Hansi managed to write only one letter to his faraway family. He felt so sad that he could not bring himself to put his feelings down in writing. He did not neglect his daily activities and the care of his family but at night, even with Sophie's emotional support, he felt overwhelmed with grief and wept a lot.

On January 4, 1941, about fourteen weeks after Móric died, Teri wrote from Losonc:

> From day to day, we hope for a sign of life from you, and we're already living in fear for you, because all our waiting is in vain. Why don't you get in touch with us, my boy? Don't you feel that we need you, that we want to hear about you, with all your pain that is the same as ours? My Hansi, how I wish I could be with you for at least a few hours to convince myself that you are bravely bearing this terrible suffering with the energy and self-mastery that you owe to yourself and all of us! If I knew that, we'd all be much calmer. It's so hard to say anything. I should be comforting you but my heart is bleeding. And yet, we all have to tell each other again and again that it was redemption for our dear Papa and we must not disturb his bitterly hard-won peace through our moaning. And then one more thing, Hansi, that absolutely must bring consolation: he was spared so much suffering and bitterness that he could not have endured. We will all have to endure a lot and that would have mentally broken our dear father terribly. You see, I am comforting you and myself again and again and trying to convince myself

that it had to happen that way if we didn't want to him to feel even more suffering! And he will stay with us forever, Hansi. He has not left, we carry him and our love within us, only his sufferings have ceased!

I know everything, my Hansi, I know that in spite of everything it is difficult to come to terms, but we must, however bitter it may be, because it would be the wish of our dear one, and it would hurt him immeasurably if we didn't carry our fate bravely or if we neglected our children and families in our suffering. Hand in hand, my Hansi, we have to fight our way through whatever may come, even if geographical distance separates us. That is in the spirit and according to the heart of our dear one who never, never gave up, no matter how terribly or however often he had to take up the struggle with life. And despite all suffering, he always found life worth living. Always think of that and I know it will help you to bear many things.

There is little to report about us. I was alone for almost four months, but now, thank God, my straw widowhood is over. Our home is beautiful and pleasant and there is nothing better for me than coming home in the evening after work. I take care of the housework myself and do it with great pleasure. Géza is great at drying dishes. Géza is an angel altogether, and because he (silly guy) says the same thing about me, you can imagine that we are not leading an unhappy life. It has to be that way, because you have to find peace somewhere and draw strength. My children, remember that we are living in concern over you, and don't keep us waiting for news any longer. I kiss Olinka and you both. With deep love, your *Teri*

Dear Hans and Sophie,

Hopefully you are fine and will notify us soon. Happy New Year. Many kisses and greetings to everyone, with true love, your Géza

167

Leika wrote from Žilina on January 22, 1941:

My very, very dear ones! Finally, finally, the long awaited letter from you, dearest Hansi, arrived a few days ago. It would have been almost two months that we have been constantly awaiting mail from you. There was not a day when we didn't talk about you, when we didn't think about it how terribly the news had hit you, Hansi. It hit you even more because you are so far away and didn't get to spend the last hours with the poor man. My little Hansi, it is a wound for all of us that will never, never heal, but we loved our dear father so much that we must not disturb his well-deserved rest with our lamenting and wailing.

We will always keep his memory in love and respect, we will always hold on to one another, just as the poor man always wished for. I have to believe that God loved our good father very much when he called to him and put an end to his torments. I told you that it was not a life for him anymore, that the poor man was very tired of life, that he no longer had any joy here. How often he said: "Why does God punish me so, why is he making me suffer so much." He often prayed to God to be released. Therefore, my little Hansi, we have to acknowledge the inevitable, we have to find the strength in order to endure this great blow of fate more easily. We would certainly not be acting in his honor if we were weak and forgot that we also have to live and work for a living.

He was talking about you a lot, and if it was so painful for him that he didn't have you here, but it was a comfort for him to know that you were safe. How happy was he to hear the news from [his friend] H. Better that you, Hansi, were working hard, and how much he liked to talk about all of you, about little Olinka, etc., etc.

For as long as we could, we went to his grave each week, and our thoughts were always with you, in our minds we were bringing greetings from you as well; we spoke of you every time at his grave, and we decided to take a picture and send it to you as soon as possible. Now everything is so covered with snow so we cannot get there.

How I would love to see the little one [Oli], I can imagine how cute she is...When I hear our Peter babble, I also see her very clearly in front of me. She always used to snuggle up to me. When I was using the typewriter, I was certainly one of her loved ones. Is she already eating better, or do you still need to dance for her, ride for her etc.? Oh, but she was a devil! Peter is also a big guy and a devil like his uncle Hans was. When you ask him where Uncle Hansi and Aunt Sophie are, he says, "there in the second room." By that he means Klári's bedroom, because your picture is in there. Recently, when something happened to him again, he said: "Yes, yes, I'm pisser Neumann." He can already sing a lot of songs and he has already learned a few words of German, but otherwise he speaks Slovak. Mama recently said to him when she was upstairs at around noon, "Petko is a good boy, he will go to sleep now," to which he answered, "No, Petko is not good, he will not sleep." Very often he asks, "Grandma, where is Grandpa?" Quite strange that the child has not forgotten him completely, either.

We are moving out of this apartment on March 31... Many people have to move out of the neighborhood, including Klári. Fortunately, we've already found another one, in Little Prague, very close to Olly Bronner and family. Klári and family also already have an apartment not far from us, across from Philiphin Pollak. Sani will have to go a little way into the studio, but a walk won't hurt him...So we are supposed to move in on April 1.

I am stopping for today. Write to us very soon. I kiss you, my dear ones, with very, very much love. Yours, *Lea*

In February 1941 (date unclear), Teri wrote: "He [Géza] is allowed to come once in a while for a few days. I have a train pass to bring him some food...We are forbidden now to work in our [illegible] jobs." She added, "I am thinking the only [illegible] is to open a kindergarten."

In a reply to what must have been Hansi's concern about her safety, she later wrote: "I have everything I need and I do feel safe... You don't have to worry...I am happy that I have the kindergarten now and [illegible] to help with the children...Please write often, I am always happy to hear from you." Teri alerted my father several months later that the family in Žilina was going through difficult times after several anti-Jewish laws and bans had been enacted. They also had to leave their home and move to a different section of town: "If you are not aware already, I am sending their new address...I do not know for how long they will be there...Géza was here last week for three days. He and I are healthy, that is most important."

Before his departure from Žilina, Hansi had promised his extended family that he would make every effort to bring them to Latin America so that all could be reunited again. True to his word, in 1941, he began the required immigration process to obtain visas for Elsa, his four sisters, and their families. He asked a close friend, also an immigrant from Slovakia, to request visas for Olga (Olly) and Anita Bronner, Julko's sister and his niece. After many years and a consuming ordeal, the Ecuadorian Government approved the applications on October 31, 1945 and June 11, 1946 and issued the visas on December 13, 1946 without a monetary deposit. Hansi was only required to provide a notarized "guarantee letter." His friend's application for Olga and Anita Bronner was approved on December 20, 1946 and the visas were issued on May 26, 1947.

In Leika's June 1945 interview, she describes how the family in Žilina became concerned about their fate after the first transport of Jewish women from Slovakia was taken to Auschwitz in late

REPUBLICA DEL ECUADOR

DIRECCION GENERAL DE
INMIGRACION Y EXTRANJERIA

Quito, a 13 . de . Diciembre . . . de 1946

SEÑOR
MINISTRO DE RELACIONES EXTERIORES
EN SU DESPACHO

En vista de la solicitud presentada
por el señor Hans Ernesto Pikler, cuyas copias acompaño, este
Departamento autoriza el ingreso al País de los extranjeros:
Zoltan LESNY,CLARI PIKLER DE LESNY, PETER NEUMANN PIKLER, GEZA
HAJOS, TERI PIKLER DE HAJOS,IVAN TIBOR HAJOS,ALEXANDER VOZAR,
LEA PIKLER DE VOZAR,FERI SLEZAK,EDITH PIKLER DEB SLEZAK, sin
la exigencia de depósito por estar amparados en la disposición
del Art. 26 letra d) del Reglamento para la aplicación de la
Ley de Extranjería, Extradición y Naturalización.

Dichos extranjeros con excepción del
primero fueron autorizados con oficios Nos. 341-S.I., de 31 de
Octubre de 1.945 y 381-S.I., de 11 de Junio último.

Estimaré del Sr. Ministro, se digne
instruír en tal sentido al Sr. Cónsul Gral. del Ecuador en Pa-
rís, a fín de que otorgue en favor de los indicados extranjeros
la visa de " INMIGRANTES".

De usted, muy atentamente,
POR LA RESTAURACION DEMOCRATICA Y LA
UNIDAD NACIONAL

Manuel Paredes Lasso.
DIRECTOR GENERAL DE INMIGRACION Y EXTRANJERIA
Es fiel copia del Original al que me remitiré en caso necesario.

Gonzalo Burbano L.

SECRETARIO DE LA DIRECCION GENERAL DE INMIGRACION Y EXTRANJERIA

Family visa for Ecuador 1

NO. B
4104408

TIMBRE
DE SANIDAD
10 CENTAVOS

C O P I A

" REPUBLICA DEL ECUADOR.- DIRECCION GENERAL DE INMIGRACION Y EXTRAN-
JERIA.- Oficio N° 341-S.I1- Quito, a 26 de Mayo de 1.947.- SEÑOR -
MINISTRO DE RELACIONES EXTERIORES - EN SU DESPACHO.- En vista de la
solicitud presentada por el señor Hans Ernesto Pikler, cuyas copias
acompaño, esta Dirección renueva la autorización de ingreso que les
fuera concedida con oficio N° 937-S.I., de 13 de Diciembre del año
próximo pasado, en favor de los extranjeros ZOLTAN LESNY, CLARI PI-
KLER DE LESNY NEUMANN, PETER NEUMANN PIKER, GEZA HAJOS, TERI PIKLER
DE HAJOS, IVAN TIBOR HAJOS, ALEXANDER VOZARD, LEA PIKLER DE VOZAR,
FERI SLEZAK, EDITH PIKLER DE SLEZAK, sin la exigencia del depósito
reglamentario, por cuanto en esa fecha, hallábanse amparados en la
disposición contenida en la letra d) del Art. 26 del Reglamento para
la aplicación de la Ley de Extranjería, Extradición y Naturalización.
Estimaré de usted, señor Ministro, se digne instruír en tal sentido
al señor CONSUL DEL ECUADOR EN PARIS, a fin de que otorgue en favor
de los citados extranjeros la visa de " INMIGRANTE ", siempre que su
ingreso esté de acuerdo con lo prescrito en el Reglamento de Inmigración.- De usted, muy atentamente.- Dios, Patria y Libertad.-
(f.) Gustavo Tamayo Mancheno.- DIRECTOR GENERAL DE INMIGRACION Y EX-
TRANJERIA ".-

ES FIEL COPIA DEL ORIGINAL QUE FUE REMITIDO AL MINISTERI
DE RELACIONES EXTERIORES, AL QUE ME REMITO EN CASO NECESARIO.-

CERTIFICO.-

HUGO SALVADOR C.
SECRETARIO AD-HOC DE LA DIRECCION GENERAL DE INMIGRACION Y
EXTRANJERIA

Family visa for Ecuador 2

172

C O P I A

NO. B
4104407

TIMBRE
DE SANIDAD
10 CENTAVOS

MOVIL

" REPUBLICA DEL ECUADOR.- DIRECCION GENERAL DE INMIGRACION Y EXTRAN-
JERIA.- Oficio N° 342-S.I.- Quito, a 26 de Mayo de 1.947.- SEÑOR
MINISTRO DE RELACIONES EXTERIORES - EN SU DESPACHO.- En vista de la
solicitud presentada por el señor José Steiner, cuyas copias acompaño, este Departamento renueva la autorización de ingreso que les
fuera concedida con oficio N° 953-S.I., de 20 de Diciembre del año
próximo pasado, en favor de las extranjeras OLGA BRONNER y ANITA
BRONNER, de nacionalidad checoeslovaca, sin la exigencia del, depósito reglamentario, por hallarse amparadas en ese entonces, en la
disposición contenida en la letra d) del Art. 26 del, Reglamento para
la aplicación de la Ley de Extranjería, Extradición y Naturalización
Estimaré de usted, señor Ministro, se digne instruír en tal sentido
al señor CONSUL DEL ECUADOR EN PARIS, a fin de que otorgue en favor
de las citadas extranjeras la visa de " INMIGRANTE ", siempre que
su ingreso esté de acuerdo con lo prescrito en el Reglamento de Inmigración.- De usted, muy atentamente.- DIOS PATRIA Y LIBERTAD.-
(f.) Gustavo Tamayo Mancheno.- DIRECTOR GENERAL DE INMIGRACION Y
EXTRANJERIA ".-
       ES FIEL COPIA DEL ORIGINAL QUE FUE REMITIDO AL MINISTERIO DE
RELACIONES EXTERIORES, AL QUE ME REMITO EN CASO NECESARIO.- CERTIFIC
               Quito, Mayo 27 de 1,947

                 GONZALO BURBANO L.
       SECRETARIO DE LA DIRECCION GENERAL DE INMIGRACION
                      Y EXTRANJERIA

Family visa for Ecuador 3

March 1942. They had made contingency plans to leave for Hungary if they felt threatened in any way. That threat came in early April 1942, and the events that took place soon afterwards surrounding the family's escape to Hungary are described in detail later in this chapter, in Leika's 1996 interview for the video archive project, Survivors of the Shoah Visual History Foundation (now called USC Shoah Foundation—Institute for Visual History and Education). Teri provided the money for this emergency travel and she also hired a guide to take the whole family on foot across the border into Hungary. They all settled in Budapest.

In a May 17, 1942 letter to Hansi, Teri described the family's ordeal and their settlement in Budapest, but she added a warning: "I will let you know when and where it may be safe for you to write to [illegible]…I will use the rail pass to visit them and Géza soon…I also will need to be careful when to write to each other." A month later, she sent a letter congratulating my parents on my birth: "We are so very happy for you. We know our beloved Papa would have been overjoyed too."

Teri's correspondence trickled off in frequency and length, as mostly postcards were found for the next year-and-a-half. She was obviously being careful what to include in them: "Everyone is struggling but healthy," was the common theme. Elsa was living with Klári and Sani, Leika and Julko were "working." It is possible that some of her 1943 correspondence was lost, because in none of them did she mention that Leika and Julko had been captured and sent to a labor camp that April.

As Leika describes in her Shoah Foundation interview, when the German army was threatening to occupy Hungary in March 1944, she and Julko escaped from the camp and crossed the border into Slovakia. They settled with false identification documents in Banská Bystrica. The rest of the family, except for Edit, escaped later and, once again, with Teri's help, crossed the border into Slovakia before the Germans won full control of the Hungarian borders on March 19, 1944. They settled in Čeklis.

On April 16, 1944, my father received a letter from Teri dated April 7. She informed him of the family's escape, their new addresses, and the names they were living under. She also warned: "You must make sure to use their different names now. Dearest Hansi, we must be careful not to write anything the authorities can use against them!"

Two months after she wrote that letter, Teri was deported from Lučenec to Auschwitz, and Hansi received no further correspondence from his family for the next twelve months.

As mentioned in the family history chapter at the beginning of this book, after the October 2008 Pikler family reunion in Budapest, Oli and I traveled with other family members to Žilina, and Oli spent the entire day talking with Leika. Oli had always enjoyed talking to her aunt and was amazed how sharp she still was at age ninety-five. "She clearly remembered so many events that went back to her childhood years. We went through a lifetime of memories," Oli later told me. We both agreed that without Teri's help, it is doubtful that the family would have survived. She took many personal risks to save them at critical times.

Leika began on that day by recounting some family memories from childhood. She also recalled the stressful financial times the family had endured, prompting their move from Ružomberok to Žilina. At the time, Leika had asked Oli if she was aware of both her 1945 and 1996 interviews. Oli told her she was not and even if she had access to them, she would not have been able to understand their contents since they were in Slovak. Leika offered to send her copies to be translated, but sadly, Oli died before she ever had the chance.

On that October day, Leika shared with Oli some of the events Klári and Teri had told her about after they were all, miraculously, released from their respective concentration camps. It was intensely emotional material which, as Oli told me during our trip home, had prompted Leika to ask her more than once if she should stop. Oli had said she was "fine" and wanted to hear "everything."

Leika chose first to share Teri's dreadful ordeal at Auschwitz because, "I listened to Teri tell this awful story many years ago, and I have carried those words in my heart since." Leika had first learned this story in 1976, when she and Sanyi were in Israel visiting their daughter, Magda and her family. They had been present at Teri's conversation with her former pupil, Peter Dansky, in which Teri also described how she managed to help the family escape from Budapest and return to Slovakia before the Germans got full control of the Hungarian borders on March 19, 1944. At the time, she told Oli that there were more details to be found in the transcripts of her earlier interviews, but Oli never had the chance to read them.

On that day in Israel, Leika heard Teri recount how she had been sent to Auschwitz, along with her mother-in-law, on June 9, 1944 but that they had been separated at the train station in Lučenec. Teri had been six months pregnant at the time. The train briefly stopped at the town of Miskolc on its way to Auschwitz, and Teri was alerted by one of the detainees in her car that Géza was standing outside on the ground along with a group of forced laborers. He spotted her as well, and she heard him shout that the train was heading to Poland.

At the Auschwitz platform, after leaving the train cars, everyone was told to line up in two columns before going through a selection procedure carried out by the SS, including the infamous Dr. Mengele. The newly arrived prisoners were either quickly found to be qualified for labor or sent to be killed immediately. Teri heard Mengele shout that pregnant women should step aside as they would get better rations. But she knew that could not be true and was able to sneak in without her pregnancy being noticed. Oli had to think hard to recount the details of the story Leika had shared with her: at Auschwitz, Teri had had the great fortune to find an inmate who was a distant relative and who worked as a room orderly in one of the blocks close to Teri's. For a while, this relative helped Teri avoid the mandatory daily roll calls, but after several weeks at the camp, Teri was exhausted and no longer able to hide her pregnancy. She was sent by Mengele to be gassed but, again "at just the right time," she met another relation, a doctor named Helena Lipscher (the niece of Regina Pikler née Lipscher) who saved Teri from that sentence, and said she would try to smuggle her into one of Mengele's pseudo-trial groups for women pregnant with twins. Teri apparently agreed to this plan, despite the fact that she was not expecting twins. In the hospital ward, she was examined by a Greek gynecologist, a Dr. Cohen, who also promised to help her and put himself in charge of her care during and after the surgery. Leika distinctly remembered that Teri had told her the "surgery" involved removing the fetus without anesthesia, and Teri had a great deal of pain and bleeding afterwards. Dr. Cohen subsequently arranged her transfer to the Ravensbrück concentration camp (see Concentration Camp Addendum for more about Ravensbrück). Leika did not know when this transfer took place, but she thought it most likely happened before she and Elsa were imprisoned at the same concentration camp in early January 1945. From Ravensbrück, Teri was then transferred to the KZ Barth camp[76] where she worked until its liberation in May 1945. Apparently, she and Géza were miraculously reunited when she was on her way back home. They went first to Lučenec and later to Košice, Slovakia.[77]

Oli also recounted that Leika and Julko, traveling together, had participated in the Slovak resistance movement. Julko had fought in several battles during the August 1944 Slovak National Uprising[78] and had lost his life in one of them. Leika had been captured by the German army and taken to Banská Bystrica but was subsequently released because the false documents she carried were believed. Several weeks later, she joined Klári, Sani, Shlomo, and Elsa in Čeklis.

Both Elsa and Klári were at the Bratislava train station on December 24, 1944 when they were outed by a member of the Žilina Jewish community. Both families were jailed by the Slovak secret police and then were sent to the Sered' transition camp[79] run by the Hlinka Guard.

At Sered', the family was split up. Sani was separated from Klári and Shlomo, both of whom were sent in late December to Terezín; Leika and Elsa were destined for Ravensbrück later that month, where Elsa perished in February of 1945. Sani was sent to the Sachsenhausen-Oranienburg concentration camp[80] where he most likely died in 1945, according to Klári's testimonial at Yad Vashem on May 31, 1956.

After the war, Leika learned what had happened to Klári and little Shlomo after the family was split up at Sered'. They were herded with many other women and some children onto a cattle car to be transported, over a period of several days, to Theresienstadt, or Terezín (see Concentration Camp Addendum). It was, at that time, the last transport, and one that did not continue on to Auschwitz because transports had been halted under the pressure of advancing Soviet and Czech troops. Klári and Shlomo were also fortunate to have been assigned housing together at Terezín and to be allowed to remain together during their five-month internment. Klári was issued a permit to work with children, and both of them were given vaccines against typhus.

When a Czech unit of the Red Army liberated the camp on May 9, 1945 Terezín was under a typhus quarantine. But Klári knew the camp's chief medical officer, Dr. K. Raška, who gave her and Shlomo a clean bill of health for the fee of 1200 Kč each, according to the documents. Dr. Raška also helped smuggle them out of Terezín on May 11 in the back of a tarp-covered army truck. It is of interest that both Klári and Shlomo were issued a document that day with a stamp from the Terezín town police station, which confirmed that they had a means of transportation and could be released from the camp.

They were back in Žilina a few days later. According to Leika's account, Klári next tried unsuccessfully to recover Sani's photo studio and equipment and also took some sort of job. During those hectic days, Klári had asked Teri, who was already in Lučenec, to take care of Shlomo for a while.

Klári's Terezin concentration camp work assignment

There is a wealth of information about Leika, not only from the life events she shared with Oli and me, her letters and the family testimonials that make up the lion's share of this narrative, but from the two interviews she completed in the wake of her experiences at the Ravensbrück concentration camp: one, with a doctor, shortly after the liberation of the camp (Statement by Lea Bronnerová at Ravensbrück, June 1945), and the other with Stephen Spielberg's Shoah Foundation in 1996. To allow for this precious firsthand material to be fully appreciated, it has been divided—but not shortened—and placed throughout this narrative. Occasionally, the reader will find that I have repeated certain images and duplicated certain events in the interest of completeness, and in mindfulness of the gravity of the words themselves. I have also interspersed in brackets pertinent information from those letters and personal conversations.

Leika's Survivors of the Shoah interview (Stephen Spielberg's

Terezin immunization record for belly typhus, Klári and Peter (Shlomo)

Clean bill of health for Klári and Peter (Shlomo); Terezín, May 11, 1945

GEORGE M. PIKLER

**Confimation of means of transport and release from Terezín,
for Klári and Peter (Shlomo); May 11, 1945**

182

project) was conducted in Slovak, in the town of Žilina, Republic of Slovakia, on August 29, 1996. It took place in her apartment (Sedláčkov sad 4). The moderator (M) for the interview was Mr. Robert Slovák (his last name simply a strange coincidence). The translation from Slovak to English of this interview is composed of four sections:

Shoah Foundation Transcript: Section One

> M: Mrs. Vozarová, could you state your full name for the record?
>
> LV: My name is Lea Vozarová, born Piklerová.
>
> M: Could you please tell us when and where were you born?
>
> LV: I was born on October 22, 1913 in Rajec.
>
> M: In which county?
>
> LV: Žilina County.
>
> M: How many children were in your family?
>
> LV: There were five of us. One boy and four girls. [Leika did not mention Wilma.]
>
> M: Have you ever told your story to anyone before?
>
> LV: No, I haven't. Well not exactly, I told... I told the story to members of my family but never to anyone in an official capacity like today.
>
> M: What was your father's name?
>
> LV: Móric Pikler.
>
> M: What was his profession?
>
> LV: He worked in lumber. He was a timber dealer.

M: And in what town was that?

LV: Ružomberok. We first lived in Rajec, but we moved later on [1917] to Ružomberok.

M: Was he a government official?

LV: No, he had his own business. He was a private entrepreneur. Back in those days trade was valued.

M: And what was your mother's name?

LV: Alžběta Piklerová, born Teichová

M: What was her profession?

LV: She was a homemaker.

M: Who raised the children in your household? Did you have a nanny, or did she do it alone?

LV: She was the one that raised us.

M: You were born in 1913, what years did you attend grammar school?

LV: I started when I was six years old, so I guess in 1919.

M: And there were four grade levels for grammar school, correct?

LV: Yes, there were four grade levels and then you graduated to a five-year Měšťanská school program. I can't remember the name of it. It was a Měšťanská.*

M: And so, you finished school in 1928?

LV: By 1928, all of us children finished school and the whole family moved to Žilina.

M: And you were in Ružomberok before that. Is that

* *Měšťanská škola* was a sort of a middle school or junior high school at that time; children would then move to a *Gymnasium* which was a preparatory school for university or a vocational school.

correct?

LV: Yes.

M: So, why did you move to Žilina? Did your father get work there?

LV: Well yes, that was one of the reasons. He did find new work. But he wasn't as young as before so he continued working for a short time in Žilina, but after that, he was more-or-less sick most of the time.

M: What sort of illness did he have?

LV: He had a heart condition and he pretty much died because of it.

M: And you stayed in Žilina?

LV: He also had cancer.

M: So how did your family make a living in Žilina?

LV: Can you repeat the question?

M: Who provided for you when you lived in Žilina?

LV: Well in the beginning it was my father, but then we children were old enough to make a living as well. Each one of us girls and our brother worked and contributed to the family earnings.

M: Would you say that your living conditions were not the most ideal?

LV: They were not good, but they were not bad either. They were average.

M: You then completed vocational training here in Žilina. What sort of training was that?

LV: It was a business school. We learned stenography, accounting...

M: That was 1929. Were you already working by then?

LV: Yes, I had a job.*

M: Where did you work?

LV: I worked for Adriatika, an insurance company. Shortly after I worked for a local builder. Friedner was his name.

M: And what sort of work did you do there?

LV: I was an administrator.

M: So, you dealt with correspondence?

LV: Correspondence, payroll, accounting, etc.

M: How did Žilina look back in those days? Can you remember?

LV: It was much different than it is today. It would be hard to describe it. Very hard.

M: Was it a multilingual city or was only Slovak spoken on the streets?

LV: Slovak was the main language. You could hear Hungarian from time to time but it was mainly Slovak. German was never spoken there. I am certain that Slovak was the dominant language spoken in Žilina.

M: Was it a tolerant city or were there elements of...?

LV: No, it was a tolerant city.

M: Was there a large Jewish community in Žilina?

---

*At age 16, Leika took a part time job as a German secretary and stenotypist in a stationary firm. The owner also had an art gallery where important Slovak painters, such as Milos Bazovsky, would hold exhibitions, and she worked there part-time as well. In the afternoons she worked as a secretary at an insurance company. But as she felt her jobs were not too stable and because there was not enough work, she started a new job at a building contracting company.

LV: Yes, there was.

M: Did you socialize in this community?

LV: Yes.

M: Did you associate yourself exclusively with the Jewish community?

LV: No, not exclusively.

M: How did the other citizens treat their Jewish counterparts in Žilina?

LV: I don't know how to answer that question. The people in my social circles were very friendly toward each other.

M: They weren't biased against Jews?

LV: No, back then I never felt any animosity.

M: How would you compare the relationships between people back then and now?

LV: I'm not sure which time back then you have in mind?

M: Let's say in 1929-30.

LV: No one talked about politics at that time.

M: Did your father follow the political situation back then?

LV: To tell you the truth, I really don't remember. I guess it wasn't that important, if I don't remember. At least in our family no one talked about politics.

M: In 1929 -1930 you were almost a 20-year-old woman. What was your life like back then? How did young people live from day to day in Žilina?

LV: Well, at that time we still went out to parties. We

were still jovial. Each of us had our own group of friends with whom we associated. We would go to the theater, to the cinema and of course we went dancing.

M: Did you like to dance?

LV: Yes, yes, I did.

M: Did you have any other hobbies?

LV: I liked to exercise. I liked sports. But my hobby of choice was gymnastics.

M: Were you in any sports club?

LV: Yes, I first attended Sokol*. And then I joined the Maccabi.

M: What sort of sports did you do?

LV: I skied, skated, I liked sledding.

M: Gymnastics?

LV: I liked gymnastics the most.

M: Did you pursue any artistic ventures? Did you play the piano or paint?

LV: No.

M: Did you participate in theater productions?

LV: I liked to do that when I was a child of course.

M: Amateur theater?

LV: When I was in Ružomberok we even were sent on an excursion to perform.

M: Were the performances for the general public or were they for certain groups of people, perhaps a

---

*Sokol was an all-age gymnastics organization based upon the principle of "a strong mind in a sound body," and Maccabi was a sports club.

religious organization?

LV: No, they were for the general public. Not for a group.

M: When you go back and reflect on these years you spent as a young woman, would you say that they were happy years?

LV: Yes, those years were good. They were very good years.

M: Were there any hardships that would keep you from calling these years the happiest?

LV: Well, the death of my father of course was sad.

M: Did he die during that time?

LV: Are you asking me what year did he die? It was in 1940.

M: Did his death hit you hard?

LV: Of course, it did. You know how that is. It was hard when he could no longer work. Well, he didn't die just because of his weak heart but he succumbed to cancer; and he suffered in the final stages. To lose a father is always painful. But in hindsight, that was a different kind of grief, knowing that at least he died a natural death.

M: When he died, were you single?

LV: No, I had a husband by then. The whole family was still together at that time.

M: When did you get married?

LV: In 1936, in December.

M: What was your first husband's name?

LV: Dr. Julius Bronner.*

M: So, you called yourself Mrs. Bronnerová. In 1936 the disturbing political climate was encroaching from abroad, namely Germany. How were you taking it in at the time?

LV: We were scared.

M: When did you first begin to be afraid?

LV: In the beginning of 1936. We decided to get married earlier, precisely because the political climate was starting to change.

M: What was your husband's profession?

LV: He was a lawyer.

M: Did he keep up with the political situation?

LV: We didn't pay much attention to it back then.

M: Not even when things got worse?

LV: When things got worse, we certainly did.

M: Did you discuss these issues at home?

LV: Yes, we did. Because these problems applied directly to us.

M: What conclusions did you draw in the family? What was the dominating opinion among your family members?

LV: What kind of opinion could we possibly have? Tell me. What sort of opinion could we have? We were unwanted.

---

*In her early twenties, Leika met Julius "Julko" Bronner, an attorney, born in Žilina in 1908, and after a long courtship they got married on December 23, 1936. They had both a civil and a religious wedding. Leika and Julko rented one room in a modern house, not far from the building where she and her second husband, Dr. Alexander "Sanyi" Vozar, would live many years later.

M: A person today could hardly imagine what you went through. But could you try to give us a glance of what it was like?

LV: From what point of view are you looking at?

M: From your own perspective.

LV: It was hard. Times were uncertain. We just didn't know what to do.

M: What did you think would happen back then?

LV: I can't give you an answer to that either.

M: Did it ever occur to you that it would result in such a vast escalation of terror as it did?

LV: No. We never thought it would evolve into such atrocities.

M: So, you were afraid. But you never thought it would end up like it did.

LV: No.

M: March 14, 1939 was the beginning of a radical change in history. The Slovak State was formed. Do you remember that Day?

LV: Yes, I remember. It was in '39. Am I right? Yes, back then my youngest sister [Edit] was getting ready to go to Bratislava. Why she was going there, I don't remember. But I just remember that she was arrested at the station and escorted to our house after which we had our home searched. They were looking for books. They were rummaging through our library. But they left us alone after that.

M: Who was conducting the home search?

LV: It was the Guardists [Hlinka Guard or Slovakian state police].

M: And did they arrest your sister in Žilina or Bratislava?

LV: They arrested her in Žilina. I don't remember if she was travelling further than that. All I remember is that they did that house search. They didn't find anything and that was the end of that phase. We were left alone after that.

M: Could you say that this experience made you more frightened?

LV: Yes, you could say that.

M: So how did things go after that? What was life like in April and May of 1939?

LV: I was working. I still had a job at that time. And that's how time passed. There's not much to say for that time.

M: Was the rest of the population acting the same way as it did before?

LV: No. People started to whisper about labor camps and how they were forming. I think that it was then we got the order to start wearing yellow stars. If I recall correctly, it might have been in '39 or possibly in 1940.

M: Did your family have to follow this order too?

LV: Do you mean did we have to wear the stars? Yes, of course. It was mandatory.

M: How did you find out about this order?

LV: They simply announced that every Jew had to wear a yellow star. Other directives and laws began to appear shortly after. Jews were not permitted to own a radio, or television. They had to turn in all their valuables, jewels, warm clothing, sporting goods. Basically, the Jews were not permitted to own anything except their living quarters. They were not allowed to walk out late at night. There was a curfew. We had a limited time window when we could go out. Jewish-owned stores had the word Jude painted over their windows. We were not permitted to enter public places. And of course, having the right to vote was out of the question.

M: When all this was happening to you—your valuables, your furs, warm clothing were being confiscated—did you try to convince yourselves that this was some kind of mistake, that this could not be happening?

LV: Did we convince ourselves to believe that this was a mistake?

M: Did they confiscate your things as well?

LV: Confiscate?! We had to bring all our valuables to them in person.

Excerpt from Lea's statement at Ravensbrück, June 1945:

I will start to recount my story from the time when the so-called "independent state" was founded. This was March 14, 1939. They immediately put into effect Jewish laws, which I suppose all of us are familiar with, and about which I need not further discuss. When they had taken almost everything from us, including our warm winter clothing, it was stated that Jews were being sent to "work." They began with the young. At the time we still believed in the "story" of work. When no news of them came after many months, they organized transports of the cruelest kind, and we realized only too well that this route led to death.

M: How did your mother react to all of this?

LV: You can only imagine how a person could cope.

M: Did you cry?

LV: I'm sure we shed a tear at that time. But then even the tears stopped. It was cruel. It was truly cruel. A person today couldn't even imagine it back then.

M: Your husband and you... Did you live with your family or did you have your own apartment?

LV: My brother saw that the situation was getting worse. He followed what was happening in Germany [and Austria]. So, he with his wife and baby daughter left in the summer of '39. We decided to move in with my parents. My father died in 1940 [September]. In 1941 [after the September 9, 1941 Jewish Codex was enacted] we received a directive that banned us from living in our place. It was on Dlabačová Street in downtown Žilina and so we had to move to Velká Okružná Street, which was by the road that led to Rajec. We lived there with my mother. We didn't have children.

M: What was the purpose of moving elsewhere? Why did you decide to exchange apartments?

LV: Because Jews were not permitted to live downtown. They assigned areas where Jews were allowed to live, it wasn't a ghetto but a rather pre-assigned part of town.

M: So, in other words, it was an apartment that was of lower grade and in a less appealing part of town.

LV: Yes, it was in a bad part of town and the apartment was not the best.

M: Who got your apartment on Dlabačová Street?

LV: Who came to live in the apartment after us is unknown to me. We never found out and we didn't even try to find out.

M: And did your husband wear the yellow star as well?

LV: Oh yes. Everyone had to. There were only a few people who managed to get waivers. They were important for the local economy. But besides them, everyone had to wear the star.

M: Your husband was not important enough for the local economy?

LV: No, he wasn't. He had to wear it.

M: How did he take it?

LV: It was humiliating to him, of course. And I think I mentioned already that we had a time limit as to when we could go out. If someone ever broke the curfew, they would be beaten severely.

M: So, by then beatings were beginning to occur.

LV: Yes.

M: Did anyone from your family ever get hurt?

LV: No, we abided by all rules and regulations. We all felt the fear and the feeling of hopelessness.

M: Did you think that this couldn't possibly last that long; that it would soon end?

LV: Yes, we believed that. We wanted to believe it.

M: Did you believe that the situation would improve in a very short period of time?

LV: No, we knew it would take longer.

M: Did you follow the events in Europe and how Hitler was systematically gaining territory all over the continent?

LV: Yes.

M: Did you sense any anti-Semitic attitudes develop in the local population thanks to the propaganda of the time?

LV: People were mainly afraid. There were no incentives for them to associate with us. Of course, some decent individuals were not afraid. But most of the time the people avoided us.

M: Up until this time, you interacted with people around you regularly?

LV: Yes.

M: Were you shunned by people who were friendly to you before?

LV: I've never experienced it with my friends. We had a few of them who even truly helped us.

M: What were your lives like at that time during the years 1940-41? There were numerous bans and laws prohibiting Jews from all sorts of things. Would you recall some of them?

LV: I already told you the ones that I remembered. You were not permitted to have a radio at home, etc. We weren't allowed to shop. We couldn't have jewelry, sporting goods. We lived a limited life.

M: Were the directives coming every month? Were they always worse than the ones before?

LV: The worst directive announced the arrival of the transports.

M: When did you realize that the transports were real, and how did that effect you?

LV: First they were taking young single girls. When my husband found out he went to plead with an official on behalf of someone. The official then stated to my husband that I was on the list as well. When we found that out, we decided we would all leave Slovakia and head for Hungary, where Hitler didn't have complete control just yet.

One day the Slovak secret police came to our apartment and wanted to arrest my husband because they suspected that he was planning an escape to Hungary with his family. They conducted a house search but found no evidence of such doings. They left the apartment and told my husband where to report the next day. The minute they left our apartment, we started packing and a friend of ours, who is no longer amongst us, lent us her documents. We managed to alert both my sisters [Klári and Edit], one [Klári] lived in Žilina. So, we left for Tepličky [a village 91 miles south west of Žilina]. We all boarded the train in Tepličky and we got as far as Lovinobaňa [a village 9 miles north of Lučenec]. In Lovinobaňa we had...

M: What was the name of the man who helped you in Lovinobaňa?

LV: Strasser. My sister [Teri] lived in Lučenec, which back then was part of Hungary and she was familiar with the area and she managed to arrange for us to cross the border that night illegally. Did I mentioned that dogs were growling around us and we had a four-year-old child with us? [Peter, whose name he later changed to Shlomo]. We sedated the child and managed to arrive in Lučenec. I would also like to add that the journey itself was terrible. The roads were muddy, and my youngest sister [Edit] left her shoe in the mud because it got stuck there. She managed to get to Lučenec with only one shoe on her foot. In Lučenec our sister [Teri] convinced us that it was too dangerous to stay and so she arranged for us to get to Budapest.

M: You stayed in Lučenec for just a few days. Correct?

LV: Yes, just a few.

M: How did you escape Lučenec?

LV: We drove out in a car. But we crossed the border to Lučenec by foot.

M: Was that dangerous?

LV: It was very dangerous. Either they would have returned us back to Žilina or we would have been put on a transport immediately.

M: You escaped from Žilina because your life was already in danger.

LV: Yes.

M: When you got to Budapest, did you know anyone there?

LV: We had family there, but they too were afraid. They weren't permitted to shelter foreign refugees. We obtained false documents and based on those papers we managed to settle in. My mother moved in with my sister's family [Klári], and my husband and I managed to find a place for ourselves. It was a very harsh and destitute life. We had to get everything on the black market and we needed money for that. My husband found a job as a worker in a brewery. And I worked as a German nanny.

[Leika recalled that only then did they begin to have daily meals and how happy she and Julius were when he brought home his first week's pay. Until then he had worked only as a lawyer and was thus doubly proud of working with his hands.]

That lasted for about a year. I can't say that it was easy. We weren't starving but we didn't always fill our bellies. After a year there was a raid.

Excerpt from Lea's statement at Ravensbrück, June 1945:

From the moment we got to Budapest, Shlomo, who was hardly four years old and understood no Hungarian, had to be trained to tell lies. He was clever enough that one could speak to him openly about why he must tell these important lies: why he had to conceal that he was a Jew, where he had lived before, etc. Once he asked his mother, "Tell me mother, after the war, will I ever have to lie again?"

M: Just to get back to your life in Budapest. Did you have to wear the yellow stars back then?

LV: In Budapest? No. We didn't have to wear any stars. But we were always afraid of raids. We were always afraid to go to a restaurant or a public place, because we had false documents.

M: And was the animosity against Jews the same as it was in Žilina?

LV: At that time, it wasn't.

M: There were no transports in Budapest at that time?

LV: No, there were no transports. Hungary was not yet occupied by the Germans.

M: So, there were no institutionalized anti-Jewish laws.

LV: I'm sure there were, but we were too busy trying to make ends meet. Our family [in Budapest] was too scared to house us. Everyone was afraid of us so there had to be some laws and orders to subjugate the Jews. There had to be a ban on things and it must have been enforced brutally.

M: Did you maintain contact with the rest of your family in Žilina?

LV: There was no one left in Žilina. At least not from my immediate family. Everyone had gone with us to Hungary. As I mentioned before, I managed to warn my family in time and so we all crossed the border together. Well, we lived in Budapest from hand to mouth for about a year with our false documents.

Then [1943] we experienced a raid in which we were arrested and interned for another year.

Excerpt from Lea's statement at Ravensbrück, June 1945:

My husband and I were arrested when we were found to be illegal immigrants and sent to a labor camp.

M: When you say you were interned, you mean you were imprisoned, correct?

LV: Yes, that is correct. Well, it wasn't a prison, but we were not permitted to leave whenever we liked. But we did get regular meals. And sometimes we got a visitor or two. But we could not leave the place. Some people managed to get privileged furloughs but we were not among them.

M: You were in the camp for about a year, correct?

LV: Yes, about a year, but when the Germans occupied Hungary, we escaped from the camp.

Shoah Foundation Transcript: Section Two

M: We spoke about your time in Budapest and then your internment in a camp for another year. You were there from April of 1943. What was it like in the internment camp?

LV: We were not permitted to work, so the days were very long and boring, but we managed to survive. When the Germans occupied Hungary, we escaped. By then it was March 1944. And we [Leika and Julko] managed to get back across the border to Slovakia, where we succeeded in getting another set of false documentation under the name Bučan and Bučanová. We found ourselves an apartment in Banská Bystrica and we managed to stay there until the beginning of the [Slovak National] Uprising.*

M: What happened to your relatives?

LV: They crossed the border back, too. Not with us. But they came shortly after and they managed to find a place near Bratislava in Cseklész [Čeklis].

M: Let's add that today, Cseklész is known as Bernolákovo. When you came to Banská Bystrica, you managed to find an apartment?

LV: Well, the landlords didn't know that we were there with false documents. My husband would get up every morning and pretend that he went to work so that it wouldn't look suspicious. I would follow him after. We would usually go to the mountains and collect mushrooms. We would be creative in finding food, because we didn't have any money. We would also get a visit from someone we knew, who would help us out financially. We were living hand to mouth.

M: Did you wear the stars when you were in Banská Bystrica?

LV: No, we didn't. We were hiding as Aryans. Our landlords didn't have a clue who we were. We lived like this until the Slovak National Uprising.**

At the time, there was a Proclamation for all former military officers to enlist for the uprising. My husband, who was a former lieutenant, enlisted and I received papers that allowed me to follow the army into the mountains as the wife of an officer. And when the Germans were advancing on Banská Bystrica, we then retreated into the mountains. The Germans outnumbered us. The army split up into separate partisan units, one of which we belonged to. It was commanded by Boris Horvath.

*According to the Shoah Foundation's official files, Leika's alias was Mária Bučanová.
**On August 28, 1944, as the Soviet Army was approaching Slovakia from the east, Slovak partisans with headquarters in Banská Bystrica initiated a revolt against the German army in Slovakia.

M: What was life like with the partisans? Were you in the mountains or were you in Banská Bystrica?

LV: We ended up with the partisans in the mountains because after the uprising, Banská Bystrica was overrun by the Germans. We survived constant fighting. The Germans were pursuing us into the mountains and they were relentless. We were shot at day and night. We had little food and we didn't have appropriate clothing. It was getting cold. Then one day, my husband was to meet a colleague at a determined location to discuss further action. The woods were infested with Germans and it was risky to be there. But they went regardless. And just shortly after they left, an intense gun battle ignited, and it lasted all afternoon and part of the night. My husband and his comrade didn't return. We waited at our post for quite some time. We lay flat on our bellies. It was cold, and it began to snow. We covered ourselves in blankets and it snowed on them and made us invisible to the Germans. It was terrible, because the shooting just continued until the morning and we were just hoping that none of the bullets hit my husband and his compatriot. We were hoping that if they were not returning it was because they didn't want to alert the Germans about our position. But morning was coming, and we could no longer stay where we were. I had to join the partisans and move on. Three days later we were captured by the Germans in the mountains. They took us to Banská Bystrica, where we were put on trial. I saw a line of people there, many of whom were my friends.

M: How did you get captured?

LV: I don't remember. They overpowered us and took us to Banská Bystrica.

M: Were they brutal? Did they beat you severely?

LV: They were brutal. There was a man with us, who was asked whether he was a Communist. He was brave and said he was. They beat him badly. As I said before, there was a line of many people that I knew in Banská Bystrica. They were all sent to Kremnicka.*

And you know what happened there. I was released because they accepted my false documents.

I managed to go back where I previously lived in Banská Bystrica. The landlords were very decent. They knew by then who I was. I lived there under my real name. They helped me and because I couldn't travel as a Jew on a train, they lent me their documents. I found out that my relatives [Klári, Sani, Shlomo, and Elsa] were in Cseklész so I went to meet them. The following day I went to Bratislava with my sister [Klári] to find some work. We were at the train station and an air raid alarm went off. During the alarm someone came to us and asked for identification.**

They, of course, suspected that the documents we had were false, so we were arrested. My sister [Klári] had all the documents for our family with her and so they brought in from Čeklis that same Christmas eve 1944 my mother and my brother-in-law [Sani], and of course their child. I can't remember where we were interrogated. I think it was in Bratislava. We spent two nights there. And then they transported us into Sered'.

M: This was one of the concentration camps. Is that correct?

LV: Yes. I remember I found work there because I knew that whoever worked received extra rations. We had a child with us and we needed the extra rations for him. I worked in the laundry. Of course, they didn't feed us that well and so we needed that extra strength that was inside of us to survive.

---

*After the Slovak National Uprising was suppressed, the German soldiers and their local collaborators—the Hlinka Guard—rounded up and massacred hundreds of partisans and even non-combatants, mostly Jews: men, women and children.
**Leika believed that a Jewish informer from Žilina had reported them at the time.

Shortly after that an SS officer, Herr Bruner, selected my mother and me for a transport to Ravensbrück [Concentration Camp].

M: How long were you in Sered'? A month, or perhaps two?

LV: I think it was about a month. I don't remember exactly. So, my mother and I were placed on a transport to Ravensbrück. My brother-in-law was sent to Sachsenhausen-Oranienburg [Concentration Camp]. And my sister [Klári] with her child was sent to Theresienstadt. The transport there was just... what can I tell you? It was a cattle car. There were about 70 of us in there. We had two buckets: one with water and the other was to urinate in. There were bars on the windows. We didn't know where they were taking us. We traveled seven days and seven nights. We arrived in a place called Fürstenberg just outside Ravensbrück.

You can imagine how cramped we were in that place. I don't have to tell you. It was almost impossible to fall asleep under those conditions. In Fürstenberg they opened up the wagon door. Several corpses were already lying there. We exited with our small rucksacks. They were cruel to us. They thought that we were all moving too slowly. They chased us through this small town and we could see curious faces pop up through the windows in the houses. But you found no compassion in those faces. They didn't care. Then we finally reached a large gate. Above the gate was a statement. I can't remember. It was *Arbeit Macht Frei* [Work Makes you Free.] The gate opened wide before us and then it shut like a wall behind us. Immediately after we got there a group of inmates at the camp came to us. And I have to say they no longer looked like humans. The fear and hunger permeated their faces. They begged us for clothes, for food. We still had our little rucksacks. And regardless of the fact that they were being beaten with batons, their hunger was much greater, and they endured the pain.

My mother and I realized that this was most likely an extermination camp. But we both tried to encourage each other to give us strength. I was one of the stronger ones and I could claim my usefulness. I told her that they needed our work, so they couldn't destroy us just yet. Then they herded us into a huge sleeping hall. We spent the entire night there. We had a little bit of food, and we realized that it was better for us to eat it while we still had it in our possession. They took our rucksacks in the morning and they dressed us in rags. You couldn't even call these old clothes. We ended up after that on Block 23. There was a quarantine in progress. They put us four to a cot so we had to take turns with who could sleep stretched out and who had to save space. Instantly we felt the presence of an enormous quantity of fleas and lice.

There was an announcement asking if we would like we could volunteer, regardless of the quarantine, to carry corpses. A woman my age who I befriended in the box car, and who had also traveled with her mother, was there. We both volunteered, because we thought we could ensure a certain amount of security. I could secure survival for my mother and myself. We would carry 70 to 80 corpses a day with our bare hands without any disinfectant. The bodies were placed in what you could call compartments. We would do this every day and it would be midnight by the time we would return to—I wouldn't call it "home"—my mother. I mean I might have done this for two to three months.

M: This would be around December 1944, correct?

LV: Yes, it was in December of 1944.

M: Was it cold, the camp?

LV: Very. We only had rags to wear. You couldn't call

those clothes.

If one had the most basic need, for example for toilet paper, one was immediately reminded that we were not in a sanatorium. How sad, my mother and I said to each other, that they need to remind us of that so often.

M: Did you experience the daily head count?

LV: I almost forgot to mention that. That was an inviolable daily activity, like clockwork whether it was Sunday or a holiday. They would herd us out into the cold after the sirens sounded and we had to lineup within a few minutes in front of our blocks for roll-call at 4 am and they would make us stand there without moving until 7 or 8 in the morning when all prisoners had been accounted for. No one was exempt from this duty, regardless of how sick one was. Some prisoners were driven to the roll-call by cudgel blows. People died during that headcount, but that did not discourage the Germans from sending another batch of sick prisoners the very next day to complete the count. They would just faint and, of course, die.

My mother was also on a work detail. She was 60 years old. She was strong and capable. One day she got the flu because her feet were wet, so she stayed "home," well, in the block. I was working, and when I returned, I found out that they assigned her to a transport into a so-called *Jugendlager* [youth detention camp]. And I knew that the *Jugendlager* was, in reality, an extermination camp. It was close to Ravensbrück, very close. I went to beg an SS nurse by the name of Erika, I pleaded with her. I told her that she knew that my mother was able to work and that she didn't have to be selected for that transport. And if the nurse insisted on sending her there, then I asked her to let me go with my mother. The nurse refused to allow me to join my mother. She started to calm me down. She was polite, I have to say. She assured me that I didn't have to worry. She told me my mother would not have to work there. She would not have to endure the head count. It was just a relief from the pain.

The 1st of February came, that terrible day when I had to say goodbye.

Excerpt from Lea's statement at Ravensbrück, June 1945:

What this meant for me you can clearly imagine. I got no news from her, although there were whispered reports that there were many bodies from the *Jugendlager* that looked quite blue and certainly had not died a normal death. They talked of roll-call lasting hours, of hunger, etc.

I could not get access to her. But once, by chance through my work, I managed to get into her camp. It was four o'clock in the afternoon and the women were just coming from roll-call in which they had stood from early morning in the cold. I started searching for her and I finally found my mother. She was huddled in a small and cold compartment filled with older women. They were shivering from the cold, from the hunger. They all accosted me, each of them asking me to help them. Apparently, they had not gotten any food for three days. After a few days, the Germans took away their coats and the women had to make do wearing light rags and were not allowed to sleep. Please don't ask me anything about that, even today it chokes me up. They too, had to stand for a head count. When I saw my mother, she wasn't that loving figure of tenderness. All I saw was terror and fear and hunger. She threw herself on me, crying, and said she thought that she would not be able to see me again. Perhaps she knew better than I did then, that this was an extermination camp. Funny, that I was still so short- sighted. I only realized afterwards where the stream of women was going, old and young, standing outside the gate without any baggage.

I was determined to help her in some way. My stay in her camp was short. I could not risk getting exposed. I was there under the radar. And if they found what I had done, I would have been sent to the gas chamber. I still remember that my mother escorted me out as far as she could. We both nodded at one another.

Excerpt from Lea's statement at Ravensbrück, June 1945:

That was the last time that I saw my mother, and that's how I still see her standing in front of me. Shriveled up, shivering from cold and with a dreadful expression on her face.

LV: That memory is terrifying to this day.

(M: Lea is visibly upset here.)

I returned to my camp and I was determined to help my mother. I must add that in her camp, their rations of bread had been cut by half. I would send my own ration of bread through channels to my mother. And through the same channels, my mother sent a letter written on toilet paper [archived at Yad Vashem].

Elsa's note to Leika, written on toilet paper at Ravensbrück's Jugendlager, February 1945:

My dear brave little girl!

I received your packet and was very happy to get it, on the other hand I felt pain, because I know you stinted it from yourself and had to keep yourself on short rations.

Honey, don't do it, you know how painful this is for me, these days one cannot make sacrifices even for one's own mother!

Right now, you need more strength than I do, I am managing well with what I get. I always have some spare bread left and am training my stomach to adapt to whatever the situation requires.

In the afternoons, those with a kerchief don't have to report on to Apellplatz, so I don't have to either, and sometimes they release us earlier in the morning. Health is the most important thing, and thank God, I am healthy and wish the same to you. If the lice didn't eat us, the situation would be quite bearable, though we never know what the next moment will bring. Aunt Rosa's shoes and kerchief of were stolen, it's a mercy that I had spare shoes and the kerchief we bought at Sered' is now on her head.

I would like to get some news from (all of) you, I am awaiting your report anxiously. Hugs and kisses, my angel, from all our company. When will we meet?

Mother

Why don't they send anything to Mrs. Sternberg either? She is cold, so thinly clad, the poor thing, and so is Aunt Rosa. [Rosa Schläfer née Pikler was Armin Pikler's wife, also known as Roza-neni or Auntie Rosa.] Urgent help is needed, to help a person bear it. I found your kind words in the parcel only afterwards. Heaven bless you and a special blessing from me. I have full confidence in you, do whatever you think right, you can judge it better from there.

Hugs, *Mother*

I kept that letter, and I managed to copy those words after the war. She wrote that she was grateful for having a daughter willing to sacrifice so much for her and that it wasn't necessary. Of course, there was no chance of getting her back. But I continued to send pieces of bread and one day the little packet of bread was sent back.

Excerpt from Lea's statement at Ravensbrück, June 1945:

From the lay preacher, Else, I learned that my mother had been selected by Dr. Winkelmann [Adolf] and had been put on a so-called transport. Since then I heard nothing more of her.

Elsa's note to Leika; Ravensbrück, February 1945

Nowadays, I believe that was because they sent my mother to the gas chamber. But back then, in my mind, I very much hoped that she was still alive.

It was then that the selections began. Like at Auschwitz, Mengele appeared in the camp. Because of the two years I spent in Hungary and the fighting in the mountains, I was never very strong, but at that time I was in worse shape and for the first time I bartered my bread for some rouge. There was a black market in the camp. You could trade your bread for something else and I traded mine for some rouge and so I wasn't sorted to the left. We had to strip naked and pass through a commission. When we were hauling the dead, we could take their bread. We would take it for ourselves or give it to others who needed it most. I don't want to boast but there were three little girls who lost their parents in Auschwitz and to this day they still attribute the fact they survived to the bread that I gave them. The morning head count, of course, continued. I can't remember what happened next.

M: You were still in Ravensbrück.

LV: Yes, I kept saying to myself that I had to survive. I had to survive because the world had to know what was going on there. Today when I was hesitating to tell my story, and let me tell you, I was hesitating very much, I reminded myself that back then I tried to survive because I wanted the world to know what the Germans had done to us. Even after so many years, you just still have to think about what to say.

Shoah Foundation Transcript: Section Three

M: You were in Ravensbrück. Is there a story that is ingrained in your memory?

LV: As I told you before, I would have to carry corpses and they would amount to 70 to 80 a day. We had to throw the bodies on a cart in a very inhumane manner. It was a cart. I remember a terrible night when a transport came from Rychlin [German labor camp]. They woke me and my friend up late at night and we had to carry the corpses onto a truck. The SS man in charge thought that the way we were handling the corpses was too humane. The soldiers brought us these stools on which they made us stand. They called them *chamarels*. While standing on them we had to toss the bodies one on top of the other. Some of the bodies were not dead and those who were still conscious knew that they were going straight for the gas. The fact that they were sent to the gas chamber was verified by the fact that the truck came back empty and we had to pile another load of bodies on it. And we saw a continuous stream of smoke from the chimney of the crematorium. We felt terrible because we were lending a helping hand to those who were sending those living people to their death. We could never forgive ourselves for doing that. But we had no other choice. We said to ourselves that we would tell our stories or write them down. But we could never describe the terror that was happening when we lived through it. In the camps I would say to myself that when my husband returned, I would tell him everything that I lived through and then I would never tell this story again. I would forget that it all happened. It is easy to say this, but of course it is never that easy in real life. Because memories in one way or another find a way back. I would also like to add that the strength inside of me can be attributed to the fact that I thought possibly that my mother by some miracle managed to survive her ordeal, and that I would be reunited with my husband. On the 30th of April [1945], the Russian Army liberated us.

M: If I may, after you carried corpses, you had one more detail that you were a part of in the camps. What was that?

LV: I forgot to mention it. I carried the sick. There were a lot of people with typhus. We had to carry them into the so-called infirmary with our bare hands and we had to sleep in the same clothes that we carried them in. I had a lot of internal strength. I wanted to survive, and that desire defeated everything that came my way. Well, that work was also not easy.

M: Were you vaccinated for this?

LV: I have to tell you that we were not. We didn't want to get vaccinated because we didn't trust anything the Germans would put into our bodies. We managed to skip the vaccinations, and we never got vaccinated despite the risks of infection. They would give us horrible food. We would get an eighth of bread and a raw beet. When we got potato peelings we considered that a holiday.

M: Did you try to avoid the vaccination because there were rumors about Mengele's experiments?

LV: We just didn't trust that the vaccinations were meant to protect us. We thought that perhaps they would decrease our chances of survival.

M: Had you heard that Mengele was injecting gasoline into human veins?

LV: Yes, I heard about that. Though I never knew anyone who went through that ordeal. I did know about the sterilization experiments, because there were several Romas with us and they went through the sterilization. I knew about that.

M: Did you ever see Mengele with your own eyes?

LV: Oh, yes. He came from Auschwitz after it was liberated. He brought with him a large number of transports from the east. The prisoners had to endure the cold and the travel. The Hungarians suffered the most, because they were not used to the cold climate.

M: Is there a story that you might remember from the time you were carrying the sick?

LV: There is perhaps this one time when I was carrying the sick and I stumbled upon a few people who I knew from my past. I could see that they realized they would not survive and they begged me to go deliver their messages: "Tell my husband to find another wife," or something like that. Those were very cruel moments. I knew that it was the end of their lives—and to have to deliver such messages. There was one who I needed to escort into the *Jungendlager*. Her parents were in Žilina and they survived. They managed to stay hidden and I had to deliver her message to them. Those are just moments that subsequently affect a person.

M: Was the sick detail harder or easier than the one that forced you to carry the dead?

LV: It was a lot easier. Just physically it was less demanding. For instance, a transport arrived once from somewhere. And that was an open train car where all the people were completely frozen. And taking apart a clump of corpses frozen together is very demanding on your body. I wasn't a big girl. I was thin. But I did what I had to do. I wanted to survive. Because I wanted to let the world know what was happening. And as you can see, I'm coming up with more stories that I would rather forget about. But I'm telling them to you.

One of the worst experiences was that after the war I found the body of my husband. I found out that back then when all the shooting started, twelve people were shot dead at once and they put them in a common grave at a cemetery. A priest buried them. But I wasn't sure that my husband was lying in that grave because his body wouldn't be marked with his real name. He had false papers on him, the same ones that I had when I was still in the mountains. He was buried under the name Bučan. When I went to Brezno [a town 28 miles east of Banská Bystrica], I showed them pictures of my husband and people who witnessed the funeral told me that there was no one who looked him among those fallen. Therefore, I requested an exhumation. I recognized his body based on his shirt. I remembered the shirt he was wearing. It was the same shirt. I also recognized his shoes. His face was no longer recognizable, but I had no doubt it was him. After that I hired some carpenters in the village to make me a coffin so I could bury him with some dignity. I've been at his grave several times. It's well kept.

M: Based on this experience you concluded that your husband died in battle. This happed in November of 1944.

LV: Yes, in November and I know that he was buried on the 16th of November.

M: And you were captured by the Germans shortly after that.

LV: Didn't I say that already?

M: Yes, you did. Let's get back to Ravensbrück. You were working as a carrier of the sick. The front was getting closer to the camp. Did any news get into the camp?

LV: I was in the camp with Dr. Nejedlá who was the daughter of Minister [Zdeněk] Nejedlý. And news of the front was coming to us through her, that the Russians were getting closer and the war would be over soon. That gave us a great boost of adrenaline.

M: And how did they get the news?

LV: I don't remember. They were Communists and they stuck together. That was obvious. There was one more person who I remember, Hanka Housková. The Communists always treated us nicely. They had certain privileges. And they could even get some packages from home. We could never get anything. Nejedlá for instance gave me her shoes. They were three sizes bigger than my feet, but I didn't have to walk barefoot.

M: Did you manage to get any information about your relatives while you were in the camp?

LV: Did I hear any news about my relatives? No, just once by complete coincidence I heard that my sister [Teri] was in another camp. It was a work camp and she was on a work detail in some factory. She was sent to Auschwitz from Hungary and she was pregnant. And in the 7th month of pregnancy, they conducted an experiment on her. And to avoid the gas chamber, there was a Czech doctor who filled out the paperwork for her to be transferred on a transport to a work camp with a factory [KZ Barth – about 100 miles northeast of Ravensbrück]. She was bleeding from the operation, but she got on the train and ended up there. It was certainly better to work in a factory than to do the things I had to do. They were under a roof and perhaps occasionally they even received a bit more bread. When I heard that she was alive, I started to save portions of my bread for her. And the strange thing about my sister was that just about that time she started saving portions of her own bread so that when we finally met, we could help each other out. It was telepathic. And it shows the true humanity that lay within us.

M: And you were hungry.

LV: We were terribly hungry all the time.

M: When did you manage to get together with your sister?

LV: That was after the war. We all met up after the war. I left Ravensbrück on the first Czechoslovak transport. We traveled by trucks.

M: So that had to be preceded by liberation. What was the camp like in its last days of German rule?

LV: Well, we saw all the bombs dropping around us. They didn't hit the camp, but they hit many structures all around it. It was terrifying to hear the explosions. And as I mentioned before, at noon we were at Lagerstrasse [the camp's main street], and two Russians were running towards us and it was then we realized we were liberated.

M: Do you remember what date it was?

LV: We had no idea what day it was in the camps. They never told us. All I remember is the hour. It was twelve noon. Lunchtime. They brought us all kinds of food. And we had to be very careful not to eat very much. Those who were not careful paid for that mistake with their lives. We were starved out. We were not used to eating larger meals. We had to hold ourselves back and not eat the food that the Russians gave us. The cans of meat, condensed milk.

But all of a sudden the gates opened up. And I remember that, because I suddenly saw greenery, I heard birds. It was a feeling that I can hardly describe. The houses in the villages around were abandoned and I must admit that we went into those houses and we took whatever we could. What we found there were enormous storage rooms filled with clothes, even children's clothes. And since we were dressed in rags, we took those clothes and put them on.

M: Would you say that it was the happiest day of your life?

LV: Certainly, the happiest. Well, I was still left behind in the camp for a while, because I was working as a nurse.

M: How did the soldiers treat you?

LV: They were very polite.

M: They weren't trying to proposition you in any way.

LV: No, not there. They would try later in Bratislava, but not in Ravensbrück.

M: Was the Russian army disciplined?

LV: I would say yes, in Ravensbrück, they were real gentlemen.

M: How long did you stay in Ravensbrück after liberation in April of 1945?

LV: It was June when the Czechoslovak Transport came for us.

M: And what did you do in between?

LV: I was a nurse. It was very sad, because we were constantly getting sick people and they were still dying. And we thought that since the war was over there shouldn't be any more casualties. We were very grief-stricken that people were still dying. I mentioned I was a nurse, but before that when the camp was still under German rule, they were transporting prisoners out of the camp. They were herding them into the transports with dogs. The prisoners had no choice but to go. Luckily, since I was carrying the sick, I was still useful to them in Ravensbrück, so they left me alone. Those who survived that ordeal have terrible things to say about it.

M: When you were a nurse in the camp, were there food shortages?

LV: Subsequently? Well, we had rations that were given to us by the Russians.

M: So, you weren't starving, correct?

LV: Well, we weren't starving, but we had to be very careful about the portions we ate. When I arrived in Prague, we lived in Krč [a district in the south of Prague] because we were still very weak. The rations did not get us out of it just yet. We were still weak. And there for the first time in a long while, we lay down in beds with white linen. And that was truly an experience that no one forgets. After a few days, they released us. Each one of us got a Ravensbrück identification card. And then everyone went their separate ways. It took time to get home. The trains were not running. Occasionally, we would catch a ride. We would sleep at the depots and then we managed to get into Bratislava. That is where my traveling companion was from. She had an apartment there that she got from a divorce, and so I moved in with her until my other sister [Klári] with her child returned from Theresienstadt. She heard that I was going to Bratislava and so she followed and found me, and that's how we arrived in Žilina. And in September [1945], as I already mentioned, I found the dead body of my husband. I realized that my mother was not going to return. I accepted a position in the Ministry of Foreign Affairs in Prague, and I worked there until February.

M: You mean February 1946.

LV: Yes. And in the meantime, my current husband returned. We had known each other before the war. We met afterward and fell in love. That is destiny. He lost his wife in the camps. She gave birth to a child there and they both perished. He waited until he received confirmation that both his wife and child were no longer living. When he heard it first-hand from a witness, we decided that we would get married.

And we were blessed with our own child.*

M: In March 1946, you returned to Žilina, correct?

LV: Yes.

M: Did you look for your relatives?

LV: Yes. None of our relatives, uncles, aunts, their children. None of them survived.

M: What happened to them?

LV: They perished in the gas chamber.

M: Where?

LV: In Auschwitz. Most of them died in Auschwitz, except for my brother-in-law who died in Oranienburg.

M: Give us a glimpse into your life at that time. On the one hand, you were happy to have survived, but on the other, you were sad to have lost so many relatives. How did you take this all in?

LV: We wanted to start a new life. We wanted to forget. But you can't just forget something like that. But a new life did start, and in my case, I was blessed with the birth of my child.

M: Was it thanks to your child that you could overcome all the trauma experienced during the war?

LV: You can't ever escape that trauma. Never. Life is not long enough to be able to do that.

M: So, you got married to Dr. Alexander Vozar on November 24, 1946.

---

*Back in 1933, at age 20, Leika briefly dated Dr. Alexander "Sanyi" Vozar, born on December 14, 1908, in Tornaja, Slovakia. He was married to Magda Vozar née Kovacs, and they had a daughter. The traumatic experience of losing his wife and little daughter in a concentration camp was a contributing factor to the episodes of depression he suffered all his life.

LV: Yes.

M: Were you living together then in your own apartment?

LV: No, we lived in a hospital for two years after that. He was an eye doctor and we were in the hospital because the house that he owned was occupied and it was difficult to get the people out of it. But after two years we managed to move here (M: her current apartment) and we have been here ever since.

M: What happened to the apartment you had in the outskirts of town?

LV: When we left, some other people, who are no longer alive, came and took everything. Nothing was left. The only things we found were our albums. Our landlady saved them for us and I was very happy that she did. The rest of our belongings were stolen.

M: What about the apartment where you lived in Dlabačová Street?

LV: I don't know who took it over after we left. But there, we were at least permitted to leave with our furniture. From the other place we had to leave with nothing.

M: Did you have any significant material possessions in the hospital?

LV: We started again from nothing. We didn't have to lock our cabinets in the hospital because they were always empty. We had only the clothes we wore. We left with nothing and we came back with nothing.

M: How did people treat the Jewish population that survived?

LV: They didn't want to believe that it was possible that these atrocities actually happened. They were in denial. Many of the people who took Jewish property were upset when they had to give it back. It was inconvenient to them. There were even comments like: "Too many of them returned." Statements like that were not a rare occurrence.

M: What about those ordinary people who didn't receive any property during the Aryanization? Were they in denial as well? Could they have been influenced by the propaganda that followed? (M: meaning Communism)

LV: Or they just simply didn't believe that something like that could ever be survived.

M: We will talk about the post war experience of you family in the next part.

Shoah Foundation Transcript: Section Four

M: Ms. Lea, we are approaching the less horrible part of your experience, the one that occurred after the war. You married your second husband, Dr. Vozar, in November of 1946. You then stayed home with a child that was born. What is the child's name?

LV: Magdalena Vozarová.

M: What year was she born?

LV: 1946.

M: And where did your husband work?

LV: Here at the hospital, in the ophthalmology department.

M: You stayed at home with your child?

LV: Yes, for a time I stayed home with her.

M: In 1948, nationalization began; were any of your family members affected by this?

LV: Nationalization didn't start in 1948. We managed to get our apartment in 1948 but nationalization took place later. I don't remember when.

M: They started to nationalize property in February of 1948 and a second wave came in 1949. Did your husband work in a state-run hospital?

LV: Yes, our house was nationalized, but I don't remember the year. I would have to look into my records. They were nationalizing large mansions. Our home was unjustly taken because it was a family home. My husband fought to get it back because it was not fair. He succeeded only when they were giving property back after the Velvet Revolution in 1989, when properties were returned to their owners and their heirs.*

M: After a while you went back to work. Where did you work?

LV: I worked as an administrator for a laboratory gear enterprise. But I didn't stay there long. After a while, most likely due to the ordeal in the camps, I started to experience trouble with my spine. And so, I was on disability.

M: In 1950, we experienced another hysteria that was caused by the Communist party. Were any of your family members persecuted?

LV: No.

M: In 1968, the Soviet Army invaded Czechoslovakia.

---

*Leika and Sanyi frequently corresponded with Hansi and Sophie (who Leika also loved dearly) and later with Hansi and Virginia. They shared, in carefully worded letters, the difficulties of living under Communist rule. After 1948, the three-story building they owned was confiscated by the government. At that time, each person was allowed to occupy only a certain square footage. They lived in only half of the second floor without paying rent and shared the rest of the space with another family. They managed as best as they could, without complaining, to live under those circumstances. The stress of the unknown, even the possibility of losing their property and Sanyi's profession, was another contributing factor for his bouts of severe depression.

How do you recall these events?

LV: The invasion was a terrible shock to us. Many people had to flee to save themselves. My husband wasn't the healthiest of people at the time and I wasn't healthy either. For us, leaving the country was out of the question. But it was sad to see our friends and relatives leaving, and we often felt alone.*

LV: My daughter, after finishing her university studies in 1970, left for Israel, where my sisters [Klári, Teri, and Edit] were living. And she went there to follow the love of her life who she met during her studies. She could work there as a doctor immediately. That was in 1970. She lived in Israel for about 14 years. And then she was invited to the US as a laboratory researcher [at the Kresge Eye Institute in Detroit], and they decided after two years to stay in the US and they have been living there ever since. They live in Detroit. We have two grandchildren—they are 22 and 20. They are university students. And they are my joy and bring meaning to my life.**

M: Was it a disappointment to see the army that once liberated you from the camps invading our country in 1968 with different intentions?

LV: Of course, it was. On one hand we were grateful to them, but then they created the totalitarian regime. After the war, we thought that we would live freely, and my sisters and I promised each other that we would live in one place. Not only did we end up living separately, but we couldn't even live in the same republic, and we dispersed again all over the world.

---

*Klári, Zoli, Shlomo and Giora made *Aliyah* in 1949. Teri and Ivan left for Israel in 1969. Leika shared these sad times in her letters to Hansi.

**Magda left for Israel in the summer of 1970 after completing her medical studies. She went first on an approved "vacation" to Italy, where Peter Bielik came to meet her according to plan, and they traveled together back to Israel where they had met the year before. Magda had been doing a summer internship at the Hadassah hospital, and Peter had been learning Hebrew in Ulpan. Magda wanted to become an ophthalmologist like her father, and she specialized in that field in Israel.

M: 1969-70 was the period of normalization, which were dark days led by the Communist party. And then came November 1989. How did you experience the Velvet Revolution?

LV: Before I answer that question, I must tell you that my daughter left the country illegally. Well, she legally traveled to Italy, but she never returned, and we were not able to see each other for six-and-a-half years. We never met our son-in-law who was already abroad. We didn't get a chance to meet our grandchild. He was two-and-a-half years old before we got to meet him. It was very cruel.*

M: And how do you see the '89 revolution?

LV: Well, we thought that life over here would finally become normal. Many things changed. We could finally travel. This was very important to us, because we could visit our daughter and they could come visit us.

M: So, did your wishes come true?

LV: They did in the sense that we could go visit them and they could come visit us.

M: Did you agree with the separation of the Czech and Slovak Republics?

LV: Personally, I was disappointed. I liked living together. I liked living in the Czechoslovak State.

---

*Magda and Peter got married in Nahariya, Israel, on March 24, 1971. Teri, Ivan, Shlomo, Yael, Gili and Peter's family were present. Peter was not sure if Klári and Giora attended the wedding. Leika and Sanyi were not allowed to leave Czechoslovakia, so they organized an alternate wedding celebration in Žilina. Leika's letters expressed their sadness at being unable to attend such an important event in their lives. Leika and Sanyi were given permission to travel to Israel for the first time in 1976, just after their second grandchild, Michael (Miki), was born. After their first visit, they were allowed to travel back once a year, and stay for about half a year or longer. Their letters to Hansi expressed the joy of being with their grandsons, Daniel (Dano) and Miki, and also spending time with Magda, Klári, and Teri.

M: And now, in 1996, we are experiencing individuals who are justifying president Tiso and his policies.

LV: I would never justify him. Absolutely not. If it wasn't for his policies none of this would ever have happened. It is unjust to defend him.

M: What would you say to people who think that he was a martyr, that he was a hero of our nation?

LV: I would say that they are misinformed, or they don't want to be informed at all.

M: Madam Vozarová, on behalf of the Shoah Foundation, I would like to thank you for sharing your experience. And since we are about to conclude our interview, what would you say to future generations who 100 years from now will view your testimony?

LV: The words of my grandson come to mind. "Why did you go there [to the camps]? I don't understand how you could allow it to happen." My answer is my testimony. The words that I wrote shortly after the war and later when I was encouraged by a Russian doctor who told me I needed to write my autobiography. I want to give him [my grandson] this testimony so that he will see that it wasn't only the sick and the weak people who went into the gas. The healthy ones like my mother were manipulated to do so as well. She was strong and didn't have a grey hair on her head. I want to give him this testimony so that he can pass it on to the next generation.

****

At last, after a wrenching year without any news, my father heard from his sisters. From Žilina, Klári wrote in June 1945 that both she and Shlomo were "healthy" but Sani, after being separated from her and Shlomo on their way to Terezín, had probably been taken to the concentration camp in Oranienburg, Germany and had not returned. She was trying to recover Sani's photo studio and equipment. "I now anxiously wait for your news...I'm closing with affectionate hugs and kisses." Two months later, Klári wrote that her efforts had been unsuccessful. "But I keep busy and have an extra [illegible] job.

Leika was working at the Czechoslovak Foreign Affairs Ministry in Prague. On October 22, 1945, she wrote about the death of their mother, Elsa, at Ravensbrück in February:

> I am healthy but quite tired and mostly very sad... Editka has come back from Budapest and is staying with me for a while...We are both so sad. We will return to Žilina soon ...For now, Editka is looking for a job...Most beloved Hansi and Sophie, write the most detailed letter you can.

From Lučenec, Géza wrote in his first postwar letter to Hansi:

> We are trying to get on with our lives, and we are going to be fine...I am confident that soon I will have a job...We are so happy that Lejka and Klárika also survived "the war" and are working on putting their lives back together. Please write soon and let us know how you, Olinka, and Georgie are doing.

The letter made no mention at all of Auschwitz. My father must have written to all of them asking about their wellbeing, because Géza replied a month later, writing this about Teri after Auschwitz: "She has migraine headaches that come unexpectedly and make her feel weak. She is home all the time." He said he had a job in Filakovo, near Lučenec, but there was no description of the job itself.

A postcard from Klári and a short letter from Teri, both from December 1945, were most likely written in response to Hansi's offer to help with anything they needed. Both replies were quite similar: "Please try not to worry about us, dear Hansi, we are managing... [illegible]" Klári added that Shlomo would be in Lučenec with Teri and Géza for a while.

Edit, circa 1946

Teri with Ivan; Žilina, June 1947

In 1946 (the date is illegible), Leika wrote that both she and Edit were now in Žilina and "so happy to be home again." I could find no reply from her to Hansi's offer of help.

On June 7, 1946, Edit wrote that some weeks earlier, she had married Ferdinand "Fero" Slezák, a shopkeeper of Tornalja, Slovakia, a town near the Hungarian border. In a postcard from Leika a month later, she expressed concerns about Edit's decision to marry, and in fact, not long after that, Edit wrote to Hansi that she was unhappy and was getting divorced.

November 1946 was an eventful month in Žilina: Teri and Géza's son, Ivan, was born on November 6 to the delight of his parents and the rest of the family. Hansi got the news on an undated letter (envelope date November 12). On November 24, Leika remarried to Alexander "Sanyi" Vozar, a man she had known in 1933 before her first marriage, and with whom she had reconnected after the war, as stated in her 1996 interview, and as she reminded Hansi when she wrote with the news a week later: "We met again earlier in the year…Sanyi lost his wife and young daughter in the camp. He waited several months for [illegible] of their [illegible]. We are very happy together."

Klári also remarried, on July 12, 1947, to Zoltan "Zoli" Löwinger, a dentist, who had been Sani's good friend. Zoli was born on September 13, 1904 in Slovakia. He, too, had lost his family in the war: his wife and a nine-year-old son. A letter announcing Klári's wedding was not found, but in one dated August 23, 1947 she wrote: "Oh, my dearest Hansi, your words of congratulation and good wishes filled my heart with happiness… Zoli loves Shlomo, too." She must have noticed that his letter was signed only by him, as she asked, "How are the children and Sophie?" Had my father not yet shared his marital turmoil with his sisters?

On June 30, 1948, in Žilina, Klári gave birth to a boy. He was named Juraj after Zoli's first son, but later changed his name to Giora. Zoli formally adopted Shlomo, and subsequently, they decided to change their family name to the Slovak-sounding Lesný.

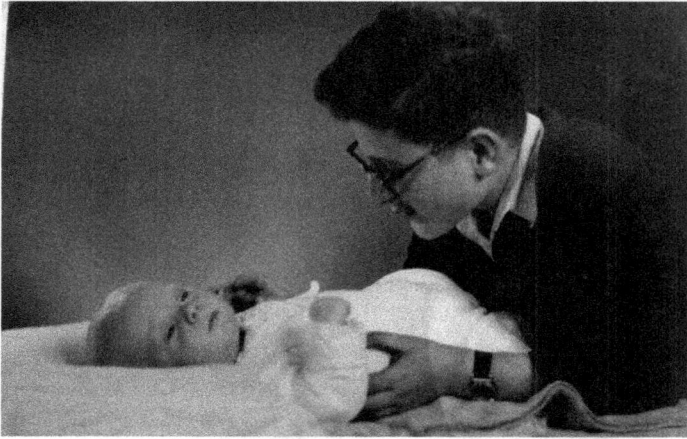

Shlomo with baby brother Giora; Žilina, 1948

In a letter written on February 19, 1949, it was obvious how painful it was for Klári to tell my father that they had decided not to emigrate to Ecuador even though he had secured Ecuadorian visas for the entire family. They had decided instead to make *Aliyah*. She included no details as to why or when they had made that decision or their travel plans.

Zoli, Giora, Klári, Shlomo; Žilina, December 1948

In a lengthy April 22, 1949 letter from Nahariya,[81] Klári explained to him that she had been afraid to mention anything "political" in her previous letter because the Communists had taken over the government the year before, and they were concerned that their emigration would be blocked. She described how she, Zoli, and Giora traveled to Israel, arriving first in Haifa on March 28, 1949 and from there going on to Nahariya. They had allowed Shlomo to join a *Hashomer Hatza'ir* youth group, which had left just before they did and traveled by train to France, and several months later by ship to Haifa, where they joined him that summer.

Teri and Géza also wrote, from Košice, that they had decided not to emigrate to Ecuador. "We [illegible] for it was not an easy decision, dearest Hansi…We can imagine how much trouble you went through to get the visas for all of us…We hope you will understand." There was no correspondence found as to when they moved to that city.

In a letter Hansi sent to all his family expressing his sadness and disappointment that they had decided not to emigrate to Ecuador, he must have also told them that he and Sophie, after a two-year process, had divorced in August 1948 and that he would retain custody of Oli and me. Correspondence from his sisters expressed disbelief and sadness about it. "We can't imagine how sad you must be and happy at the same time to have the children with you," they wrote. His sisters had always been very fond of Sophie. In letters Oli and I received from our aunts, they always asked us to convey their greetings and good wishes to our mother.

In subsequent correspondence, Klári related their experiences in their new life in Israel: they were quite happy to have chosen Nahariya: It was a small resort town where they felt safe; they lived in a small house but it had a large front yard. Giora had adapted well, they were all healthy and happy, she and Zoli were now employed, she was a bookkeeper for the Social Welfare Department and Zoli was a driver for a paint manufacturing plant owned by a kibbutz. Shlomo had arrived in September and was not living with them, but rather, at a kibbutz midway between Tel Aviv and Haifa. Klári would bicycle to work, a common mode of transportation in Nahariya.

Shlomo, Klári, Zoli, and Giora; Nahariya, 1949

Klári's letters, sent over the course of several months after they settled in, did not exclusively focus on their everyday family life. She also kept in close contact with her sisters and shared news she had received from them: Leika and Sanyi's cryptic correspondence that described their living conditions under the Communist regime and Sanyi's bouts of depression; Teri's struggles with severe intermittent headaches and Géza's role as a high school math teacher and the university math courses he was taking in Bratislava[82] and Edit had written that she was planning to emigrate to Israel. Hansi had only received sporadic letters from Edit, one of them mentioning that she was thinking of joining Klári and her family "soon."

According to Klári, Edit, a divorcee, arrived in Israel alone in late 1949; she found work as a cook, and later remarried a widower with two children who worked as a prison guard in Ramla. Edit and her family lived in Lod, about three hours from Klári. They saw each other a couple of times a year, either for High Holidays or on other special occasions. In a subsequent letter, Klári commented that Edit seemed "too strict" with the children.

Magda, Leika, Géza, Teri, and Ivan; November 1949

In other correspondence, Klári described her close relationship with Olga "Olly" Schwartz and her daughter, Anita. Olly had previously been married to Julko's brother (Ladislav "Laci" Bronner), had also been in Terezín, and had lived in Žilina. Now she and Klári lived in the same housing complex. Olly was a great help to Klári, picking up Giora from the nearby kindergarten and bringing him home when she was at work. Klári also mentioned the close friendship they had with Itzhak Patish (Alice Pikler's son, a second cousin of Hansi and his sisters) and his family in Kibbutz Kfar Masarik[83] north of Haifa. She told Hansi that Itzhak had helped her and Zoli find a place to live when they arrived in Nahariya and had also helped Zoli find his job. In an undated letter, she mentioned that she was working at the City Hall accounting department.

1950-1960

Klári and Zoli wrote a lovely congratulatory letter after receiving news that Hansi had remarried to Virginia Salvador in Quito on April 21, 1951. Leika, Teri and Edit sent similar letters addressed to both. They all wanted details about Virginia. Leika wrote on May 7, 1951: "We are all so very happy for you...How are Olinka and Georgie reacting? [illegible] to this new life? You must be careful, dearest Hansi, to make sure they do not feel estranged from Sophie."

Zoli with his 1950 Chevy

In a 1952 letter, Klári wrote that Giora had brought home a little dog, a mixed fox terrier, and they had adopted her because he was so happy with the puppy. Later that year, Klári mentioned that they had begun to look for a larger and more comfortable home. They finally found one in 1954, she wrote, a duplex in a new neighborhood. They were quite pleased with its location and the fact that now they could plant fruit trees around it. A year later, Zoli was promoted to sales representative for northern and central Israel. She wrote about Zoli's "passion" for cars. He could not wait to own one. So, he "got rid of the truck" and bought a 1950 Chevy which he drove for his business all over the Galilee.

On school vacations, Giora would accompany him. Klári was happy that they could now occasionally drive to visit Edit and her family as well as their friends. In an undated letter, Klári mentioned that she was now "responsible" for caring for a new dog in the house. The previous one apparently had unexpectedly died.

In 1953, Géza wrote about Ivan's admission to a children's sanatorium for a "possible" heart condition. In two subsequent short notes, he reported: "Terka has severe pains in her face and headaches. She will need an evaluation in Prague…Ivanko will be discharged in several weeks; they found nothing. He is fine." Later, Géza added: "Teri is back home with no relief from her migraines. She has been diagnosed in Prague with trigeminal neuralgia.[84] Ivanko will be in Žilina with Lejka for a while until Terka feels better."

During the October 1956 war between Israel and Egypt, Shlomo was in the military, but Klári reassured my father that the family was safe and he had nothing to worry about. In that letter, she also wrote "We have not received any news from you in two months. Is something wrong? Please write soon, Hansi." At the time, he was recovering from a massive heart attack he had suffered that summer and was unable to write to any of them. He would most likely never have shared the news with his sisters, but for the fact that he received similar letters of concern from all of them, and finally had to tell them what happened. I believe Klári suspected something about it and decided not to worry him further about the fact that Edit was not feeling well, waiting several months before she wrote to tell him. Klári and Leika both sent letters in mid-1958 in which they shared their concern about Edit's failing health.

In the fall, Edit was diagnosed with ovarian cancer after an evaluation for lower abdomen pain, bloating, and fatigue. In two letters, one dated November 22, 1958 and the other from late December, Edit acknowledged feeling weak but said she was still working as a cook. As usual, she tried to allay Hansi's concerns. None of the letters from Israel mentioned anything about the care she received.

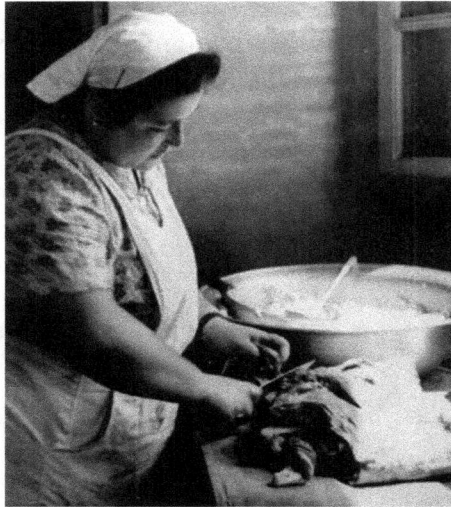

Edit cooking; Israel (date unknown)

Shlomo completed his military service in February 1959, and his parents wrote to say how happy they were to have him home. He had decided to go to Hebrew University in Jerusalem, his mother wrote later, and would start classes that November.

In late March 1959, Klári wrote to Leika, Teri, and Hansi that

Edit had been hospitalized at the Assaf Ha'Rofeh Hospital. Klári would visit Edit several times even though the hospital was far away. On April 22, 1959 in an emotional letter, Klári told Hansi that Edit had died. She expressed her profound sadness of losing her beloved sister but, typical of her caring and protective nature, she tried to console him by reminding him that Edit was no longer suffering. Correspondence he received from Leika, Sanyi, Teri, and Géza brought similar sentiments. I recall how devastated my father was when he learned of Edit's death. Even though he was not a practicing Jew, he followed the thirty days' traditional ritual mourning period of *shloshim*.

That year, Klári reported that Zoli's car had been hit by a biker. He was fortunately unharmed, though the biker was hurt. Zoli had brought home a new car, a BMW 700.

As noted in Chapter Two, from time to time, Virginia and Hansi sent to his sisters small bags with coffee beans, often with a small gift hidden inside. In one of those bags, Giora received a Doxa watch. They were all happy with those small packages and each time wrote thank-you notes in return.

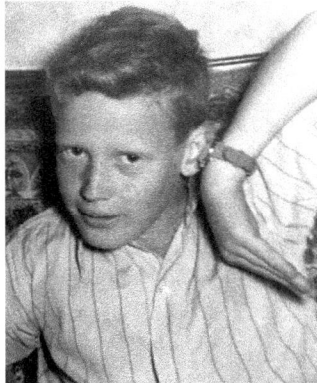

Giora with the Doxa from Hansi

1960-1970

After Edulka was born in Quito in February 1960, Hansi and Virginia received letters from Slovakia and Israel with effusive congratulations. The family were all so happy that the baby had been named after their sister and asked for photos.

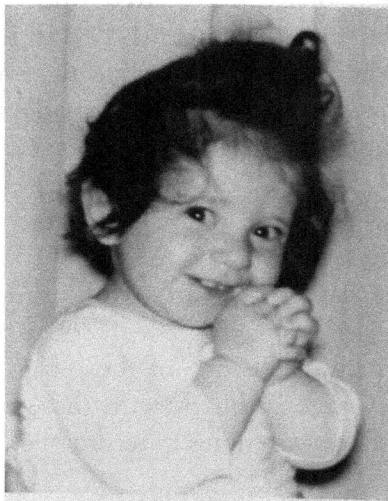

Edulka; Quito, circa 1961

Klári, in a short note dated May 15, 1960, asked for news from me, as I had not written to the family while preparing to take my high school final exams. She also let me know she was sending for my upcoming birthday, a "very nice remembrance of the liberation day of the western Galilee. I got it just now and hope you will enjoy it…Tell Virginia and father they may write to me. Many kisses to you all and a very big one to little Edith. Yours, Klári."

In 1961, my father found out from Leika that Klári was having back pain, which she thought was probably sciatica, in addition to the rheumatoid arthritis that she had suffered for many years. He must have insisted that she seek medical care because she wrote back that she had been diagnosed in Haifa as having a ruptured disk and that she had agreed to have a surgical procedure for it. A month later, another letter brought this news:

> I am feeling better every day and recuperating nicely… Both Zoli and Giora are a great help at home…We also have a Hungarian woman who lives around the corner and comes to clean and prepare meals…I will soon be going back to work full time.

In September 1962, Klári wrote: "We have decided to sell the house. We want to live closer to my work and Giora's school." She described their new apartment and wrote it was unfortunately in the third floor of a building with no elevator. "We are not happy going up and down, but this is a good place." Zoli, she added, was also having back pain and had to wear a metal back brace which was not helping him much.

In a letter dated December 12, 1962, Leika told Hansi that Géza had died in Košice on November 26, having probably suffered a heart attack: "We are not only saddened but worried about Terka and Ivanko…She has the headaches but also depression and we know from Sanyi how debilitating that can be." No correspondence from Teri was found until a brief note dated February 22, 1963, in which she spoke of the sadness of having lost Géza. "It was so sudden…Ivanko is with me now." A month later, she wrote, "Thank you, dearest Hansi and Virginia, for your loving letter and for the gift." In an undated note she described how wonderful it was to have Leika and Sanyi "nearby…We are with them in Žilina now."

Leika's letters of April 2 and May 25, 1963 related her concerns about Teri and Sanyi. Teri had worked for a short while as a secretary at a university in Košice but had to stop because of her migraines, and Sanyi was having one of his episodes of depression: "Dearest Hansi, it is so sad to witness this, but I know it will be temporary, hopefully for both of them." In 1963 came the news that Zoli had been placed in a body cast which he wore even while driving. Shlomo had finished his studies at the Hebrew University and had plans to go to a university in California starting in January 1964. Leika added "Life must go on and we must always think about what is best for our children. We are sad that he will be living so far away."

Teri wrote in September 1964 that Ivan was a student of mathematics at Charles University in Prague: "He likes and excels in that subject. I am very happy for him."

In an undated letter from sometime that year, Klári and Zoli shared their excitement at the news that Shlomo had met Yael Boritzer that September, and after a five-month courtship, were engaged to be married in New York in January 1965: "He sent us lovely pictures of her...He wrote that he is so happy...We are also happy for them, but sad we cannot be there for the joyful event." My father wrote to ask Oli if she would attend the wedding as the representative of the Pikler family. She did. Afterwards, Klári wrote that she and Zoli had celebrated the wedding at Kibbutz Yagur along with some of Yael's Israeli relatives.

In late May 1965, Hansi learned that Zoli had had a heart attack two weeks earlier. He had been in the hospital for a few days but was now home doing well. He was planning to return to work full time.

The following year, Hansi received a photograph of Klári and Zoli with Shlomo and Yael along with a note sharing their happiness after meeting Yael. They had all just returned from a tour of northern Israel.

That same year, Klári wrote that Giora, after graduating high school had "volunteered" for military service and had left home for basic tank training.

"We are not too happy with his decision, but we must accept it," she wrote.

As time went by, Klári's letters only mentioned that he was doing well and by March 1967, he had finished his training. But two months later, with news about an impending Arab-Israeli war,

Klári told Hansi: "We are very worried and afraid about Giora's tank unit deployment." Leika wrote that Zoli was "not taking the news well."

Another letter from Klári, posted in early June, brought very sad news. Zoli had had a second heart attack, which he had not survived. She stated that Giora had been sent home and was now with her. She was hoping he would not have to go back if there was a conflict. After Israel won the Six Day War, she wrote that Giora had left to join his unit. Shlomo had come home for a visit and she and Shlomo had toured the liberated Old City of Jerusalem.

Hansi retired in the spring of 1967, but Virginia continued to work at Casa Ortega's cosmetics department for several more months. Leika wrote to him:

"Dearest Hansi, you worked very hard all your life, and now is the time for you and Virginia to slow down and enjoy every day to the fullest." Familiar as she was with Sanyi's episodic depression, she most likely began to worry it might also happen to Hansi.

I received postcards from Leika and Sanyi, Teri, and Klári, all sent in July 1968, congratulating me for my medical school graduation. They wrote: "We were so happy to receive Hansi's letter with the news of your recent graduation. You can be very proud of your accomplishments...We can feel in his letter how proud he is of you as well."

Klári's visit to Ecuador in August 1968 is related in Chapter Two. I recall the "happy anxiety"' in my father's letters preceding his sister's visit. After she returned to Israel, her letters described her overwhelming joy at having made the trip to see her beloved brother and meet Virginia and Edulka. She had also been reunited with Oli, who was two years old the last time Klári saw her in Žilina. Oli had traveled to Quito with her daughter, Vivian, for this special family get-together. From Ecuador, Klári made brief visits to Miami to see Sophie and Sam, and then to Baltimore to meet Elaine, Vanessa and me. We could easily identify her as she walked off the jet bridge. We were thrilled to meet her and told her how grateful we were that she had come. We spent the whole day catching up before she left for California to join Shlomo and Yael. She related how wonderful it was, after twenty-nine years, to see Hansi and Oli again and also to meet Virginia, Edulka and Vivian. When she got home, Klári also wrote to express her happiness at the opportunity of meeting us.

On January 27, 1969, Hansi and Virginia, with the help of a friend of theirs at the telephone company switchboard, were able, to have their very first short phone conversation with Leika and Sanyi. I was an intern at Johns Hopkins in Baltimore, MD when he wrote to me that he had had a hard time holding back his tears while talking to his sister. He had told her he was worried he had not heard from Teri for a while, and Leika had hinted that Teri might be moving to Israel in the spring and had asked my father not to worry, to be patient, that soon he would hear from her. Also, he said the lack of news from Oli was too much for him to bear.

The fact that he had not heard about Teri's plans to emigrate to Israel was most likely due to the fact that she had to be careful not to disclose any such information that could be used against her by the Communist government. Three weeks before Hansi placed his first call to Žilina, the newly elected First Secretary of the Communist Party of Czechoslovakia, Alexander Dubček, had proposed a series of political and economic reforms that would grant additional rights to citizens. Though the revolution known as the Prague Spring was squelched on August 21, 1968 when the Soviet Union and other Warsaw Pact members invaded the country, Teri and Ivan must have taken advantage of the political liberalization that had begun in early January and decided to emigrate to Israel. Teri arrived in March and Ivan four months later. On April 7, 1969, Teri wrote:

> My dearest Hansi, you don't know how sad I felt when Lejka told me you worried about the lack of my news...I had been preparing myself to leave home and travel to Israel and have not been myself for a

while...Leaving Lejka and Sanyi was very [illegible]...
Ivanko is coming in several weeks [illegible] safer to
travel separately...I am now close to Klári and that
brings me so much joy and comfort...Please write
soon, I want to hear from all of you, thousand kisses,
Yours, *Teri*

Klári's correspondence two weeks after Teri's arrival expressed both
happiness to have her close by and concern about Teri's health
and state of mind. There were no words of complaint in Klári's
letters but there was a sense that she felt overwhelmed. She again
described how thankful she was to Olly Schwartz for helping her
get Teri settled in. On June 16, 1969, she wrote to me:

First of all, belated birthday wishes, my good boy. May
your residency at the [Mayo] Clinic be the first step to
a happy and successful career. Enjoy your work, your
lovely family, and be very happy. Let us hope that in
two years, when you have to do your military service
(your father wrote to me about it) there will be no
war anywhere...My sister, Teri, is still with me... Ivko
is still waiting for his permit to get out of the CSR. I
think he intends to stay with us, although we too are
in a precarious situation and in constant war. Let us
hope that this war too will end one day and our sons
will study instead of carrying guns.

Best wishes from Giora too. He comes home almost
every Saturday for 48 hours but he is very tired and
not able to write...You are getting ready for the visit
of your father and the whole family. I am happy they
can afford this journey. I am sure they will enjoy it
very much, too.

Your mother wrote to me but I do not like the sound
of her letter. How do you find her? Is she well? And
how about Oli?...I got nice pictures of all of you in
Quito. Elaine, you look lovely. I would be very glad
to hear from you. Many kisses, a big one to the little
devil [Vanessa]. Yours, *Klari*

In the back of that letter Teri wrote, "I also send my best wishes for your career and hope you had a nice birthday. Many kisses to all of you, love you, *Teri.*"

In several letters Leika wrote in 1969, 1970, and 1971, she mentioned that she and Sanyi were shipping Teri's personal effects to Israel and asking friends they knew were traveling to Israel to take small parcels for her.

Teri after her arrival in Israel; 1969

1970-1979

After the February 1970 death of Mr. Levy, Hansi's typist and friend, there was a break in my father's customary correspondence with his sisters—he usually wrote at least one letter a month to each of them—and their letters reflected their concern that he might be ill. In May, he managed to find a temporary typist and was able to share the news about his friend's passing. Only later that year did he again find someone to type for him, but still not on a regular basis. In the meantime, his family only heard from him sporadically.

In August 1970, a month after our son, Jason, was born in Rochester, MN, Elaine and I received congratulatory letters from Klári, Teri, Leika, and Sanyi. They sent similar correspondence to Hansi, Virginia, Sophie and Sam.

In a September 22, 1970 letter, Leika told Hansi that Magda had arrived in Israel that summer. She was again cautious not to write any details that the government could use against them. That letter also brought news that Klári was not well: she was having coughing spells and abdominal discomfort, but there were no other specifics about it. Leika was worried and thought that Klári might not have written to Hansi about her health issues—and in fact, there was a gap of about two months where I could not find any letter from Klári to Hansi.

Ivan wrote to me from Nahariya on October 3, 1970:

> The situation here remains unchanged. Klári was back home for a couple of days for Rosh Hashanah. She looks very bad, lost 8 kg of weight this month. She is again very yellow [jaundiced], mostly in the face and in her eyes. On the other hand, she is in relatively good mood and I dare to say, she doesn't know, what is happening with her and believes probably they didn't find the diagnosis yet. Yesterday she had strong pains and we had to take her back to the hospital. Peter hired a taxi and went with her. Today they will do a bronchoscopy (in Haifa) and then will return to the Carmel hospital.
>
> According to my information they are sure she has cancer in the left part of the lung and there is serious suspicion of liver metastasis. It is impossible to foresee, the doctor said, how long it could take, but there is absolutely no hope for her to survive. As far

as my mother is concerned, she does not know about it and I have my reasons not to tell her. Although her physiological condition is o.k. according to the doctors (and I believe them) her psychological condition is not so good and we are seriously concerned because I am going to study in Tel Aviv this year and it is a big problem how to arrange things so that I could feel safely about what she is doing, what is happening with her during the week when I am not at home.

In his letter, Ivan also stated that after Géza died in 1962, his mother's psychological condition got "worse and worse" and that she was taking multiple medications (analgesics, barbiturates, etc.) "that leads to situations very similar to psychological illnesses."

His concerns about her wellbeing are obvious, more so with the fact that in his letter he also stated:

It is absolutely impossible to talk seriously about psychiatric care with her. It is very difficult even to live with her, for the whole world seems hostile to her (except me, perhaps) and daily life is hardly bearable that way. Lejka and Klári know about it. We are discussing the situation with Peter and Yael and we all hope we'll come to a solution.

Finally, he stated that he was planning to talk to a psychiatrist once more that week. He also reported that Madulka had arrived that summer and was taking a Hebrew course in Haifa and would be marrying her fiancé, Peter Bielik—also an émigré from Czechoslovakia—who was taking his B.A. in chemistry at the Technion. Shlomo was to begin work at the Vulcani Institute in Rehovot the day he wrote the letter. The Neumans had rented a flat in that town. Giora had moved with them and stayed for a while. For three months, they were also happy to take Ivan in and provide moral support. Ivan was happy to have Shlomo, Yael and Gili close by.

Most likely in response to Hansi's concern, Klári wrote in mid-

October that she was under evaluation at the Carmel hospital in Haifa for both the coughing spells and the abdominal pain. As usual, she dismissed the seriousness of her condition. According to Ivan's October letter, she did not know her diagnosis at the time. I do not know how my father learned that Teri had been hospitalized in Nahariya and Klári had been diagnosed with cancer and hospitalized in Haifa. After her October letter, he did not hear from Klári again. I called to notify him of her death in November 1970 (I was then a medical resident at the Mayo Clinic in Rochester). The family felt I would be best suited to break the sad news to him.

Klári had made every effort to help Teri and Ivan settle in after their arrival in Israel. After she died, Shlomo, Yael, and Magda took over this task with a great deal of generosity and love. According to Leika, at that time, Ivan was unable to cope with Teri's health issues. Magda, who thought of Ivan as a brother, was of great support to him during these difficult times.

On December 7, a few days after Klári died, Leika wrote to

Ivan, Teri, Klári, and Magda; Israel, 1970

247

me, grieving about Klári's fate and expressing her sadness at being unable to get a travel permit to be at her bedside during her illness:

> The wound that affects us all is too deep and unfortunately will remain open forever. Time should at least alleviate the pain and for all of us who have hung on to our Klárika with so much love, it should serve as a consolation that she has been released from so much suffering. With her rational, caring, and practical views, she would certainly have only one wish, that our life should continue undisturbed, that we should be a support for those who need us so much. And there are really many of them. Ivko wrote to me about her serious situation but I had so much hope that she would pull through with proper care; unfortunately, nothing changes the sad fact that she left us forever.
>
> You were lucky enough to get to know her, even if only briefly, to know what a valuable person she was, what a mother, sister, relative. She wanted to tell me all about you when I came, how happy she was to visit our dear Hansi and his family, and to be with Sophie and all of you.
>
> A great concern for me is Hansi. He called me for my birthday but his voice seemed so sickly. Since his last letter of October 12, we have not heard from him. Is there a serious reason for it? Please write to me openly and sincerely the actual reason for such a long silence. I am also of the opinion that you should hide the whole thing from him for the time being. I wrote to him recently but made no mention of it. My brother clings to each and every one of us with an incredible amount of love, and I know too well what this loss will mean to him. But if you decide to write the truth to him, let me know, I will then try to give him strength so that he can bear fate more easily. For Terka, it is also twice as hard a blow, since she needs my presence now. Fortunately, she has Olly, my former sister-in-law, nearby to help her, if needed.

Leika also mentioned that Magda wanted to get married in December, but since there was a possibility that Leika might come, she postponed it. As usual, she sent greetings and kisses to Sophie and Olinka. "I often think of them. We kiss you with lots and lots of love, yours, *Lea and Sanyi.*"

A day later, before she mailed her letter, she wrote to me again, this time acknowledging that she had just received news from Hansi:

> He congratulated Sanyi on his approaching birthday, and reassured me that he is healthy, but just very, very nervous. The fact that he has no report from Israel worries him very much and he is full of fear and concern. I want to withdraw my opinion of yesterday and believe that Hansi can no longer be left in this uncertainty. He feels that something serious is going on, he knows his sister far too well for that, knows that it is not normal for her to leave him without any news for so long. Perhaps this uncertainty is even more nerve-wracking and we all want to help him bear this stroke of fate more easily. If you decide to take this step, if you think it is the right one, write to me right away. [Leika was obviously unaware that I had spoken with my father about Klári's death soon after it happened.] Then I want to write to Hansi immediately and make it clear to him that we shouldn't think selfishly, that it was a relief for our Klári. I have an old letter from Klári when our poor Edit closed her eyes, which literally says we should have a good cry, but then dry our tears and thank the Almighty that He has freed her from this torment. If she [Edit] had gone right away and not suffered, she wrote at the time, it would have been more calming to her. It should also serve as consolation for Hansi that Klári was not aware of her serious illness (our dear ones in Israel are of this opinion), and even made plans for the coming winter. We have to be grateful that she still had a chance to see her children and grandchildren. You have to look

for and find consolation, where and how you can. Hansi still has to live for all of us who are so lovingly attached to him.

Judging by this letter—I don't know whether my assumption is correct—it seems to me that it was a matter of depression. Even if this condition is very unpleasant, I unfortunately have plenty of experience with it [Sanyi]. It is not incurable. It does come back and has to be treated again on a case-by-case basis. In any event, my dear ones, I ask you very strongly to write to me sincerely if this is the situation. When I know everything, maybe my words will also be able to achieve a certain result. Is his pension enough to live on without worry? He mustn't worry that he can't send anything to Madulka, for example [after she and Peter get married]. They are young and healthy and will certainly find their livelihood. What must reassure Hansi is that he can help out Terka, who really depends on it, he must be happy about it and find many other joys in life. How terrible this distance is, how different it would be if one could get close to him and perhaps calm him down. Kiss the children from us.

I kiss and hug you both with a lot of love. Yours, *Lea*

Two-and-a-half months later we received a lengthy letter from Leika:

My very dear ones! This time I haven't written for a long time. I often feel bad and then find it harder to focus my thoughts. It is difficult to come to terms with such a loss [Klári's] and whenever I think of it, I feel like I'm choking. I wrote to Hansi again and at least tried to instill strength in him with words, often it seems to me as if I wanted to give myself courage with my words. If we could at least see each other, I think it would be easier for each of us. I don't even want to count how many years it has been since I saw my brother when I accompanied them to Genoa.

Olinka was 2 years old; we never imagined so much time would pass when we wouldn't be able to see each other. But you must never look back, we must live in the present and the future.

I can't shake off the thought that Hansi is probably dealing with some kind of depression, even if he thinks none is imminent. Those who have it are seldom aware of it, and if one still has many obligations ahead, as my brother does, who still has to bring up his daughter, and if he finds no joy in life and gives himself completely over to his feelings, that is a mistake. I myself spend sleepless nights, feel an inner restlessness, yes, that's is all justified, but as always I pursue my obligations and think about how much I am still needed. It isn't always easy to overcome your nature, but a healthy person can do it. I don't want to talk Hansi into it, but it would calm me down if he went to see a psychiatrist before it gets worse. Perhaps I am speaking like this because I have been burned before. I still remember how Sanyi's illness began ten or twelve years ago, I couldn't believe it myself, that it could be a depression; Terka was the one who drew my attention to it. It is worth getting an evaluation and so important, in case the doctor is of the opinion that this is not the situation. It is actually not at all clear to me and I don't want to ask Hansi such detailed questions, like whether he is apathetic, disinterested, or on the other hand, whether he is irritable, quick-tempered, and whether he has lost his self-confidence. With Sanyi, if he is in a depression, he has no interest in anything or anyone. He sees everything as black, is afraid of life, and has no confidence in himself. I sit next to him for hours and instill courage and strength in him. The last depressions were not that deep and long-lasting. He was lying at home for a week, and then slowly started working again.

In the meantime, you have probably received Madulka's invitation to the wedding. What should

I tell you—that I am not at all upset that I or we can't be there? You wouldn't believe me at all, but we don't want to be sad, there is no reason for it, if two loving hearts have succeeded in uniting their lives. Whether we are present or not, it should not change their happiness. However, we want to raise our glass at the same hour and toast their happy and contented future. Our friends and acquaintances want to be present and we want to be in their thoughts. Madulka will unfortunately take it hard as she is sensitive and unfortunately closed-off. It's just sad when you don't even know your future son-in-law. He writes nicely and loves Madulka above everything, which is, of course, mutual. It will be doubly painful for everyone that our dearest Klárika's place is empty. Terka is supposed to take our place, as well as Sanyi's brother, who lives nearby. On the evening of the wedding, they want to call, Madulka insists on it; she wants to pay for it from her first salary.

Terka isn't feeling good about it either; it's a double blow for her too. I don't know how they [Terka and Ivan] can solve the financial side now, that gives me a lot of headaches and I know how much this awareness weighs on Hansi. The last thing he wrote to me about it was that he didn't know how to give his support to Terka and wants badly to do it. There is also a lot that weighs on Ivan; the child has not seen much pleasantness since his early childhood. I love him a lot, he has a good heart and is a valuable person. At the moment his studies are so difficult that he can't work at the same time, and then he tries to be home on Wednesday evening so as not to leave his mother alone, because he is everything in her life! They haven't had any news from you or Hansi for a long time. Giora has moved back to Nahariya and works in a knitting factory, but he wants to start his studies soon.

Georgie, I've asked so often about your dear mother; I know that she wasn't well. We always got on well and I ask you to convey my greetings and kisses to her, as well as to Olinka, about whom I haven't heard anything for a long time. I think of them all a lot!

For today, my dear ones, we greet and kiss you many times, in Sanyi's name, too, who is still at work and besides, I don't want him to read what I wrote in this letter, either. With love, yours, *Lea*

Hansi and Virginia received Leika and Sanyi's letter of March 2, 1971, announcing Magda and Peter Bielik's impending wedding. As noted earlier, it took place in Nahariya on March 24. They wrote that they would not be allowed to travel to Israel and join them at such an important and happy family affair. Instead, they were planning a celebration in Žilina, on that date, with their closest friends.

On September 26, 1971, Leika wrote: "I am always thinking of Hansi and hoping his spirits will lift." He had had a short phone conversation with Leika and Sanyi a few days earlier, and Leika had been concerned that he "sounded down and got very emotional when we spoke." She also said that Magda seemed very interested in the field of ophthalmology after she worked in an ophthalmic outpatient clinic at the Rotschild Hospital in Haifa. "She has not made a final decision or written anything in more detail about it…Sanyi would of course be happy if she wanted to choose his subspecialty, but we don't want to influence her."

On a trip to Quito in early 1972, I also thought my father exhibited signs of a mild depression. For several years thereafter, in letters from home, I would find short notes from Virginia and Edulka saying that he was often quite anxious, very protective of Edulka and worried about the lack of news from Oli.

The family received news of Giora and Judith Pál's wedding on January 20, 1972 in Nahariya. Attendees from the family included Teri and Ivan, Magda and Peter, Shlomo and Yael. Olly Schwartz was there with her husband Emil, their daughter Hanna, and her daughters. Also present was Rachel Vrublewska, Klári's close friend, who had survived Auschwitz and made *Aliyah*.

From Nahariya, Ivan wrote on October 5, 1972 that Teri had been hospitalized at a psychiatric hospital at the beginning of July and discharged in mid September. She was now home and being treated as an outpatient. She wanted to make sure Hansi was not informed of this. Ivan at the time was working on a movie for the Israeli TV and on October 22 would be starting a six months military deployment.

I was terribly sad to learn of Teri's health situation but I abided by her request. Still, I couldn't stop thinking that during my parents' multiple travails after leaving their loved ones in Slovakia, Teri had been the one who tried to cheer her brother up in every card and letter. How sad that my father never had the opportunity to do the same for her, when she had suffered so much because of Auschwitz and after losing her beloved Géza.

Our aunts never forgot our birthdays or those of our children; they would write in advance with their heartfelt congratulations and best wishes. Such was the case with Leika and Sanyi's letter of May 29, 1974, which then continued:

> Hansi called us not so long ago. It's fantastic when you consider that you can talk to each other from such a distance and know at the moment what he or she is doing at the time. Despite this great joy—I know that both sides are very excited to hear each other's voices—unfortunately, Hansi didn't understand me too well. Sanyi thinks it was a kind of nervousness that made me so hoarse that I could only manage a crowing voice. It was still good that Sanyi could speak, and since we have two phones, I was also able to understand well every word Hansi spoke to Sanyi. We also spoke with Edulka and Virginia. Everyone's voices rang in my ears all night long. Will we have the opportunity to see each other again? Unfortunately, at the moment there are no exit permits for us, even if we could manage the funds. Hopefully it will happen one day, as will a visit to our children, a hope we will

not give up.

Our children report punctually every week and in such a detail that we can experience everything with them, even if it's after the fact. Peter is already back at home, so we breathed a sigh of relief and now we really hope that peace will prevail and that our lives will be calmer as a result. Peter is working in his old position.

A few weeks ago, after a long time, I finally had a report from Terka and Ivko. He is working five hours a week at a film archive and is also attending a 3-year university course in Mathematics/English. He very much hopes to finish his studies and that no financial difficulties will prevent him from doing so. Just as Petko wrote to me, it is not easy for him in life and my greatest wish would be to see him cross the finish line standing on his feet and to create an independent home for himself. He really didn't have a nice childhood or youth. Frequent illnesses, worries about himself, everything has left its mark; his nerves, even if he doesn't write about it, are very unstable. Terka also works thirteen days a month, her work is difficult and she has back pain from it, but I'm still happy she can do it. Her abnormal weight gain worries me. Even if they never complain, I know that it is not easy for them from a financial point of view and I am therefore very grateful for Hansi's assistance. Unfortunately, I can only help out with small packages, whatever I think will help. Every penny they can save for themselves still makes a difference with so little income.

As Hansi writes, they want to visit you in August. Did I understand it right on the phone, that you have already bought a house in Rochester? I wish for you, my dear ones, that all your plans come true and I believe that you, dear Georgie, will have a bright future. I wish you much joy and success in your work! I would very much like to know something about

Olinka and her family. I know that she is lazy about writing. And, of course also about Sophie, who I've wanted to write for so long. I always think of her with love. Send many greetings and kisses. I would also like to know how things are with her health.

Recently, we also got a photo of Hansi with Virginia and Edulka. Hansi looks much better than before and I was completely surprised how Edulka has developed for her age [fourteen at the time]. She is a pretty, bold girl, and how good that Hansi and Virginia are not alone after all. For today, my dear ones, I kiss and hug you all, everyone, everyone, and give an extra kiss to the children. Yours, *Lea*

On August 17, 1974, Teri wrote in a postcard: "I received a lovely birthday card from Sophie and Oli …It was very nice to hear from them."

Leika's letter of October 30, 1974, acknowledged the letters she had received from Vanessa, Jason, and Elaine and me, wishing her and Sanyi a happy birthday:

Above all, thank you very much for your birthday wishes, as well as for those sent by Vanessa and Jason, they were very sweet. I really like that you are so devoted to the family and that you keep also a record of our birthdays in this way. We appreciate your love and are very grateful to you for it. Without wanting to flatter you, your children are lovely indeed and I always like to look at the pictures you sent me a long while ago.

We received your letter, dear Georgie. We were worried because we hadn't had any news from either you or Hansi for a long time. I was very happy that Hansi and the family were able to spend some time with you in Rochester and also with Olinka. You are both really good children, but it is the normal course of life that children, like parents, live their own lives; you have the future ahead of you, and the past is for us. Of course, it would be very good if it were possible for Hansi and the family to live in the same city with you, and perhaps this would also bring more contentment to Hansi about his life and family.

As for the assistance for Terka, I've already written to Hansi and thanked him for his plans to continue sending it, because unfortunately, they are very dependent on every penny, even though they never complain. They wrote to me about your separate birthday presents for her. Unfortunately, Terka hasn't written to me for months and only recently did I find out the truth, that she is in the early stages of Parkinson's. Her hands and feet tremble, she has difficulty writing. She just wrote to me very briefly for my birthday. She does not know her diagnosis and should not find it out either, since she has had enough without it. She had to quit her little job, too, so this small income is also missing. She was given medications to which she has reacted well. She should keep taking them and then return to Madulka's hospital for a check-up. Ivko wrote to you, Georgie, and I hope everything will work out in the future for him too.

Sanyi has not yet accepted a temporary summer holiday job, because we have tried again to submit a request to be able to visit our children. We don't want to get our hopes up and prefer to be surprised. Under no circumstances would we fly, but we could take a train to Athens, which we can pay for ourselves, but then continue by ship which we would also have pay. Our longing is great, of course, and even if it weren't the best time of year, the main thing for us is to be with our loved ones.

Olinka and Sophie wrote to me for my birthday. I can't tell you what joy it gave me, and I wrote to them, too. They promised me to write in more detail and send pictures. I am hoping that Olinka is happy.

My dear ones, for today I am closing, and I kiss and

hug you all with much love. Your, *Lea*

Later that evening, Leika and Sanyi got a call from Quito:

> We talked to Hansi for a long time. Virginia also came to the phone. Their voices are still ringing in my ears. If only Hansi didn't get so upset all the time. He wanted to have flowers sent for my birthday. I wouldn't have been happy. I told him I would only have been offended that he was spending so much money and was glad he didn't argue with me about it. For days I will think a lot about our conversation. I am sending you one more kiss, *Lea*

Leika and Sanyi often wrote, in carefully worded letters, of their disappointment at being unable to leave the country to be with Magda and Peter in Israel for the birth of their two grandsons, Dano and Miki. They were overjoyed when they received government permission to travel there in the summer of 1976. "Oh, dearest Hansi, we waited so many years for the happiness of hugging our loving daughter, and Peter, and kissing our grandsons, they are adorable boys."

As I have recounted in Chapter Two, Hansi died in May 1978. Oli, Elaine, and I returned to the US three days after his funeral: Oli went home to Miami, Elaine to Rochester, and I had to return to Houston for my fellowship, due to end in July. Before we left Quito, Virginia and I discussed her immediate needs as well as Edulka's, and made plans for Virginia to apply for Hansi's social security payments and ongoing reparations from the German government. It was obvious that the house would have to be rented out while they were searching for a buyer, so Virginia and Edulka could have a steady income. They would need to rent an apartment, too, hopefully one nearby in the same Mariscal neighborhood where we had lived since the early 40s, which, (until twenty years ago) was a safe and wonderful residential area.

Leika's condolence letter is included in Chapter Two. In Teri's loving condolence letter of June 2, 1978, written in Slovak and translated by Ivan, we read the following:

> You can well imagine how the knowledge of your father's death has afflicted me. I can hardly accept the fact that he is no longer living. I know that you are sad, but on the other hand, I believe that you are strong and will be a strong support for our Virginia and Edulka. And for this, I want to thank you. I am not strong enough to write more today, just one more thing: when I was in Auschwitz, I promised myself that I would never cry again when someone died in his bed and among his relatives and family. Give my special love to all the children, love to all of you and your mother, *Teri*

The following six months were quite stressful for all of us. I remained in close contact with Virginia and Edulka, but for several months, aside from notifying the rest of the family about Hansi's death, we were unable to continue a close correspondence with them. Leika and Sanyi wrote on June 24, 1978:

> Thank you for your caring lines, which had double meaning in the face of all the pain and loss. We want to do everything possible to make sure we are always in contact; that's how Hansi brought you up, and that's what we were taught as children, with love and devotion. That has remained with us all, and you know the mutual love we felt for Hansi and the other siblings.
>
> I would like so much to make it easier for you in your pain, but it's hard to find the words. I very much long to be with you to talk about all the past years that I have not been able to spend with Hansi. I always lived with the thought that it would happen one day, but unfortunately it was just a dream! It may be of some consolation to you, dearest Georgie, that your father had a lot of joy because of you and was always happy with you; he always wrote so lovingly about all his

children and even if Olinka wrote to him less often, he frequently remarked that she had a big heart and felt well loved by her.

I had a few lines from Terka. They have already told her the sad news. In the meantime, she was in the hospital again where Madulka works, probably with another seizure? They wrote that she is fine again, and was with Madulka for a few days, who took her back to the old-age home. For myself, dearest Georgie, I want to thank you for offering to continue helping Terka now that Hansi is no longer with us. You can't even imagine what it means to her.

That is all for today, my dear ones. Many kisses and hugs for you and the children. Love, *Lea and Sanyi* P.S. Terka's birthday is July 31!

After I completed my fellowship at the MD Anderson Hospital in Houston, I joined Elaine, Vanessa, and Jason in Rochester, MN the first week of July, just in time to witness the 5th of July flood, one of the worst ever in Rochester: one third of the city was covered with water. Our basement was flooded as well. We managed to save most of the furniture, but the whole thing was a mess.

As planned, Virginia rented out my parents' house while looking for a buyer, and she and Edulka moved into an apartment a few blocks away from the house. We moved to Tulsa, OK in mid-October, where I had accepted the position of chair of the Oncology/Hematology department at one of the university hospitals and was also establishing a private practice.

Leika and Sanyi as well as Teri kept up a regular correspondence with Virginia, Edulka, and me. On November 21, 1978 Leika wrote this to me:

Before we got your news, we could not explain your long silence, which made us very sad. It is very difficult for me to bear the loss of my beloved brother and to realize that he is not alive anymore. He loved his family and raised you to love your family, and even if he is no longer among us, I am convinced that the attachment will continue on your part.

We have to thank God that Hansi experienced so much joy with you, dear Georgie—after all, he was so proud of you. You made his life more beautiful in many respects. I wish that Olinka could be happy. But as I can see from your letter, Georgie, her marriage has not succeeded too well. Even if she doesn't write to me, which I understand because she isn't very happy, her life and her children are still of considerable interest to me.

I always remember your mother, Sophie, with love. How much would I enjoy getting together with her again one day, and how happy I'd be if she would write again in detail. It is certainly not easy for her when her mother is so ill. I only have her old address and don't know whether they have moved in the meantime, otherwise I would have written long ago.

Thank goodness I have better news from Terka. Madulka picks her up frequently for lunch, then takes her back to the home in the evening. If things could continue like that, then Ivko would have it easier. He has now accepted a better-paying job. I am expecting to hear from him, since he has not written for a long time. I am glad Edulka could finish her first year of medical school. I am concerned with their daily existence but as Virginia wrote, she is supposed to receive a pension after Hansi.

Until we hear from you again, kiss the children from us, I embrace you my dears and kiss you with great love, *Lea*

It was also in the autumn of 1978 when Sophie began to describe a sensation of facial fullness that concerned her and led to the diagnosis of recurrent breast cancer. She and Sam came to Tulsa for a short visit in the spring of 1979 after she had completed a course of radiation therapy at the Mayo Clinic. Chapter Two contains the details of her medical history, subsequent treatments, and events leading to her death.

Virginia and Edulka were our first guests at a house we bought in 1979. Giora, in his first visit to the US, also stayed with us. Ivan's letters acknowledging receipt of my father's contributions for Teri would include news about Teri's health and some of the work he was involved with. In one of his letters, he mentioned Teri's diagnosis with early Parkinson's disease.

1980-1989

Ivan and Yaffa got married in Nahariya, Israel on February 6, 1980. At the wedding were Teri, Leika and Sanyi, Magda and Peter with their two boys, and Yaffa's parents. In an undated letter to us, Teri wrote: "It was a very happy and wonderful day for me. I wish Hansi, Klárika, and Editka, as well as all of you, could have been with us. I missed them dearly.

Teri with teh Vozars and teh Bieikes at Yaffa and Ivan's wedding Israel;
February 1980

In October of that year, Ivan wrote that, at last, Teri had begun to receive a Social Security pension from the German government and was no longer in need of Hansi's financial support. According to Ivan, she was living at a comfortable home for the elderly and had made new friends. That month we also heard from Leika and Sanyi:

> Thank you very much for your invitation to our dear Vanessa's bat mitzvah. We would like so much to attend this joyful event but, unfortunately, in our circumstances, it will be impossible for us to do so. So, we want to express at least in writing our congratulations and send you all hearty hugs and kisses. We wish you, dear Elaine and Georgie, much pleasure from your children and that you should be able to go on raising them in good health and happiness.

My mother, Sophie, died on June 3, 1981. I notified Leika and Sanyi as well as Teri of her death. In spite of my parents' divorce, my aunts and Sophie had exchanged sporadic greetings over the years, and their condolence notes expressed the deep feelings they had for her, and their sorrow that Oli and I had lost our mother.

A year later, in June, Teri wrote a short note from Haifa during the Lebanon war:

> I wish you would not to worry about me too much. True, it's not nice here right now, but we hope it will all end soon and well...Ivan and Peter are away... Jonathan [Teri's grandson] is now seven months old and not only has his mother [Yaffa] but also Yaffa's mother to look after him. I am so sorry I can't be of much help. Magda's parents are here so it is all easier to bear...Dani and Miki are lovely...I hope all of you are well. Please write and send me photos of the whole family. With love, your, *Teri*

Leika and Sanyi, also from Haifa, wrote to Virginia on July 19, 1982 and asked her to forward the letter to me afterwards. They were concerned with the lack of news from all of us:

> First of all, we want to thank you, dear Virginia and Edulka, for the coffee you sent to Israel. It arrived safely and we are enjoying it very much. It has been such a long time without a sign of life from you.
>
> We arrived here last November and have to return on October 12. We are happy we have been here to help with our grandchildren, as Madulka is busy at the hospital and now has private office hours twice a week, coming home late at night. When the war broke out, Peter left but was able to visit the family a few times. We hope Ivan will be home tomorrow. Giora is well and at home. We hope peace will be restored soon. We visit Terka often, now at last she has her own room at Bet Avot. She has a lot of pain in her legs and feet, they get swollen. We are happy to be together and at our age we like to remember our youth, when we were children and the whole family was together.
>
> Please write sometime as we are so interested to hear about everyone in the family. We want to stay in contact; we know this would have been Hansi's wish, too. Much love and kisses to all of you, from *Lea* and *Sanyi*, also from Madulka, Peter, Dani, and Miki.

From Haifa, Teri wrote to us in English on January 24, 1984:

> I was so happy to meet Vanessa last summer. She is a very lovely and pleasant young lady. I had the feeling I've known her from childhood and although I could not speak with her (I have forgotten almost all English) her eyes spoke for her.
>
> I know you must be very proud of her and so am I... We had a lovely time together...About me only a bit... Last year I was more in the hospital than at home. I

had pulmonary edema many times and I am suffering with arthritis in both legs, so walking is very difficult.

Please write soon. I love you all, *Teri*

Our daughter, Vanessa, went to Israel that summer on a Tulsa Temple Israel *midrasha* confirmation class program. She was sixteen years old at the time. She told us that Magda met her in Tel Aviv and spent the day with her: "She went out of her way to be with me all day." She then took the train to Haifa with Kelly, a classmate, and met Giora and his family at their home. They spent the night and had a wonderful visit. The next day, Vanessa visited Teri:

> Teri was very sweet and I felt loved by her even though I had not met her before. She had framed pictures of our family. We had ice cream on her balcony and we had a wonderful afternoon together.

Teri died in March 1984 of heart failure, three weeks before her second grandson, Nadav, came into the world. I had received a loving letter from her dated February 23, 1984:

> I was very happy with your letter and to learn that you are all well...So glad you sent the pictures. You all look wonderful...It would fill me with great happiness to have you visit me. Write soon.
>
> Hugs and kisses, *Teri*

In the last three years of her life, Teri had felt better, and had enjoyed being with Ivan, Yaffa, and her first grandson, Jonathan, as well as Magda and her family. Leika's letters at the time mention Teri's improvement and the happy moments she and Sanyi shared with Teri when they visited her. Leika recounted many years later that she and Teri had always been "very close."

We learned from Leika the following year that she had been diagnosed with osteoporosis. She was 71 years old, quite active, and otherwise in fairly good health. I had neglected my writing responsibilities for a while, and she was quick to point that out to me. She also lovingly insisted that it was time for Elaine and me to visit her and Sanyi in Žilina.

Elaine and I decided in 1986 to travel to Europe (the "back to roots" trip) and visit Leika and Sanyi that summer. Jason, who had been on the same Temple Israel *midrasha* program his sister had attended, had returned from Israel a few days earlier, in time to go with us. We traveled first to London and then to Prague, where Leika and Sanyi waited for us at the airport. As Elaine, Jason and I walked out after clearing customs (which seemed to take an eternity), I experienced an overwhelming feeling of joy at fulfilling my dream of meeting them. As they embraced us warmly, I felt I had known them all my life. Words could not possibly express our rush of emotions. They were amazed at how many suitcases we had brought. Leika was seventy-three years old at that time.

On the evening of the next day, we all traveled by train from Prague to Žilina. We arrived past midnight and our luggage filled the only taxi around, so we walked to Leika and Sanyi's apartment. They were wonderful hosts and made us feel very welcome, in spite of the language barrier (Leika spoke no English and I did not speak German, though I understood a bit). I quickly learned that my aunt did not require the outdated European manners I had learned when growing up. In quite a diplomatic way, she let me know I didn't need to pull out a chair for her, or carry her dishes after a meal, or open a door for her.

I brought with me a small box of photographs I had found, along with the documents I had inherited from my father. I wanted Leika to help identify any Pikler relatives in them. We sat around the dining table and watched Leika laugh aloud as she looked at the photos. As it turns out, in most of them there were not relatives but Hansi's girlfriends! Leika also reminisced about "the good old family times" and I taped those conversations, hoping to have them transcribed and translated one day.

Sanyi and Leika at the Tatras. 1986.

Jason, Margo, George, Elaine, Sanyi and Leika; Budapest, 1986

Sanyi spoke some English. He was a meticulous organizer, and planned all of our excursions: a tour of Žilina (we looked for the house Oli was born), a visit to the Jewish cemetery, a hike to the Tatra Mountains (Leika was seventy-three and Sanyi seventy-eight) where both took off and hiked faster than we could; a tour of Rajec, our ancestors' home town (including the site where the Pikler's house stood in the town's square) and a few days later, to Budapest, where I was scheduled to attend the International Oncology Congress. On the way there, we got off the train in Bratislava, where we met Tante Fini.[85] In Budapest, we met Sanyi's sister, Margo.

We had such a wonderful trip that summer! A lifetime dream for me became a reality—meeting my aunt and uncle. I wrote to let them know how much the three of us had enjoyed our visit and being with them. They wrote back on September 23:

My very dear ones!

I wanted to write to you immediately after our return from Budapest and to share with you how pleased and happy I was with your visit. I cannot express in words what meeting you meant to me. You left me with a warm feeling of togetherness, warmth and love. From the first moment, I felt as if we had always known each other. I think a lot about my dear brother, how happy he would have been if it had been possible to see us again.

It is a pity that we couldn't talk to each other, but our hearts spoke for us. A lot remained to be said, and I hope that you will learn German to the point where we can talk. I can't promise I will learn English; my brain is already too old now, and because of the war years, I missed learning that language.

I am glad that you also left Budapest with good impressions. At the airport, I wanted to say goodbye sooner so as not to burst into tears. In our thoughts, we accompanied you in your long journey back home.

We spent a few more days with Margo, which was very pleasant. Now we are back at home and in our daily life. Recently, we got permission to travel and visit our children, and we intend to go to Israel via Vienna and Switzerland, around mid-November. Obtaining visas takes time.

We have regular mail from the children saying that everything is in order and that they are very much looking forward to our visit. Fini wrote and asked for your address. She was overjoyed that you wanted to meet her.

A new year is coming. We wish to you all good health. It should bring only joy and satisfaction. It will be very difficult for nine men to come together to say the New Year's prayer. Every day there are less of us.

I have a guilty conscience that I haven't yet thanked Virginia and Edulka for the presents. I want to do it soon. Hopefully everyone is well! If you write to Oli, please pass on our warmest regards and best wishes for the New Year. I've already worn the jacket you brought me, it's nicely warm and I think of you every time I wear it. So, thank you once again.

I'm already looking forward to the photos that you promised to send us, dear Georgie. When you see them, you'll experience everything all over again. I remain, with a lot of kisses and a lot of love, yours, *Lea*

Sanyi added in English:

My very dear ones,

First I want to acknowledge your nice letters of August 31 and September 14. We were overjoyed that we were finally able to meet each and spend such lovely moments together. We were also happy with your loving comments about your stay with us, that your return trip was uneventful and that you found everything back home in order. We hope you will come back again, hopefully this time we won't have to wait too long for that to happen.

I hope to hear from you soon. Many hugs and kisses for you, and best wishes for a healthy and prosperous New Year. Love, *Sanyi*

We received a handwritten letter from Leika and Sanyi, dated February 25, 1987:

My dearest ones,

We have been in Israel since last November 21. Madulka, Peter, and the boys were expecting us, so we all felt great joy for each other. Ivan came to greet us that same evening. The next day we went to Nahariya to be with Giora's family and a few days later Ivan visited us again with his whole family. Shlomo also intends to come this summer...We have already been to Danko's bar mitzvah. We were happy that we were able to experience this. It was very solemn. Danko got a flight ticket to London for 10 days from his parents. A friend of Madulka sent her an invitation, so Peter and Madulka will travel with him. We will stay with Miki. We were happy that we were able to persuade Madulka also to travel. Hopefully they will have a nice time and will be a wonderful memory for Danko.

We think often and very happily of the days we spent with you last summer. We look forward to the promised photos. Many thanks also for your letter and the check sent with it. Do not forget that you were our guests and therefore not debtors at all. So once again, thank you!

In the meantime, a letter from Shlomo arrived and described Michal's bat mitzvah...We know you were there, too. Unfortunately, our family is so small by now, but at least the few who remain stick together.

I have a guilty conscience that I haven't written to Edulka and Virginia. Hopefully they are fine, and Olinka, too. I send best regards and kisses to everyone.

I hug you both along with Vanessa and Jason and kiss you all with a lot of love. Yours, *Lea*

Fini often mentions how happy she was with your visit!

In the spring of 1987, I called Israel and spoke with Leika and Magda. It was a lovely conversation. Magda was happy that she had chosen to follow in her father's footsteps with a career in ophthalmology. She was very busy at the hospital. I told them we had considered a trip to Nahariya to meet them, but unfortunately, my call schedule was quite busy, too, and it would have been impossible for me to get away. They were obviously disappointed with this news. They wrote on June 1, 1987:

My very dear ones!

Above all, I want to congratulate you, dearest Georgie, on your approaching birthday. From the bottom of my heart, I wish you a lot of health and joy all your life.

It was a good feeling to hear your voice on the phone again. I am very sorry that nothing came of your planned trip to Israel. But I can understand that you, dearest Georgie, can hardly get away, and it really doesn't pay to make such a big trip, with so many associated expenses, for less than two weeks.

I am grateful that I have been given the opportunity to be with you at all, those were really beautiful, unforgettable days that I will definitely never forget in my life.

Petko should arrive on the 16th with his family. We all want to do a three-day stay at Kynareth with Madulka, Petko, Giora, Ivan and their families. That way, nobody will be burdened with work and it will be nice that at least the small family that remains can be together again. For me, of course, it is painful, that of the five siblings who were so close, I am the only one still alive.

As Madulka mentioned to you, they have plans to go to America for two years. She could not speak very openly on the phone because the children were present and they still don't know anything about their plans. Madulka has been assured of receiving a scholarship. Peter has no job yet, but he hopes to have

found something by the time he gets there. Madulka thinks that they will not leave before September 15th. We will stay until then. We are happy and grateful to be able to spend such a long time with our children, and I can only repeat what a good, self-sacrificing child Madulka is, we get so much love and attention from her that I can't even express it in words. I am glad that I can take care of the household for them and relieve Madulka of some of her chores, and that the little ones can always find an open house.

I get together with Ivan more often, unfortunately I can't talk to his children; they are beautiful, healthy children and Ivan is a happy father. Jaffa is working again for two-and-a half days a week.

I often look at the photographs of when we were together and think of the nice days we spent together. I am glad to have heard about Edulka. Is Virginia in Quito? Write again soon and also about the children. I send a lot of loving kisses and hugs to you.

Yours, *Lea*

In early September of 1987, I wrote to them about my recent conversation with Charlie Pikler and details of how Elaine and I had first met with him in Rochester, MN, back in November 1971. I told them about the Pikler family documents he had sent to me and specifically about the letter his father had written to him after he was born. I asked Leika to help me find more information about our branch relatives.

Magda and her family left Israel on September 13, 1987. Their itinerary was Amsterdam, Toronto, and then Detroit, MI, their final destination. Leika and Sanyi left the same day and flew to Vienna, and from there went by bus to Bratislava. After a two-day stay with Sanyi's brother and niece and Fini, they went home.

Leika wrote on October 24 that the farewell, as always, had been difficult for both sides and this time, it was somehow more difficult to be part of their everyday lives. They were welcomed home very kindly and with love by all of their friends and neighbors, which felt twice as good after having to say goodbye to the children. Magda was happy working at the Kresge Eye Institute. Peter had found work in his field and the children were happy at school. Leika also wrote that when she met with Fini, she had asked her about the family tree. Fini "couldn't tell me anything in more detail about it, and most likely, you already have that information from your father." Fini was still doing well, considering her age (84 at the time). She sent many greetings and kisses and told Leika that she had received the two letters I wrote to her that year.

I called Magda and Peter to welcome them to the US and to invite them to visit us anytime. They had settled in, rented a small house, and bought a used car. They were hoping Magda's parents would be able to visit them next year.

Leika and Sanyi made their first trip to the US in 1988 to visit their children and grandchildren, and they happily accepted an invitation to visit us in Tulsa that summer. Magda came with them. Oli, Virginia, and Edulka also came for this special occasion. Virginia and Edulka met Leika, Sanyi, and Magda for the first time.

During their Tulsa visit, Leika sensed that Oli and I were eager for her to share her memories while growing up with her brother and sisters. It was during one of those conversations that she related her parents' decision to allow Elsa's sister, Margit, to "adopt" Teri and move her to Poltár to live with Margit and her husband, Elemer

Krausz. I remember the sadness in Leika's voice as she related this memory. Móric's finances had suffered the impact of the war, but her aunt and uncle had had no children and had been financially secure. Leika claimed that her aunt had asked Elsa to give up one of her daughters, who she would love to raise as her own. Leika was the one her aunt chose, but Elsa suggested Teri instead. Leika recalled how Hansi, who was still living at home when Teri left, had consoled his sisters. "He was always such pillar of emotional strength for us," Leika said. Then she lamented the fact that she never got to hug her brother again. Oli broke down in tears and nothing more was said. It was a short but wonderful family reunion spent around the pool, around the dining room table, and touring the city parks.

Elaine, Leika, Oli, Sanyi, and Magda; Tusla, September 1988

1990-1999

In 1994, Magda and Peter organized a family reunion in Cape Cod to celebrate Sanyi's 86th birthday. A year later, on March 9,

1995, Sanyi died while attending a luncheon given in his honor by the ophthalmology department at the Žilina hospital. After all his colleagues' speeches, Sani rose up to give his own, and collapsed from a heart attack.

In April 1997, Shlomo and Yael invited the whole family to share Passover at their house in Tucson, AZ. Both were wonderful hosts. It was an enjoyable family get-together with so many languages spoken in one room at the same time. Virginia and Edulka were there along with Leika, Oli with her granddaughter Michelle, Shlomo and Yael's daughter Michal, Elaine's mother Lillian, and Elaine and me with our children, Vanessa and Jason. The Seder spoke to all of us. We also did a lot of sightseeing.

Virginia visited Edulka for a month in Brazil in 1998, five years after Edulka had been admitted to a plastic surgery fellowship in Rio de Janeiro. Due to her rigorous training and on-call schedule, I received only sporadic correspondence from her during those years. Upon returning to Quito after her 1998 visit, Virginia wrote: "Not understanding the language was hard for me…Edulka was frequently on-call so I did not see her much.

Family Passover at Shlomo and Yael's Tuscon Home; 1997

2000-2009

As detailed in Chapter Two, Virginia moved to Brazil in 2003. After that, I hardly received any correspondence from her. We occasionally spoke on the phone and it was obvious she was not happy being there. We learned years later that she had never been sure she wanted to stay there permanently.

On November 29, 2003, the family was again together to celebrate the wedding of Kenny Lugo, Oli's son, to Odalys Carrasco in Miami Beach. It was quite a festive event. Leika, who was in the country visiting her family at the time, also attended. Magda and Peter organized a luncheon to celebrate her 90th birthday, giving Oli and Leika another opportunity to spend time together. Oli told me later that this time, Leika wanted to learn details of Oli's life after she left Ecuador in 1957. Leika was sad that Sophie was not alive to enjoy her grandson's wedding, and she told Oli how much she had loved our mother in the years after she married Hansi.

Leika's 90th birthday luncheon; Miami Beach, November 2003

**Family get-together for Kenny and Odalys's wedding;
Miami, Beach November 2003**

Jason and Leika; Miami Beach, November 2003

On January 3, 2006 the family attended a twenty-first birthday party for Noam, Giora and Judith's son, on a Caribbean cruise. Five of the six first cousins were present. All around, it was a fun celebration, but we all missed Ivan and Yaffa; and Virginia was mostly wheelchair-bound and had a catatonic appearance. The family had a hard time establishing a conversation with her. It was sad to see her that way, as she had always been very social. Five months later, she died in Brazil.

First cousins at Noam's birthday party cruise; 2006

2010-2013

In 2010, at age 97, Leika fell at home and broke a hip. In spite of her age, she consented to undergo surgery. She recovered very well, although she had to use a walker. In the winter of 2011, she fell again, and a second surgery was performed, but this time she was too weak and was unable to recover. She died in Žilina on December 25, 2011 of heart failure, one day after her first great grandson, Aaron Bielik, was born. Leika was a down-to-earth, very practical and decisive, strong and independent person. She was unpretentious and quiet, a thin woman, not quite five feet tall, with a witty sense of humor. According to her sisters and brother, she was the pillar of the family. All of them looked up to her for advice and support. I found her letters to be inspirational and filled with many words of wisdom which have enriched my life.

With Leika's death at age 98, the journey of the fifth generation of the Móric Pikler branch came to an end. In spite of the geographical distances that kept some of them apart, and the struggles and terrible ordeals each had to endure, they demonstrated with actions the devotion and unquestionable, unselfish love they felt for each other. The importance of strong family bonds, always emphasized in their home as they grew up, kept them linked together throughout their lives, as a loving example for all the generations to follow.

Leika; Žilina (date unknown)

Notes

Chapter One

[1] This was one of the most consequential battles in Central European history between the forces of the Kingdom of Hungary, led by Louis II, and those of the Ottoman Empire, led by Suleiman the Magnificent. The Ottoman victory led to the partition of Hungary for several centuries between the Ottoman Empire, the Habsburg Monarchy, and the Principality of Transylvania. This battle marked the end of the Middle Ages in Hungary.

[2] In 1867, the Austro-Hungarian Compromise was signed, under which the House of Habsburg agreed to share power with a separate Hungarian government. The territories of the former Austrian Empire were divided between them creating the Austro-Hungarian Empire in which the lands of Austria and Hungary became independent entities enjoying equal status. [11] The territory of Slovakia came under Hungarian administration.

The Habsburg monarch ruled as Emperor of Austria over the western and northern half of the country that was the Austrian Empire with Vienna as its capital, and the King of Hungary ruled over the Kingdom of Hungary with Buda as its capital until 1873, when Budapest became the new capital. The governmental division was so marked between Austria and Hungary that there was no common citizenship: a person living in Austria- Hungary was either an Austrian citizen or a Hungarian citizen, never both. [11] They did share a common currency, but they were fiscally sovereign and independent entities. [24]

The Austro-Hungarian Empire lasted fifty-one years and ended on

October 28, 1918, following the end of World War I. On that date, the Czechoslovak Republic was created after the historical Declaration of Turčiansky Svaty Martin [37]. The peoples of Bohemia, Moravia, and Slovakia joined together in a peaceful revolution under the leadership of Thomáš Garrigue Masaryk, the most profound writer and thinker of the late nineteenth and early twentieth centuries. [25]

My father admired Masaryk's "humanism, profound social justice and ethical convictions" [25] and, although he may not have necessarily agreed with his religious convictions, he felt Masaryk was respectful of the Jewish people.

The Czechoslovak Republic under Masaryk's leadership gained worldwide esteem as the only democratic and most enlightened state in Central and Eastern Europe because of its democratic parliamentary rules safeguarding personal liberties and, in no small measure, because of its liberal attitude toward the Jews. [26]

Slovakia remained part of Czechoslovakia except for the years of the Second World War, when if functioned as a separate Slovak State under the tutelage of Nazi Germany. [9] Following World War II, Carpatho-Ukraine, the easternmost region of Czechoslovakia was annexed to the Ukraine. In 1993, Czechoslovakia peacefully divided into the Czech Republic and the Slovak Republic.

[3] Jews settled in Jihlava (a town between Prague and Brno in today's Czech Republic) in the thirteenth century (1262). They were expelled in 1425 and from other Moravian royal towns in 1454. They were allowed back in 1709 to participate in commerce after paying a hefty fee.

[4] In 1683, hundreds of Moravian Jewish families fled to Slovakia seeking refuge from the Kurucz riots and the living restrictions of Moravia. Most of these immigrants settled in western Slovakia bordering Moravia.

⁵ Before the Khmelnytsky uprising, magnates had sold and leased certain privileges to arrendators, many of whom were Jewish, who earned money from the collections they made for the magnates by receiving a percentage of an estate's revenue. By not supervising their estates directly, the magnates left it to the leaseholders and collectors to become objects of hatred to the oppressed and long-suffering peasants. Khmelnytsky told the people that the Poles had sold them as slaves "into the hands of the accursed Jews." With this as their battle cry, Cossacks and peasants killed Jews and Polish-Lithuanian townsfolk, as well as members of the legally privileged noble class and royal officials. They massacred them all, sparing neither women nor children. They pillaged the estates of the Jews and nobles, burned churches and killed their priests, leaving nothing whole. [12]

⁶ Eszterházy was a Hungarian noble family with origins in the Middle Ages. Since the seventeenth century, they were among the great landowner magnates of the Kingdom of Hungary during the time it was part of the Habsburg Empire and later Austria-Hungary. During the history of the Habsburg Empire, the Esterházys were consistently loyal to the Habsburg rulers. [15]

⁷ Kojetín is a Moravian town in the Olomouc Region of today's Czech Republic. The first documentary evidence that Jews lived in this town dates from 1566, when 52 families lived on the Judengasse (Jewish street). Records of the cemetery's consecration date to 1574. The synagogue, which had a seating capacity of 300, was renovated in 1614, and again in 1718. During the late seventeenth century most of the Jews of Kojetín worked as peddlers and cattle growers. The Jewish community absorbed many refugees from the Khmelnytky massacres of 1648 as well as some of those who were expelled from Vienna in 1670.

[8] The series *Monumenta Hungariae Judaica* or *Magyar-Zsidó Oklevéltár*, is a documentary collection based on state, county, and municipal archival sources relating to pre-1780 Hungary and published by the Hungarian Israelite Literary Society in Budapest. The first of 18 volumes appeared in 1903, and three other volumes were published prior to 1938. After 1959, another 14 volumes were issued, the last one in 1980.

[9] The *Familianten* Law applied only to a part of the monarchy, and limited by quota the number of Jewish families to 8,541 in Bohemia, 5,106 in Moravia and 119 for Silesia but not including Hungary (Slovakia was a part of Hungary). Originally intended as a temporary measure, the *Familianten* Law ceased to be effective after the March Revolution of 1848 and remained so until its final repeal in 1869. To enforce this quota, a so-called *Familianten* order was issued. It stipulated that men who had children at the time of the legislation were deemed "heads of families." They were given a *Familiant* number (familiennummern) which was inherited by the eldest son at his father's passing, who was then permitted to marry and carry on the family name upon attaining the age of 24, while younger brothers could either remain bachelors the rest of their lives or emigrate. A younger son (but not a daughter) could inherit the number only after the death of an older brother. If the grandfather was still alive, the firstborn grandson could not marry. If a *Familiant* had only daughters, his "number" expired. In addition, Jews were permitted to reside only in places to which they had been admitted before 1726, and within these they were limited to special quarters, streets, and even houses. Violations of the regulations could be punished by flogging and expulsion. The permits could also be sold if there were no sons to inherit them.

The *Familiant* system underwent some changes: from 1726-1749, the state sought to reduce the size of the Jewish population. From 1749-1780, which was marked by the reforms of Empress Maria

Theresa, a fanatical upholder of the *Familianten* Law, the state—under threat of financial crisis—was forced to shift from restriction to regulation. Marriage permits were issued to the second and third eldest sons of families paying a hefty price in taxes. These alleviations tended to favor the upper and professional strata in Jewish society. Immigration to Bohemia and Moravia was eased, making it possible—for a price—for an "expired" Family's status to be transferred to other applicants. Later, the numbers were increased to 8,600 for Bohemia and 5,400 for Moravia. From 1786, a certificate to prove that the applicant had attended a German or Jewish-German school was required, and from 1812 he had to take an examination in the catechism from *Bne-Zion,* a textbook published in 1812.

These laws were a constant source of communal strife and discord. They led to tensions in Jewish society, which had before been relatively homogeneous despite the social differences. There were lawsuits before secular authorities, denunciations, bribery, and sale of expired family numbers to higher bidders from outside the community. Many Jews were not able to settle anywhere permanently so they wandered about the country and contributed largely to developing a Jewish beggar group living virtually outside the law, deprived of any economic status or regular means of livelihood. The Law was sometimes circumvented through conversions to Christianity. The system forced many Jews to marry secretly. The children of such couples were considered illegitimate by the authorities and had to bear their mothers' names. It was not until 1847 that the fathers were permitted to acknowledge their fatherhood in the records and thus establish a quasi-legitimacy for their children.

In disrupting Jewish family life, the *Familiant* system became one of the causes of assimilation. It also led to large-scale emigration from these areas. In fact, whole Jewish communities relocated themselves to neighboring Hungary (Slovakia). Many of those communities were founded by the younger sons of Moravian or Bohemian Jewish families. These might have included Pikler family ancestors. Rajec at the time was in a Habsburg Hungarian province. [27] By 1900, for example, almost half of the Jews in Hungary were of Bohemian or Moravian descent.

One fringe benefit of the *Familianten* Law was that the government kept very good records of which families lived in which towns. The lists of *Familianten* were collected in the *Book of Jewish Familianten* in Moravia. Each record comprised the name of county, registration number of the family in the whole land, the registration number of family in the county, name of the father, his wife, his sons, and a few other family details. *Familiant* status was noted in the Applicants Book. Also stipulated was the compulsory amount of the dowry, measured according to place of origin and means of subsistence.

The *Familianten* Books provide an excellent tool for genealogists and lay people trying to trace their family roots.

For Moravia, the surviving books are not collected in one place, but are available from the various regional archives, such as in Brno or Olomouc (Czech Republic), or in the Czech National Archives or the Jewish Museum in Prague.

An index of all Bohemian towns with *Familianten* records in the Czech National

Archives is available for review at: http://www.jewishgen.org/austriaczech/familianten.html.

There is also an index of all persons mentioned in the *Familianten* Books at: http://www.toledot.org/kraje.html.

[10] Joseph II was the Holy Roman Emperor of the German Nation from 1765 and ruler of the Habsburg lands from 1780 to his death

in 1790. He was the eldest son of Archduchess Maria Theresa and her husband, Emperor Francis I, and the brother of Marie Antoinette.

After November 12, 1787, by decree of Joseph II, all Jews within the Empire were required to adopt German surnames. From 1848 onward, especially after 1867, Hungarian Jews increasingly adopted Magyar (Hungarian) surnames and given names. Although the Emperor also, required the rabbi in each Jewish community to maintain registers of births, marriages and deaths, the rule was often ignored before 1848.

[11] The *Toleranz Edikt* was most likely drafted by Joseph's visionary minister Joseph von Sonnenfels, the grandson of a rabbi but a convert to the Catholic Church.

[12] The gulden (German) or forint (Hungarian) was the currency of the lands of the House of Habsburg between 1754 and 1892 (known as the Austrian Empire from 1804 to 1867 and the Austro-Hunarian Monarchy after 1867). In Austria, the gulden was initially divided into 60 kreuzer, and in Hungary, the forint was divided into 60 krajczár. The currency was decimalized in 1857, using the same names for the unit and subunit.

[13] "RAJ" means "Paradise" and can be traced back to biblical times. The first written record about it was in 1193 as Raich, in a document issued by King Bela III. The first mention as a town comes from 1397.

Rajec lies at an altitude of 1,483 ft above sea level and covers an area of 12.1 sq. mi. It is situated between Strázovské vrchy and Malá Fatra mountains, in the Rajčanka river valley, around 12 miles south-south-west of Žilina.

In 1900, per JewishGen, Rajec's Jewish population was 218. Before 1938 there were about 200 Jews in town (~10% of the population).

According to the 2001 census, the town had 6,074 inhabitants, 96.86% were Slovaks and 0.68% Czechs. The religious makeup was 92.79% Roman Catholics, 3.42% with no religious affiliation, and 1.89% Lutherans. The last census of 2010 showed a fairly stable population of ~ 6,000.

Currently there is no synagogue. At one time there were two. The oldest was razed a long time ago. The other one was razed not long ago to build a parking lot for an adjacent small shopping center. The current city mayor and the city council are unsympathetic to the Rajec Jewish history.

[14] Located in central Slovakia with population 84,919 inhabitants, it is the sixth most populous city in Slovakia. It is a popular winter and summer tourist destination with an easy access to the surrounding mountains.

Its Slovak name includes two roots: the adjective *Banská* from Slovak – *baňa* – *mine*, and the name of the local river *Bystrica* (from Slavic *bystrica* – swift stream). From the 15th to 18th centuries, it was Slovakia's main area for the exploitation of its copper deposits (and to a lesser degree iron, silver and gold). The mines were exhausted by 1900.

During World War II, Banská Bystrica became the center of anti-Nazi opposition in Slovakia when the Slovak National Uprising, one of the largest anti-Nazi resistance events in Europe, was launched from the city on 29 August 1944. After the partisans were defeated on 27 October, it was briefly occupied by the German forces before it was liberated by Soviet and Romanian troops on 26 March 1945. After the war, Banská Bystrica became the administrative, economic, and cultural hub of central Slovakia.

It has been a university town since the 1950s. Its largest, Matej Bel University was founded in 1992. A synagogue in Banská Bystrica built in 1867 was demolished in 1983.

[15] Town in northern Slovakia. Located around 41 miles west from Žilina. Population: Census 2001: around 30,000 (45,000 with nearby villages)

From the second half of the tenth century until 1918 it was part of the Kingdom of Hungary. The first written mention about the settlement was in 1233. The town was established by Germans who named it Rosenberg. It got its town rights in 1318.

In the nineteenth century, it was one of the centers of Slovak national movement. It slowly became one of the industrial and financial centers of the Kingdom of Hungary. Many factories emerged: paper and pulpwood works, brick works or textile industry.

After the breakup of Austria-Hungary in 1918, it became part of Czechoslovakia. When Czechoslovakia was split in 1939, it was incorporated into the first Slovak Republic. It became part of Czechoslovakia again in 1945. In 1993, after the dissolution of Czechoslovakia, it became part of Slovakia. In 1995 it became a district town.

[16] Zilina is located in north-western Slovakia about 120 miles from the capital Bratislava, close to both the Czech and Polish borders. It is the largest city in Slovakia and its third most important industrial center. It is the seat of the Žilinska university.

The latest census, carried out at the end of 2014, reported a population of 81,155 inhabitants. Per Pavel Frankl, chairman of the Jewish Community and co-author with his brother Peter of the book Jews of Žilina [6], there are currently 40 Jews in Žilina with a total of 55 in the Žilina district. All belong to the Reform Movement.

Jews first appeared in Žilina in the nineteenth century; there were only two Jewish families living in Žilina in 1789. The town was not willing to allow more Jews to settle. They could come during the day to do business, but they had to leave the town for the night. The fact was that Žilina, with mainly Christian tradesmen, guilds, and merchants, was not willing to accept Jewish business competition, and therefore the Jews settled in neighboring villages. The first synagogue was built in 1850 and served until 1928. According to the 1851 census, 261 Jews lived in Žilina.

Following the schism in Hungarian Jewry, the Žilina community opted for the *Neolog* movement; Orthodox Jews eventually established their own small separate community in 1921.

In the first third of the twentieth century the number of Jews grew to the point that the need of a new synagogue became urgent. Its construction was completed by the end of 1931. It was the most modern and most beautiful Jewish building in Slovakia, and the one Elsa would attend. In 1930 the Jewish population had risen to 2,500. By then, Peter and Pavel Frankl's book describes Žilina as having a 'very rich' Jewish community life.

The orthodox synagogue on Daniela Dlabača street no. 15, built in 1927, is a simple building with a meeting-house Salem and adjutant rooms. This synagogue was also renovated after the war and a Judaica Museum was established and is visited by school children for their education about Judaism and the Holocaust. Religious services in this synagogue stopped in 1987 due to the poor condition of the small building, and also because there were no more members of the community that could carry out the religious services.

In 1942, there were 3,500 Jews living in Žilina and its surrounding areas. 3000 of them were Jews originally from Žilina, and 500 Jews were those who relocated themselves to the town from the small cities and villages after the adoption of anti-Jewish legislature from 1938 to 1941. They could not stay in their hometowns or did not feel safe there anymore. A detention center was established in Žilina from where many train transports were dispatched to the concentration camps beginning in 1942. The city did not forget the fellow Jews killed in concentration camps during the WW II and built the "Road of No Return" Memorial on the premises of the old detention camp. This memorial was unveiled in 2004 in the presence of the President of the Slovak Republic. From this place, 18,223 Jews were transported to Nazi concentration camps between March and October 1942. Only 700 Jews came back from the concentration camps. 500 of them emigrated shortly after the end of the WWII in the first wave of emigration between 1948 and 1949. After that, emigration was forbidden by the Communist regime. In the beginning of the '50s about 200 Jews lived there.

Žilina's Road of No Return memorial stone

There were about 150 Jews living in Žilina at the end of the '60s and the Jewish religious community kept their ancestral traditions even under the stressful political atmosphere of the Communist regime.

Žilina's Road of No Return memorial

The last dramatic change in the life of the Jewish community was the emigration between 1968 and 1969 of its young generation. The membership of the Jewish religious community dropped to 100, made mostly of elderly people.

Partial revival of the Jewish religious community took place with the change of the political system in Slovakia after 1989. The old Jewish cemetery was renovated, hundreds of tombstones were put or straighten up again, many of which laid down on the ground. Some of the tombstones had been damaged in 1958 by unknown offenders.

The Jewish Cemetery, founded in 1852, is located in the west side of town. Near the gate is a large building, the Hall of Remembrance, a memorial to Žilina's victims of the Holocaust. It was unveiled in 1952. The central motif is a steel shaped pyramid, 5.5-meter-high, covered with Swedish black granite. At the bottom of it are stone renderings of Moses's Ten Commandments. On the Hall side walls, are white marble tablets with the engraved names of the 2,642 Jews from the Žilina area, victims of the Holocaust, including the names of Julius Bronner and Alexander Neumann. On the front side, there is a list of 42 names of fallen combatants of World War II.

Žilina's Jewish cemetery gate

Žilina's Jewish cemetery Wall of Remembrance

Elaine and I visited Žilina on August 28, 2018. This was her second visit, my third one. The cemetery back in 1986, had wild vegetation in many areas covering and destroying or damaging the graves, despite the generous work of Christian volunteers who tried their best to take care of this problem. This time, with regular gardening we were happy to witness a well-kept cemetery. This is among one of the best kept Jewish cemeteries in Slovakia.

In this cemetery is the grave of Móric Pikler, Elsa Pikler née Teich, Alexander Neumann and Géza Hajos, which was restored in 2018 thanks to Ivan's efforts, as well as the grave of Alexander Vozar, Lea Vozar née Pikler, and our cousin, Magda Bielik.

Móric, Elsa, Sani, and Géza's gravestone at Žilina's cemetery

Vozars and Magda Bielik's gravestone at Žilina's cemetery

The Jewish community is also taking care of its senior citizens with the cooperation of other Jewish organizations, to ensure a peaceful and pleasant retirement for them. However, Žilina's full religious life has not revived. There are, however, still some regular activities going on. Every year there is a commemoration ceremony organized to pay honor to those killed in World War II, with a reunion meeting of all Jewish natives of Žilina the day before. Almost one hundred people from all over the world take part in this meeting. A small celebration party on Chanukah as well as a Seder dinner on Pesach also take place.

Today, about two hundred synagogues and 620 Jewish cemeteries remain in Slovakia. [28]

[17] The name of a small town about 12.4 miles north of Bratislava, the capital of Slovakia. After World War II it was renamed Bernolákovo after Anton Bernolák.

Chapter Two

[18] Bukovina is a historical region in Central Europe, divided between Romania and Ukraine, located on the northern slopes of the central Eastern Carpathians and the adjoining plains. Its name is derived from the abundance of beech trees.

Bukovina was originally a part of the principality of Moldavia. It was occupied by the Russians in 1769, and by the Austrians in 1774. From 1774 to 1918, it was the easternmost province and an administrative division of the Habsburg Monarchy, the Austrian Empire, and Austria-Hungary. After World War I, Romania established its control over Bukovina. In 1940, the northern half of Bukovina was annexed by the Soviet Union and currently is part of Ukraine. Southern Bukovina remains within Romanian jurisdiction.

Pâltinoasa, Kimpulung and Câmpulung Moldovenesc are all located in the historical region of Southern Bukovina (Suceava County). Câmpulung Moldovenesc, the largest of the three, is a city with a population of 16,105 inhabitants (2011 census). Its economy: dairy products, lumber and ecotourism.

Bukovina

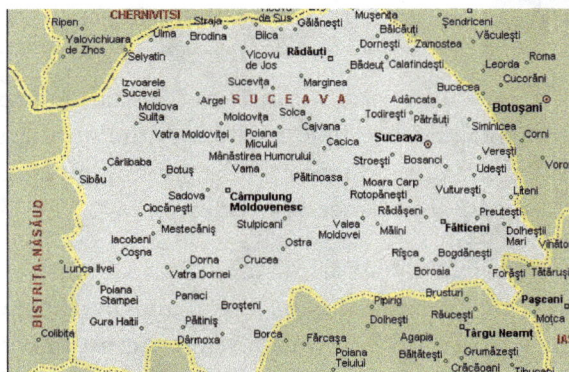

Bukovina's Suceava region

[19] Oli and I never heard him mention his baby sister, Wilma. I learned about her for the first time from an email I received from Katalin Pikler [Abraham Pikler branch] on December 7, 2007. She stated that Leika had told her about baby Wilma when Katalin visited her in Žilina several years earlier.

When Edulka was born in 1960, Hansi and Virginia named her Edith Wilma for both of Hansi's sisters. So, he must have known about Wilma.

[20] The law was an important instrument of social administration. The domicile of origin was the home that a legitimate child acquired at birth during the lifetime of his father in the country in which the father was domiciled at the time of the birth. The law also applied to his wife who was given the domicile of her husband. An illegitimate child or a legitimate child born after his father's death had his domicile of origin in the country where his mother was domiciled at the time of the birth.

Citizenship was also determined by the domicile law during the Austrian Empire and after 1918 in the constituted Czechoslovak state, a person would be Austrian or Czechoslovak, respectively.

Üdvözlet Rajeczröl. — Gruss aus Rajecz.   Vásártér és templom — Ringpla

Piklers' house (4th from left). 1910.

2018 view of previous Piklers' house in Rajec's central square.

[21] *Gymnasium* is the equivalent of high school. It prepared students for higher education at a university.

[22] *Matura* is the equivalent of a high school diploma.

[23] The assassin was Gavrilo Princip, a nineteen-year-old student and aspiring poet, who belonged to a faction of militant Bosnian Serb nationalists. Living next door to the independent nation of Serbia, they dreamed of a Greater Serbia encompassing all Serbs, and wanted to reverse the formal annexation of Bosnia by the Austrians in 1908. Princip had plotted with others to carry out the assassination but, at the last minute, he was the final trigger: he fired twice at point blank range. The first bullet hit the Archduke in the neck, while the second tore open the stomach of his pregnant wife, Sophie, the Duchess of Hohenberg, as she tried to protect her husband. It was poor timing for the royal couple, as it was also their 14th wedding anniversary. [70]

Outside the Balkans, the assassinations made the headlines for a few days, then dropped from sight. Nothing seemed to change in Rajec and daily life seemed to go on in the same fashion.

During the following four weeks, however, moves and countermoves and multiple ultimatums succeeded each other ever faster. In Vienna, Emperor Franz Joseph seemed unperturbed by the death of the nephew he disliked. What he and his advisors saw in the assassination was something they had long sought: an excuse to attack Serbia.

With the strong backing of the Kaiser and after overcoming all difficulties to mobilize an army during the Summer, on July 23, the Austria-Hungary envoy presented Serbia with an ultimatum which they knew Serbia could not and would not accept. On July 28, Austria-Hungary declared war on Serbia. A day later, Austrian gunboats on the Danube began shelling the Serbian capital, Belgrade.

France at the time was bound to Russia by treaty. Tsar Nicholas II waffled, issuing contradictory orders, but ultimately also began to mobilize troops despite a German ultimatum demanding a halt to this mobilization. On August 1, Germany declared war on Russia and on the same day, France began preparing for a German attack that clearly was inevitable. On August 3, Germany declared war on France. Britain asked both France and Germany for guarantees that they would honor Belgian neutrality. France said yes but Germany did not reply. So, after German troops crossed the Belgian frontier on August 4, Britain delivered to Germany an ultimatum: halt the invasion by midnight or Britain would declare war.

The United States joined the war on April 6, 1917, after Congress voted to declare war on the Kaiser and his allies. On December 7, 1917, Congress declared war on Austria-Hungary. More than two million American soldiers fought in the battlefields of Western Europe under the command of General John Pershing. About 54,000 Americans (including those missing in action) were killed in battle, over 63,000 died from accidents and disease (including the deadly influenza epidemic of 1918), and over 200,000 were wounded.

The toll of this awful war: over 38 million military and civilian casualties with over 17 million deaths and 20 million wounded. [70,71,72]

The war ended with the signature of the Treaty of Versailles in the Hall of Mirrors in the Palace of Versailles, on June 28, 1919, five years after the assassination of Franz Ferdinand. It took effect on January 10, 1920.

[24] After five years working with Móric in the timber trade business, he went to work for one of the largest lumber companies in Romania, where forestry had a long tradition and for centuries timber had been one of the country's primary exports. The company

was located in the town of Brezoi, in a region called Oltenia in the Valcea County of South Romania, towards the Danube and in the border with Bulgaria. The company's name derives from the Carpathian Mountains, the largest range of mountains crossing Romania.

[25] On January 30, 1933, Adolf Hitler became chancellor of Germany. Two months later his regime moved swiftly to implement its anti-Jewish policies. On April 1, 1933 the Nazi Party announced a nation-wide boycott of Jewish businesses [75,76]. In addition, Jews were expelled from political, cultural, and professional life. On April 7, 1933, the Law for the Restoration of the Civil Service was promulgated. It eliminated, by virtue of its "Aryan" clause, all but a handful of Jews and half-Jews from public office. Several months later, news reached Czechoslovakia of the Nazis instigating public burnings of books by Jewish authors and those opposed to Nazism.

[26] On August 2, 1934 the German President, Paul von Hindenburg, died. Hitler combined the offices of chancellor and president and declared himself *Führer* of the Third Reich. [73]

In May 1935, the Reich's office for statistics stated that approximately 90,000 Jews and 20,000 non-Jewish political emigrants had fled Germany since January 1933.

September 15, 1935, the Nuremberg Laws were decreed at a Nazi party rally. They contained two especially important provisions: (1) the Reich Citizenship belonged only to those of "German or related blood", (2) the Law for the Protection of German Blood and German Honor prohibited marriage and extra-marital intercourse between Jews and persons of "German or related blood."

The First Ordinance to the Reich Citizenship Law on November 14, 1935, specified that "a Jew cannot be a Reich citizen." It also enacted a classification system to define various degrees of

Jewishness. One was defined as a full Jew if "descended from at least three grandparents who are fully Jewish by race," or if "descended from two fully Jewish grandparents" and subject to other conditions specified by the ordinance. A grandparent was defined as fully Jewish if he or she "belonged to the Jewish religious community."

[27] Czechoslovakia's ZB weapons, primarily its machine guns and rifles, were highly regarded for their quality and were exported to many armies all over the world including the Haganah in Israel's 1948 War of Independence. Ecuador also bought the ZB rifles (Mauser) and during my ROTC senior high school year we were trained in their use and maintenance.

[28] On March 12-13, 1938, the *Anschluss* took place: Hitler's armed forces annexed Austria into Nazi Germany with full political and military control. Austria was no longer an independent state. Some 185,000 Jews were now subject to the same policies that had been enforced on German Jews [75,76].

That day began with an outpouring of popular devotion to Hitler and anti-Semitic slogans throughout the streets of Vienna as well as in neighboring provincial towns. The Jews were the major victims of squads of swastika-bearing Austrian storm troopers as well as unofficial gangs of private citizens (*Rollkommandos*) and street mobs who bullied or forced their way into and invaded, searched, appropriated, plundered and looted Jewish homes, businesses, and institutions with virtually no opposition or hindrance from local officials or the police. Jewish shops were pillaged in Vienna night and day, not only in the Jewish districts but in the city's main business areas as well. All types of stores, large department stores as well as modest and small stores and restaurants were attacked and looted. The official guardians of civil order, the police stood by, offering no help to the victims and frequently facilitating the pillaging or joining in to share the loot; they arrested Jews who filed complaints or denounced their victimizers. In addition, Jewish shops were forced to put identification signs in their windows, inscribed "Jewish Enterprise," or "Non-Aryan Enterprise" or "Aryans do not buy from Jews." Many stores had the word "*Jude*" scrawled in red paint on their windows or doors [31].

A short while after the annexation of Austria, Adolph Eichmann arrived in Vienna, opened the *Zentralstelle für Jüdishe Auswanderung* (Central Bureau for Jewish Emigration), and almost immediately made it known to Austrian Jews that there was no future for them in that country. His brutal dealings with Viennese Jewry brought Eichmann his first distinction in the Hitler regime. [36] A policy of forced Jewish emigration was proclaimed by the new masters of Austria and carried out with the outmost speed and severity.

All matters concerning the departure of Austrian Jews were handled by a central government office, located in the Rothschild Palace and staffed by Gestapo agents under Adolf Eichmann and Treasury officials. This central office examined the personal and financial status of all emigrants, with particular emphasis on the taxes they still owed; and when all formalities were completed, emigration papers were granted [32]. Jews left Austria at a much quicker pace than was the case in Germany.

Approximately 110,000 Austrian Jews succeeded in leaving (65,000 departed in 1938, and over 40,000 during the first nine months of 1939 when the European war broke out). [32]. Sophie's parents were among this latter group of refugees.

[29] On September 29-30, 1938, the infamous *Munich Agreement* was signed by Germany, France, England, and Italy. The Soviet Union and Czechoslovakia were not invited. It followed a conference held in Munich on September 28 among the major powers of Europe, where Germany insisted that western Czechoslovakia, the Sudeten border area where the majority of that country's German-speaking

inhabitants lived, was part of Germany. These people had been pressing for union with Germany.

The British and French ambassadors accepted Hitler's terms and then put enormous pressure on the Czech government to yield—basically to sign its own death warrant. The Sudeten area contained the mountainous approaches and Czech fortifications, so that its loss left Czechoslovakia militarily defenseless. The country also lost the banking and heavy industrial districts which were situated there. The region was thereafter named *Sudetenland. I*n November 1938, as a consequence of this agreement, southern Slovakia, including the town of Lučenec, was cut off Czechoslovakia and fell into the region occupied by Hungary.

[30] Czechoslovakia, forsaken by France and Great Britain, was invaded by German troops on October 1, 1938, and they occupied the Sudetenland. The Munich Pact had sealed the fate of some 25,000 Jews in the Sudeten region annexed by Germany. Expulsion of Czechs and Jews from the region took place daily. Human beings were treated like hunted animals. The German authorities drove groups of refugees from the Sudetenland to the Czech frontier; some of these managed to pass illegally into Czech territory and proceeded to Prague or Brno, but others, both Jews and gentile anti-Nazis, were turned back by Czech border guards. Since they could not reenter the German-occupied territory they had left, they remained stranded in no-man's land. At last, early in March 1939, as a result of British representations to Berlin, the expulsions stopped and most refugees from the Sudetenland were granted temporary asylum in Czechoslovakia. But this reprieve was hardly relevant, for on March 15, 1939, Hitler's armies marched into Bohemia and Moravia. [26]

Hansi learned firsthand the struggles some refugees had to endure before they made it to Brno.

[31] On October 5, 1938, the travel documents of all German Jews were declared invalid. Their passports had to be handed in within two weeks and were marked with a large red "J", for *Jude*. Hansi's passport was issued in Žilina on December 29, 1938 [#1/994/1938] and was not marked. I could not find Sophie and Olga's original passports.

[32] On October 5, 1938, in Žilina, Slovakia, politicians set up an autonomous Slovak government. The power was in the hands of the *L'udova Strana* (People's Party) founded by Andrej Hlinka and led by Monsignor Jozef Tiso [33]. Both Hlinka and Tiso were Slovak Catholic priests. This was a right-wing conservative political party with strong Christian and nationalistic orientation. From 1938-1945 it also maintained a militia, the Hlinka Guard, the party's military arm for internal security, which willingly helped Hitler with his plans. It operated against Jews, Czechs, Hungarians, left-wing politicians, and any other members of the opposition.

In 1942, the Guard supervised the mass deportation of Slovak Jews to Auschwitz. It would regularly make roundups of Jews in the spring and summer months. It was the secret police who attempted to round up the family in Žilina in early 1942 but they were able to evade their capture and fled to Hungary. Deportation of the Jews by the Hlinka Guards lead to confiscation of Jewish property, some of which was distributed to individual members of the Guard.

Tiso was overthrown by the Red Army and the Czechoslovak Partisans in April 1945. He was tried and convicted for treason, suppression of freedom, and crimes against humanity, and was executed in 1947.

[33] Milena Jesenská described with great poignancy the plight of the refugees and the assault on Czechoslovakia as a whole. She took up the most sensitive issues plaguing her nation and became the voice for human rights and for the persecuted. She had previously served

as a correspondent and later had written the fashion and domestic affairs column for the Czech-Jewish liberal newspaper *Tribuna*. Her command of German was total; as a translator of Franz Kafka's work into Czech, she had an essential grasp of his images, symbols, and human concerns and was deeply conscious of his genius.

In 1937 she joined the staff of *Prítomnost* ("Present"), the prestigious Czech magazine for politics and culture. Her early articles, drawn from everyday life, psychological inquiries, and the like, soon turned to weighty issues, exploring the various aspects of the refugee problem. Most of her articles dealt with the lives of the German fugitives who reached the borders of Czechoslovakia, their sad plight, and the generous assistance given to them by the local populace [34].

After the Munich betrayal, Jesenská dealt with this issue, too, with scorn and disdain: "In France and England funds are raised to assist the democratic German refugees, but no one in our generation could feel grateful for this act" [34]. She pointed a relentless finger at their betrayal: "You stood by the cradle of our newly established state and after twenty years of independence now you yourselves have become its ill-advised Fates" [34].

Between 1938 and 1939, she became the editor of the magazine after its founder and editor Ferdinand Peroutka was removed by the Nazis. As the political situation grew more serious, so did the depth, foresight, and power of her writing.

After the occupation of Czechoslovakia by the German army, Jesenská, who was not a Jew, helped many Jewish and political refugees to emigrate. She herself decided to stay, however, despite the consequences. On November 11, 1939 she was arrested by the Gestapo. She spent 11 months in two prisons before being deported in October 1940 to the Ravensbrück concentration camp in Germany, where she died on May 17, 1944 three weeks before

D-Day and nine months before Elsa Pikler died at the same camp.

[34] The First Vienna Award, which was a result of the Munich agreement, was signed on November 2, 1938. It resulted in the partition of Czechoslovakia. Germany and Italy forced Czechoslovakia (later Slovakia) to cede its primarily Hungarian-inhabited southern territory (which included Lučenec) to Hungary. Poland gained a small northeastern territory which included Techen -where Sam Luftig's family lived. [73] The rest of Slovakia was guaranteed autonomy within a federal state named Czecho-Slovakia.

[35] Herschel Grynszpan, the son of Polish Jews, moved to Paris in early 1938. When he learned that his parents were being deported from Germany in October 1938, he decided to assault the German ambassador in Paris in order to arouse public opinion in the West against the Nazi persecution of Jews. On November 7, 1938 Grynszpan shot Ernst vom Rath, the Secretary of the German legation in Paris. The Germans accused Grynszpan of being a tool of world Jewry and, while the embassy official lay mortally wounded for two days, the German government stirred up feelings of hostility and retaliation against German Jewry. The official died on November 9.

[36] In retaliation for Grynszpan's actions, on November 9-10, 1938, the infamous Kristallnacht pogroms (often referred to as "The Night of Broken Glass" in English) erupted in Germany and Austria. They were instigated by Josef Goebbels, the Nazi minister of propaganda, and though the German Government attempted to present the actions of Kristallnacht as a spontaneous protest on the part of the Aryan population, it was in fact carefully planned, incited, and unleashed at the order of the Nazi leaders. The Gestapo chief at the time, Heinrich Müller, sent a telegram to every police unit in Nazi Germany. "In shortest order," it read, "actions against Jews and especially their synagogues will take place in all of

Germany. These are not to be interfered with."

No complete tally exists of the destruction which took place during Kristallnacht. What is known is that at least 20,000 Jews were arrested and hurried off to concentration camps at Sachsenhausen, Buchenwald, and Dachau, and many were beaten by Nazi thugs. According to Nazi estimates, 815 shops were destroyed, 29 warehouses and 171 dwellings were set on fire or otherwise destroyed. Within a day, at least 91 Jews were killed. Firefighters stood by as synagogues and Jewish-owned homes, schools, and businesses burned to the ground. 119 synagogues in Germany and Austria were set on fire, including Vienna's Temple Brigittenauer, where my parents were married 25 months earlier (October 11, 1936), and 76 more synagogues completely demolished. Offices, cafes, and thousands of private homes were ransacked or destroyed by fire. Jewish owners had to repair, at their own expense, the damage done to their businesses and dwellings, and the Nazi authorities confiscated the insurance claims of the victims. In addition, a fine of one billion Reichsmarks was levied on the entire Jewish community. Drastic decrees, completely undermining what was left of the economic life of the Jews, followed these savage outbursts. A decree of November 23 ordered that by January 1, 1939, all Jews were to be barred from operating retail stores, artisans' workshops, and mail-order businesses. The pogroms marked the beginning of the end for the Jews still in greater Germany. Many Jews fled, dashing illegally across the borders and pouring into Western Europe. [36, 37]

In Slovakia, a boycott of Jewish shops was organized, and Christians were warned not to shop in Jewish stores. In early December, a mob badly damaged a synagogue in Trnava. The most gruesome plight was that of the "stateless" who had been born in the territory ceded to Hungary, among whom were many Jews. These people were forcibly taken from their houses in the middle of the night, placed on trucks, and sent to the Hungarian frontier, but the Hungarian authorities refused to admit them. Several hundred families, including small children, had to remain for weeks on the borderline between the two countries, inadequately clothed and without food. The only profound human protest came, once again, from a non-Jew, Milena Jesenská, who traveled to the Slovak-Hungarian border, and in her article, "In No-Man's Land" in Pritomnost on December 29, 1938, gave a moving description of the anguish of the Jews trapped there [19,34].

[37] On April 18, 1939, the Slovak state enacted its first anti-Semitic legislation. Ordinance 63, Section I, defined who was a Jew, and Section II restricted the number of Jews to be permitted in certain liberal professions, primarily attorneys and physicians. Jews could not become notaries nor could they serve as newspaper editors, except of Jewish publications. [38]

[38] The first practical results of the intensified anti-Jewish policies soon became evident in a spate of anti-Semitic legislation. On September 3, 1940, the Slovak parliament adopted Constitutional Law 210, which authorized the government to take whatever action it deemed necessary in matters of Aryanization. The laws affecting education and school attendance of Jewish students constituted a particularly severe hardship. A decree enacted on June 13, 1939, restricted the number of Jewish students at public schools to 4 percent of the total student body. Later, a law was passed excluding Jews altogether from the country's schools. Jews were also barred from training schools for apprentices, and they could no longer have the Slovak authorities validate report cards or certificates issued to them by schools or other educational institutions outside the country. Eventually, Jewish children of school age were permitted to attend only Jewish elementary schools or classes, which had to be maintained by the Jewish religious communities [38].

[39] On August 21, 1939, an economic agreement between Germany

and the Soviet Union was signed, and two days later, a non-aggression pact followed, in which the two countries agreed to take no military action against each other for the next ten years. It also contained a secret protocol dividing northern and eastern Europe into spheres of influence. The German High Command, however, began planning an invasion of the Soviet Union in July 1940 which Hitler authorized on December 18, 1940 [73].

[40] Without a formal declaration of war from Germany to the general public or the world, World War II began on September 1, 1939 with Germany's surprise invasion of Poland. In spite of the overwhelming German armor, Poland fought bravely but its forces were overcome. Poland's pledged llies, France and Great Britain, did not come to its rescue [73].

World War II was fought between two groups of countries. On one side were the Axis powers, including Germany, Italy and Japan. On the other side were the Allies, including Great Britain, France, Australia, Canada, New Zealand, India, the Soviet Union, China, and the United States.

[41] The two laws were 1) The Reich Citizenship Law *(Reichbürgergesetz)* which deprived the Jews of German citizenship, confining them to the status of "subjects." Only those of German or related blood were eligible to be Reich citizens. A supplementary decree outlining the definition of who was Jewish was passed on November 14, and the Reich Citizenship Law officially came into force on that date. The laws were expanded on November 26 to include Romani people and Afro-Germans. 2) The Law for the Protection of German Blood and German Honor *(Gesetz sum Schutze des deutschen Blutes und der deutschen Ehre)* which forbade marriages and extramarital relations between Jews and Aryans and prohibited Jews from employing female Aryan servants under thirty years of age.

In the next few years, some thirteen decrees supplementing the

Nuremberg Laws would outlaw the Jews completely [76].

[42] There were several non-sectarian committees that dealt with refugee problems: in Germany and Austria the *Hilfsverein der Deutschen Juden* organization was in charge of helping Jews to emigrate, help which included traveling subsidies. It also prepared a pamphlet in Berlin for Jews emigrating to Latin America (*Jüdishe Auswanderung nach Südamerika*). In Czechoslovakia, the Social Democratic Refugee Relief Committee was established in March 1933 to help refugees of racial and religious persecution. There were also various political relief committees formed to help political refugees.

The American Joint Distribution Committee, the Jewish Colonization Association, and HICEM provided guidance and assistance to the above committees and helped Jews from Germany, Austria, and Czechoslovakia emigrate overseas [24,37].

At the suggestion of the Czech Government, all relief committees merged to form a National Coordinating Committee to which, later on, the Committee for Austrian Refugees was added.

[43] The lion's share of the funds for refugee aid in Czechoslovakia came from wealthy individuals and public figures, from religious and relief organizations in England, and from the Quakers in the United States. The Freemasons and even the "Red Help" in Moscow regularly sent donations. Generous sums were donated by Czechoslovakia President T.G. Masaryk and his successor Eduard Beneš. The British and French Governments supported this effort by guaranteeing a loan of 8 million pounds sterling to be floated in England by the Czechoslovak Government, and, in addition, making a contribution of 4 million pounds each. The money was to be used both for the relief of refugees and for their emigration [44].

[44] Neville Chamberlain, British Prime Minister, announced to

the nation on September 3, 1939, that a "state of war now exists between Great Britain and Germany." By the afternoon, the French had also formally declared war. There was no strong public backing for war in either country, but the invasion of Poland changed public attitudes. They were joined by Australia, India, and New Zealand [73].

[45] As Polish resistance to the German invasion neared its death throes, the country was faced with a wholly new threat. On September 17, 1939 Soviet troops invaded eastern Poland with the clear intention of joining in on the benefits of victory, as already promised in the German-Soviet Non-Aggression Treaty of August 23. German forces occupied Warsaw. The *Blitzkrieg* was over in one month. [73].

[46] After months of ultimatums, Soviet attacks on Finland began on September 29, 1939. Without a formal declaration of war, on November 30, 1939, the Red Army crossed the Finish border three months after the outbreak of World War II and ended with the Moscow Peace Treaty on March 13, 1940 [73].

[47] A historical fact which few, if any, immigrants were aware of: "Quito was the name of the country before and after Christopher Columbus' voyages. Before, it was the land of the Quitus aborigines. Under the Spanish rulers it became the Royal Audience of Quito, also called *La Presidencia de Quito* [47].

In the first half of the eighteenth century, a French scientific mission arrived there, with the purpose of clarifying whether it was Newton, the Englishman, or the French astronomer Cassini, who was right in the controversy about the true shape of the earth. Newton maintained that the earth bulged at its middle, and as a result of its rotation was flattened at the poles. Conversely, Cassinists believed that the flattening occurred at the equator and that the globe lengthened towards the poles, as a preliminary measurement made in France of an arc of the meridian seemed to indicate [47]. After several years of geodetic studies, the French emissaries, comparing their survey data with others collected in boreal regions, concluded that full credit was due to Newton's viewpoint [47]. Their calculations of the distance from the equator to the North Pole became the basis of today's metric system (a meter was originally defined as one ten-millionth of the distance between the North Pole and the equator).

Today the curious traveler will find at the village of San Antonio de Pomasqui, 15 miles north of the capital, Quito, a monument which marks the spot where the imaginary line of the equator divides the two hemispheres of the world. An inscription reads, *Latitude 0o 0' 0"*, and the visitors may have their picture taken, with one foot placed in the northern and the other in the southern half of the planet [47]. The new Mitad del Mundo (Middle of the World) 100-foot-tall monument was built in 1979 (it was actually built in the wrong place - several hundred feet south of the true Equator as determined by modern GPS technology!) The site's elevation is 8146 feet and its longitude 78 degrees, 27 minutes and eight seconds west. The "true" equatorial line is located at the near- by Museo Solar Inti-Nan and marked with a red line (a yellow one is painted at the monument).

Ecuador's Mitad del Mundo monument

At the Mitad del Mundo monument. 1972

Vanessa and Jason standing between Earth's south and north hemispheres

The name *Ecuador* came to life in Europe when those early groups of scientists used this name to refer to the domains of the Spanish crown where they conducted their studies. At a later time during the wars of independence, when the liberator Simón Bolívar had established the union of Great Colombia (1819), a legal document included the name *Ecuador* for the first time. The name was officially adopted in 1830 [47].

[48] The Guayaquil-Quito Railway *el ferrocarril del Sur* was inaugurated in Quito in 1908 after ten long years of construction, linking by rail four of Ecuador's five largest cities (Guayaquil, Riobamba, Ambato, and Quito). Ecuador's President, Eloy Alfaro, in 1895 declared his intention to complete the construction of the railroad, to take it to the Andean heights, which at the time ran only from Duran, a small city across Guayaquil (on the left bank of the Guayas river), and Yaguachi to the Chimbo River Bridge, at the edge of the mountain chain. The government of President Alfaro hired engineer Sigvald Müller to complete the studies for the railroad's route which would climb the Andes up to the top of Sibambe, considered a very difficult engineering project and an obstacle at the time. Müller took more than two years to finish his report to the President, considering the projected railway to be "perhaps the most difficult one in the world." [60]

To finance the construction of the railroad, Alfaro found Archer Harman through his foreign minister in New York, an audacious, enterprising, ambitious and visionary man who had worked on an American railway project but was also a promoter and speculator. Archer's bother, Major John Harman, joined the construction team. He was a highly qualified engineer, spirited and disciplined, able to confront any technical difficulty. John Harman had graduated from West Point and was educated to believe in challenging the impossible. [60]

The Guayaquil-Quito Railway sets out on its journey at sea-level from the Duran station, but about 54 miles farther on begins to climb so sharply that on completing the next 50 miles it comes to an exhausted stop at an altitude of 10,600 ft. To reach this place, John Harman engineered the rail line to ascend the mountain at a gradient of 5 1/2% along a zigzag (switchbacks) cut out of solid rock. So, to get through it, they brought four thousand Jamaican workers, experts in handling dynamite. The figure of the mountain and the controversial connotations of the project derived by conservative politicians from the Sierra, made this section to be known as "the Devil's Nose."

The famous "Devil's Nose" section of the Duran-Quito train route.

To this day, the Devil's Nose remains one of the wonders of the modern engineering world. It requires several switchbacks, including one length where the train reverses direction and heads backward as it gingerly stair-steps down the highlands. After that, two more Andean ranges had to be crossed, rising and descending all the time, with the highest point along the whole line at Urbina, 11,841 ft above sea level, right at the foot of Mt. Chimborazo which towered still another 10,000 ft above. The next highest point, 11,600 ft, offered a view of Mt. Cotopaxi. The train had to descend from there to Quito, which lay "only" 9,350 ft above sea level.

At the "Devil's Nose" railroad section: train No. 5 above heading for Riobamba; train No. 58 below posing for pictures.

To count the hairpin bends, the 309 bridges, the tunes, would keep a traveler more than busy along the extent of 288 miles, which was covered in a little more than 14 hours [55].

Unfortunately, one year before the railroad reached Quito, Major John Harman joined the thousands of workers who had given their lives to build the railroad. He died of yellow fever, quite prevalent on the Coast [60]. His brother, Archer Harman, died in an equestrian accident in Virginia in 1911. And, only a year later, fate would come to Alfaro himself; after his mandate ended, he tried unsuccessfully to regain power by force from the conservatives from the Sierra. He was captured, imprisoned, and murdered, his body dragged through the streets of Quito up to El Ejido Park (across from which we lived from 1953-1962), where he was incinerated along with the bodies of other leading members of his Liberal Party [60].

[49] With the arrival of the Spaniards in 1534, the Roman Catholic Church became the center of religious instruction and the largest patron of the arts. As part of the acculturation of the indigenous people, the Spanish established painting and sculpture schools where Spanish artists trained the indigenous population in the arts. As a result, the *Escuela Quiteña* (Quitenian School) became famous in Latin America for its talented artists. Scholars considered their contributions to colonial art some of the most valuable in America. Thus, UNESCO declared Quito a World Cultural Heritage Site in 1978.

[50] The book describes the presence of a population of poor, hard-working, industrious, Spanish people that settled in that area after the Spanish conquest of those lands led by Captain Don Juan Salinas de Loyola and the foundation of La Inmaculada Concepción de Loja on December 8, 1548, later known as Loja. They taught what they knew to local aborigines, trades that were typical and almost exclusive to the Spanish peninsular Jews. Not all their neighbors spoke well of them and they were often put down, suffering constant humiliations perhaps because of their lack of iconography or religious symbols of the Christian type. They, however, worked quietly, with dignity, and would congregate to pray in small "synagogues."

[51] At the January 31, 1935 meeting of the *Comité Internacional de Inmigración* several months after the election of President José María Velasco Ibarra, the government signed a preliminary agreement with a group of Jewish activists in France, offering the group a

concession of 1,200,000 acres of rural land to be developed by European immigrants in a largescale colonization project [48,67]. The agreement was ratified by the Ecuadorian Congress. In its first article, the government undertook to grant "free entry into the country to immigrants of the white race, coming from Europe and America, without distinction of nationality or religion" [41]. Unfortunately, the agreement was never put into practice.

[52] On January 18, 1938, an executive order by the dictator Alberto Enríquez Gallo decreed that all Jews then living in the country—barely 300—who did not work in agriculture or industry were to leave Ecuador "for the good of the country" within 30 days. This decree was never published in the Official Registry and soon after its promulgation the dictator renounced his post before the National Assembly. The law was repealed with the intervention of Julius Rosenstock, diplomatic representation, and the World Jewish Congress (WJC) [61,67].

In 1952, another law was passed requiring every foreigner to supply proof that he was engaged in the occupation stipulated in his entry visa. This legislation was counteracted by the intervention of the World Jewish Congress [39,61]. The organization tried to help those Jews who were primarily engaged in business activities but were only supposed to be in the agricultural sector. However, their attempts at agricultural settlements were unsuccessful in Ecuador and Bolivia.

[53] Weiser Varon, Benno (1913–2010), was a journalist, author, diplomat, and university lecturer. He was born in Czernowitz (Austro-Hungarian Empire, currently a city in the Ukraine). After the outbreak of World War I he moved with his family to Vienna. In 1938 he had almost completed medical studies at the University of Vienna but after the annexation of Austria by the Third Reich, he had to stop his studies. He left in the autumn of 1938 for Ecuador and settled in Quito where he succeeded in obtaining visas for his

family, his fiancée, and 150 European Jews.

In Quito, as one of the only European refugees to be proficient in Spanish, he was hired in April 1940 as a political editor by the leading newspaper of Quito, *El Comercio*, to cover the events in Europe, on which he had a daily column, "El Mirador del Mundo" ("Observer of the World"). He also wrote columns for *Ultimas Noticias* (which Hansi used to learn Spanish)—the evening edition of the newspaper.

My father knew both Benno and his brother Max but was a closer friend with the former. Benno, a lifelong Zionist, was invited in the spring of 1946 by the American Zionist leadership to join the Jewish Agency for Palestine's political efforts and to establish a regional Agency office in Bogotá, Colombia. In June 1947 he was called to New York where he headed the Latin American Department of the Jewish Agency. His main mission was to create and maintain Latin America's support at the UN for the Zionist cause and later for the State of Israel. Weiser succeeded in securing Ecuador's crucial vote, on November 29, 1947, at the special session of the UN General Assembly, in favor of the UN decision for the partition of Palestine and the establishment of a Jewish state which was declared on May 15, 1948.

In 1960 he was asked to take over the Israel Ibero-American Institute of Cultural Relations in Jerusalem and moved with his family to Israel where he lived for four years. He reported on the Eichmann trial for several newspapers. His name, Benno Weiser, was Hebraicized as "Benjamin Varon." From 1964 until 1972, he was Israel's ambassador to various Latin-American countries, first the Dominican Republic, then Jamaica and finally Paraguay. Weiser Varon terminated his diplomatic activities for the State of Israel in 1972.

In 1973, he moved to Boston, then to Brookline. He wrote articles for publications such as *Commentary, Midstream*, the *New York Times*, and the *Boston Globe*. In 1986 he was appointed professor in the department of Jewish Studies at Boston University, retiring in 2001.

In addition to the newspaper columns, Weiser also wrote poetry, essays and novels in German, Spanish and English, as well as Polish, Yiddish and Hebrew. Among his writings are *El Mirador del Mundo* (1941), *Yo era Europeo* (1942), *Visitenkarte* (1957), and *Professions of a Lucky Jew* (1992).

[54] In Quito, where eighty percent of the Jews in Ecuador lived, they formed an organization handling cultural and religious affairs, relief, and community life. They established a court of arbitration, a *Chevra Kadisha*, a women's league, a young people's organization, and an athletic group. A cooperative bank was founded, supported by the Joint Distribution Committee (JDC). They built a theater, a cemetery, a kosher restaurant. In addition, they had two newspapers, a fortnight in German and a weekly in Spanish. The large hall of the *Asociación de Beneficiencia Israelita* was rented ninety-three evenings a year for Jewish cultural events. [65]

At the beginning of the 1970s, in the course of the oil boom and thanks to easier-to-obtain entry permits, Jewish families from other Latin American countries arrived in Quito, first from Chile during Salvador Allende's presidency, and towards the end of the twentieth century, many arrived from Argentina.

In 2005, the Jewish community in Quito (pop 2M) numbered ~ 200 families, or 550-600 members. In Guayaquil ~ 20 families or some 70 members.

On June 7, 2017, I interviewed Rabbi Max Godet in Quito. At the time, the Jewish community in Quito had 150 families, or around 500 people, and Guayaquil about 20-30 families or about 100 people. Rabbi Godet, who has since left Ecuador, characterized the community as "Modern" where members participate actively in the synagogue.

55 The children's prayer, *Müde bin ich, geh' zur Ruh*, was written by Luise Hensel (1798-1876), a widely-read Catholic poet and hymn writer. It was published in 1869. The prayer is dear to the heart of many Mennonites who grew up in German-speaking homes.

Müde bin ich has found its way into many Lutheran and Mennonite hymnals, in addition to being passed down through family lore. It first appeared in a songbook for nursery school children compiled by Theodor Fliedner in Kaiserswerth, Germany in 1842.

The hymn appears in several German variations, and a number of English translations of the prayer exist. I have included Margaret Loewen Reimer's translation from the article she wrote for *The Conrad Grebel Review* in 2009. She is a Waterloo, Ontario writer and editor who has written extensively on Mennonites and the arts.

56 Pablo Better, whose parents also immigrated from Czechoslovakia, was one of my childhood friends. We took swimming lessons together during the summer and attended the same high school although we were not classmates.

Pablo became Minister of Economy in 1991 and Chairman of the Central Bank of Ecuador in 1999. I interviewed him in Quito on October 15, 2015 and on July 18, 2018.

57 On April 9, 1940, German tanks and troops swarmed into Denmark at 5:00 a.m. and into Norway late that afternoon. The pretext was "indisputable evidence" that the Allies were about to end Scandinavian neutrality. By day's end, Germany had triumphed. [73]

On May 10, 1940, Winston Churchill became Great Britain's primer minister. Before dawn on the same day, Germany invaded

Belgium, the Netherlands, and Luxembourg (the Low Countries). Nazi propaganda asserted that German troops were coming to protect the three small nations against a French and British invasion. The German invaders arrived before their excuse did!

Hitler gave no respite. Two days later the *Blitzkrieg* swept into France. German flanking movements surprised everyone by driving through the supposedly impassable Ardennes Forest which virtually broke the French Army.

Throughout the First World War the Netherlands had firmly opted for neutrality and had planned to do the same for the Second World War. Hitler realized as early as October 9, 1939, that this country was strategically lodged between Great Britain and Germany and was the ideal location for an air and naval base from where Germany could attack the British Isles.

At that time, he ordered his military to begin preparations for an invasion of the northern flank of the Western Front crossing Luxembourg, Belgium and the Netherlands. The invasion began in the early hours of May 10. The German air force, the *Luftwaffe*, attacked the Netherlands with an aerial bombardment of Rotterdam, also known as the Rotterdam Blitz, on May 14, 1940.

Germany's bombardment, in addition to causing massive destruction of the city, dropped paratroopers near the Dutch seat of government and the Royal Palace in The Hague, starting the Battle for the Hague. The Dutch army was able to temporarily slow down the German invasion but the invaders military superiority prevailed. The Dutch capitulated the morning of May 15. [73] The German army initially moved into Belgium on May 10, part of Hitler's initial western offensive, and sustained eighteen days of ceaseless German bombardment. The Belgian forces fought on, courageously, but were continually overcome by the invaders. Despite some support by British forces, the Belgians were simply outnumbered and outgunned from the beginning.

The King of Belgium asked for an armistice, the Germans demanded unconditional surrender. Belgium's government in exile, stationed in Paris, repudiated the surrender, but to no avail. Belgium had no army left to fight. King Leopold surrendered on May 28 but refused to flee the country and was taken prisoner by the Nazis during their occupation and confined to his palace. [73]

Jealous of Hitler's successes, Italian dictator Benito Mussolini, without telling Hitler, entered the war on the side of Germany on June 10, 1940. Franklin Roosevelt, the United States president, aptly described this perfidy: "The hand that held the dagger has struck it into the back of its neighbor."

The Soviet Union annexed Estonia, Latvia and Lithuania (the Baltic states) on June 15, 1940. [73] German soldiers marched into Paris on June 14, 1940, and on June 22 the French government signed an armistice with Nazi Germany. "Hitler insisted on the armistice being signed in the Compiègne Forest, where, in a railroad dining car twenty-two years earlier, Germany had been forced to sign the armistice ending World War I. The Nazis removed the rail car from a local museum and transported it to the site of the 1918 armistice for the signing." Under its terms, the Germans occupied France's northern two thirds ("occupied zone"). The French government, led by pro-fascists and German collaborators, set its capital in the town of Vich, located in the lower ("unoccupied free") zone, 220 miles south of Paris.

On July 16, 1940, Hitler's Directive 16 set out the plans for Operation Sea Lion—the invasion of England. A day later, the battle of Britain began. This battle was fought entirely by air forces with the Royal Air Force (RAF) defending the United Kingdom against the German Air Force (Luftwaffe). The RAF proved superior and lost less planes (915) than the Germans (1,733). Hitler was forced to postpone indefinitely the invasion of Britain. The battle lasted three and a half months. The Germans continued to bomb Britain's larger cities (the Blitz) [73].

58 There is a discrepancy about Móric's actual date of death: Edit's letter points to September 29 while his gravestone has September 27, 1940 inscribed on it. George found out that he died on Saturday, September 28 at 3:45 am—on Shabbat—and was buried on Monday, September 30.

59 On April 6, 1941, the Germans attacked Yugoslavia and Greece. Operation *Castigo* (the word for *punishment* in Spanish) began with the bombing of Belgrade by the German air force. It resulted in the death of 17,000 civilians—the largest number of civilian casualties in a single day since the start of the war. [73]

60 Operation Barbarossa, the German assault on the USSR was unleashed on Sunday, June 22, 1941, without a formal declaration of war. In this, his greatest gamble of the war at that point, Hitler achieved the principal advantage in the battle—surprise: the German move came as a shock to Stalin [99]. Three great army groups with over three million German soldiers, 150 divisions, and three thousand tanks smashed across the frontier into Soviet territory. The forces invading Russia represented the finest army to fight in the twentieth century. Barbarossa was the crucial turning point in World War II, for its failure forced Nazi Germany to fight a two-front war against a coalition possessing immensely superior resources. [73]

61 One day after the Japanese attacked Pearl Harbor on December 7, 1941, the Congress of the United States entered World War II by declaring war on the Empire of Japan. Great Britain and other Commonwealth and Allied nations joined the United States in this declaration. Franklin Roosevelt did not include Germany and other Axis nations in his announcement. Four days later, Hitler and

Mussolini declared war on the United States. The United States then responded with its own declaration of war against Germany and Italy, and Congress empowered its armed forces to operate anywhere in the world [73].

[62] On January 29, 1942 Ecuador was sacrificed at the PanAmerican Conference in Rio De Janeiro and forced to sign the infamous *Protocolo de Rio de Janeiro* by the group of foreign ministers of Brazil, Argentina, Chile, and the United States who called this the "Protocol of Peace, Friendship, and Boundaries between Perú and Ecuador." According to this agreement, Ecuador renounced its rights to 77,000 square miles of its southern and eastern territories which included a large portion of the Amazon (*Oriente*) and agreed to withdraw its long-standing claim for rights to direct land access to the Marañon and Amazon rivers.

With its recent entry into World War II, the United States was eager to present a united American continent and was instrumental in imposing its will and influence on these foreign ministers; it forced Ecuador into signing the agreement and acquiescing to the Peruvian demands.

[63] Isidro Ayora graduated as a surgeon at the age of 26 from the Central University of Ecuador in Quito. He obtained a postgraduate scholarship in Germany and for four years he studied at the universities of Dresden and Berlin, where he specialized in obstetrics and gynecology.

Upon returning to Ecuador in 1909, he was appointed professor of obstetrics at the Central University and Director of the Maternity of Quito, a position he held for twenty consecutive years. By that time he had founded, along with doctors Angel Suarez and Ricardo Villavicencio, the Surgical Clinic of Quito on May 1, 1911, which was later called *Clinica Ayora,* where I was born.

In 1918 he founded and directed the Nursing School. He created the first Cuna House, directed the hospital San Juan de Dios, was elected Dean of the School of Medicine and subsequently President of the Central University.

In 1916 he entered politics and was elected to the National Congress by the province of Loja. Later, in 1924, he was appointed President of the Municipal Council of Quito and later that year he was elected Mayor of Quito, a position he occupied between January 1 and December 31 of 1925.

In January of 1926 while he was President of the Central University he was called by the Army to integrate the Second Provisional Junta of Government as Acting President of the Republic, and from 1929 to 1931 he was its constitutional President.

After renouncing the presidency of the Republic on August 24, 1931, he returned to the practice of medicine and also devoted himself to agriculture. He resided for six years in the United States and, in 1957, returned to direct the Maternity hospital in Quito which today bears his name.

He enjoyed gardening and taking long strolls. In the mid fifties, during one of his walks along the park across our home, my father introduced him to me as we walked by.

In 1966 he retired from professional activity and moved to the city of Los Angeles, California, where he died on March 22, 1978.

[64] On May 8, 1945 Germany surrenders. The war in Europe ends. [73] Victory in Europe Day, generally known as VE Day (Great Britain) or V-E Day (North America), is a day celebrating the formal acceptance by the Allies of World War II of Nazi Germany's unconditional surrender of its armed forces on May 8, 1945. The instrument of surrender was signed a day earlier and stipulated that all hostilities had to stop at 23:01 (CET), 8 May 1945, just

an hour before midnight. Small pockets of fighting still continued into the next day. German and Soviet forces confronted each other in Silesia on May 9. The Soviets lost 600 more soldiers before the Germans finally laid down their arms.

Upon the defeat of Germany, celebrations erupted throughout the western world, especially in Great Britain and North America. Tempering the jubilation somewhat, both Churchill and Truman pointed out that the war against Japan had not yet been won. Japan didn't surrender until August 15, 1945. Their surrender became official on September 2, 1945.

Seventy million people fought in WWII. The Soviet Union lost 7.5 million soldiers, the most of any country involved in the war. Other major players in the Allied powers saw massive casualties as well. The U.S. lost 400,000, Great Britain lost 330,000, and China lost 2.2 million. Among the Axis powers, the German army saw 3.5 million casualties, Italy lost 77,000 and Japan lost 1.2 million.

While the war was coming to an end, survivors of the concentration camps continued to suffer. When they returned home, they found their former lives destroyed and their communities gone. Many survivors lost their entire families and had no home to return to.

[65] In March 1969, Sophie, Oli, and Vivian traveled to Quito to attend, along with Hansi, Virginia and Edulka, the Central University of Ecuador School of Medicine ceremony in which I was awarded the 1968 summa cum laude Gold Medal. They all stayed at Hansi and Virginia's home. During their trips to the US, he, Virginia, Edulka, and Oli, visited Sophie and Sam at their home.

Over the years, in their letters, Hansi and Virginia always asked me to convey their regards to both Sophie and Lillian. They also on a few occasions exchanged New Year's greeting cards. In 1970, Hansi wrote to Sophie, thanking her for the "two wonderful children she had with him."

Hansi, Vanessa, Elaine, Sophie, Oli, Virginia, Edulka and Vivian. Quito, 1969.

Hansi with Vanessa. Quito, 1969.

Hansi with Edulka and Oli. Quito, 1969.

Sophie and Hansi at her Miami home. 1972

My father on a few occasions called and wrote to Sophie about Oli. In June 1971, when he learned that Oli and German Lugo were getting married, he called Sophie to inquire about German. He knew nothing about him. Sophie assured him. Soon after the wedding he learned they would be moving to Venezuela. In his letters George could feel the overwhelming concern he had about this move. And, after it took place, several weeks went by without him receiving any news from Oli. In his desperation, Hansi wrote to Sophie several times asking her to share any news she might have. He did not always receive a reply and Oli would drop a few lines which helped somewhat with his anxiety and depression.

[66] Sam was born on October 5, 1919 in Teschen-Poland (a town that was half Polish and half Czech). He was the youngest of five siblings: two brothers, Leopold, fifteen years older and Sigi, twelve years older; and two sisters, Berta, thirteen years older and Rosa, four years older.

He was trained as a furrier and by 1938 he was working in this profession in Prague. That year, after the Anschluss, the three brothers bought visas for the whole family to go to Ecuador. Sam was 19 yrs old at the time. He decided not to travel out of Europe with his brothers, and instead went to Teschen after Germany invaded Poland on September 1, 1939. He wanted to convince his father to leave but he refused.

In late 1939, Leopold and Sigi went to France by train and from there to Ecuador. Leopold became a money lender and also sold cars. He was in Ecuador from 1939-1946 and then emigrated to the United States. Sigi was a hat maker and lived in Ecuador from 1939 through 1947 and he emigrated then to the United States settling in New York City.

Sam remained in Teschen to protect his father and was soon captured by the Gestapo and was sent to the Mienkiñea concentration camp and transferred in the following five years to four other camps (Dembica, Plaszow-Krakow, Gross-Rosen and finally Buchenwald. His father and sisters perished in the Holocaust.

After Buchenwald was liberated by the U.S. Army in 1945, Sam was sent to a field hospital in Germany (Bad Salzungen). After his discharge, he went first to Canada but was not allowed to remain in the country because he was a Jew. Then he went to Paris for a year and in 1947 traveled to the US with a visitor's visa. When the visa expired, he had to leave as he could not get an affidavit to stay. Since he had an Ecuadorian visa, he traveled there in 1947 to visit Sigi just before he left for the US.

For many years, Sam refused to talk about his concentration camp experience. He later acknowledged that he lost his faith after witnessing the murder of so many children during the Holocaust. He could not understand how God would allow that to happen.

After my mother died in 1981, Sam became an active member of Temple Zion Israelite Center, serving as *Gabbai* and Haftorah Chanter every other week, as well as *Chazaan Sheni* for several years. He was a member of Bet Breira Samu-EL Or Olom synagogue for several years prior to his death.

Sam enjoyed the weekly Sunday morning services and breakfasts with synagogue buddies during his many years at Temple Zion. He was a frequent speaker on his Holocaust experiences at various public and private schools throughout the county. He very much enjoyed interacting with and educating the students. After his death, Kenny and I found a large suitcase filled with letters and postcards from students wishing him well and thanking him for his presentations. He was very proud to have been interviewed for Steven Spielberg's Survivors of the Shoah Foundation.

Sam Luftig at Karen and Jason's wedding; August 2006

Virginia; Quito, December 1970

[67] Virginia was born in Manta, Ecuador on March 26, 1918 into a Catholic family. She had a younger brother, José Salvador Moreira, who lived with his family and their mother in Guayaquil, Ecuador. She was in charge of the cosmetics department at an import-export firm (Casa Ortega) in Quito, owned by a second cousin of hers. This was the same firm Hansi joined in 1952.

[68] These joyful trips, particularly to El Tingo, also had a downside and often could be quite miserable: there were plenty of mosquitoes that throughout the day—but mainly during summer evenings or dewy mornings—tracked you down and left you with itchy red welts where they punctured your skin and sucked blood. There was no place to hide. They would find you, even indoors. There were no insect-free areas and no effective insect repellent measures.

[69] Every year, for example, he received an invitation from the United States Embassy to attend its Fourth of July reception. Elaine, a US Citizen, never got such an invitation. Hansi would invite her to come along.

[70] In 1973, during my two-year US Army tour, my father sent me a newspaper clip about Chile's former military attaché to Ecuador, who had just become Chile's president after the death of Salvador Allende and the military takeover of September 11, 1973. He was the commander-in- chief of the Chilean army from 1973 to 1998. He had been a guest in our home several years earlier. I recognized his photograph. It was Augusto Pinochet!

[71] In 1964, a mammogram showed a suspicious mass in her left breast. She underwent a modified radical mastectomy. The pathology report stated that all axillary nodes were negative. Hormone receptor studies were not available at the time. She was considered to have Stage I breast cancer and no adjuvant therapy was recommended.

[72] Superior vena cava syndrome is a group of symptoms caused by the compression of the vena cava, a major vein. It carries blood from the head, neck, upper chest, and arms to the heart. The syndrome occurs when this vein is partially blocked or compressed, and usually develops slowly. Common symptoms include: difficulty breathing or shortness of breath, coughing, swelling of the face, neck, upper body, and arms.

Chapter Three

[73] Lučenec [Slovak], Losonc [Hungarian] is a town in the Banská Bystrica region of south-central Slovakia. In the 19th and 20th centuries, new industries like brickworks and tanneries were built, giving the town industrial recognition. In 1871, it was connected to the railway between Budapest and Žilina. After WW1, Lučenec became part of Czechoslovakia, and, briefly in 1919, part of the Slovak Soviet Republic.

On November 2, 1938, southern Slovakia, including Lučenec and towns around it, were annexed to Hungary as a result of the Munich Agreement. On November 10, 1938, the Hungarian army occupied the city. The Jews were targets of agitation, and as the time passed, they lost their fundamental rights. They were accused in inflammatory articles in newspapers. Some Jews were arrested and tortured. In 1941 many Jewish youths were impressed into forced labor battalions. Some 18,000 Jews randomly designated by the Hungarian authorities as "Jewish foreign nationals" were kicked out of their homes and deported to Kamenets-Podolsk in the Ukraine, where most were murdered. In early 1942, another 1,000 Jews in the section of Hungary newly acquired from Yugoslavia were murdered by Hungarian soldiers and police in their "pursuit of partisans."

In March 1944, when the Germans occupied Hungary, other harsh laws, both economic and general decrees, were levied on the Jews. A *Judenrat* was established in Lučenec at the beginning of May 1944 with an order to concentrate all of the area's Jews in a ghetto. In June 1944, many Jews were concentrated into a local brick factory, and from there they were transported to Auschwitz. After the war, in 1945, Lučenec was returned to Czechoslovakia. Finally, when the peaceful split of the country took place on January 1, 1993, Lučenec once again became part of Slovakia.

[74] *HaShomer HaTza'ir* was the name of the political party of the Jewish community in the pre-1948 British Mandate of Palestine. It is the oldest Zionist youth movement still in existence.

[75] Starting in 1938, Hungary under Miklós Horthy passed a series of anti-Jewish measures in emulation of Germany's Nuremberg Laws.

The first, promulgated on May 29, 1938, restricted the number of Jews in each commercial enterprise, in the press, among physicians, engineers and lawyers to twenty percent.

The second anti-Jewish law (May 5, 1939), for the first time, defined Jews racially: individuals with two, three or four Jewish-born grandparents were declared Jewish regardless of the religion they practiced. Their employment in government at any level was forbidden, they could not be editors at newspapers, their numbers were restricted to six per cent among theater and movie actors, physicians, lawyers and engineers. Private companies were forbidden to employ more than 12% Jews and most of them lost their right to vote as well.

The "Third Jewish Law" (August 8, 1941), known in Hungarian history as the racist ("race protecting") law, prohibited intermarriage and penalized sexual intercourse between Jews and non-Jews.

[76] This satellite camp was designed from the outset, in 1943, for

both men and women prisoners. The first known prisoner transport arrived at Barth in November 1943. Overall, it is estimated that its prisoner population reached 7,000 men and women from more than 20 nations and included Jews, Gypsies, and "asocials" (those considered to be living outside of social norms, like prostitutes, homosexuals, and drug addicts). They had the toughest living conditions, with 12-hour forced labor in the aircraft assembly lines, the harassment of SS guards, and hunger. Hundreds of prisoners died of starvation or were shot for sabotaging their work. More than 5,000 women and men had to work there in a branch of the Rostock Heinkel aircraft factory from November 1943 to April 1945. While the women worked in the production of parts on the assembly lines, men performed more sophisticated assembly work on aircraft components.

On April 30, 1945, the SS forced those prisoners capable of marching to do so in several columns in a westerly direction. Around 300 seriously ill and completely exhausted male prisoners stayed behind and were liberated by the Red Army on May 1, 1945. [81]

[77] Košice is the largest city in eastern Slovakia and the second largest in the country. Prior to World War I, the town belonged to the Austro- Hungarian empire. After that war it became part of Czechoslovakia.

Following the Viennese arbitration of November 2, 1938, Košice wa annexed to Hungary for more than six years. Soon after the annexation, anti-Semitic legislation hit the Jewish community hard. Jews were deprived of jobs and their property. Every year afterwards, the Hungarian authorities deported thousands of Jews for alleged lack of citizenship to camps where they were killed.

After the German forces occupied Hungary on March 19, 1944, the deportation of Jews to Auschwitz began. Some 15,707 Jews were deported.

In 1945, Košice became part of Czechoslovakia again until 1993, when the Czech Republic and Slovakia peacefully split.

[78] On August 29, 1944, 60,000 Slovak troops and 18,000 partisans organized by various underground groups and the Czechoslovak government-in-exile, rose up against the Nazis and its collaborators. The insurrection became known as the Slovak National Uprising.

A number of Jewish partisan groups operated across Nazi-occupied Europe, some made up of a few escapees from the Jewish ghettos or concentration camps, while others, such as the Bielski partisans, numbered in the hundreds and included women and children.

Many individual Jewish fighters also took part in the partisan movements in other occupied countries. In all, the Jewish partisans numbered between 20,000 and 30,000.

The partisans engaged in guerrilla warfare and sabotage against the Nazi occupation, instigated ghetto uprisings, and freed prisoners. In Lithuania alone, they killed approximately 3,000 German soldiers. They sometimes had contacts within the ghettos, camps, Judenrats, and other resistance groups, with whom they shared military intelligence.

The Jewish partisans had to overcome great odds in acquiring weapons, food, shelter and evading capture. They typically lived in underground dugouts and camps in the forests. Nazi reprisals were brutal, as they employed collective punishment against their supporters and the ghettos from which partisans had escaped, and often used "anti-partisan actions" as a guise for the extermination of Jews.

The partisans operated under constant threat of starvation. Those who managed to flee the ghettos and camps had nothing more than the clothes on their backs, which often were reduced to rags through constant wear. The forests also concealed family encampments where Jewish escapees from concentration camps or ghettos, many of whom were too young or too old to fight, hoped to wait out the war. While some partisan groups required combat readiness and weapons as a condition for joining, many noncombatants found shelter with Jewish fighting groups and their allies. These individuals and families contributed to the welfare of the group by working as craftsmen, cooks, seamstresses, and field medics.

Ultimately, the 1944 uprising was crushed by the Germans and their Hungarian and Ukranian collaborators. [84,86]

[79] Sered' is located 34 miles east from Bratislava. It was the site of one of three forced-labor transit camps for Jews established in the Slovak state, a Nazi client state during World War II. The Slovak authorities utilized the camp as a detention center for Jews and as a staging ground for deportation to eastern concentration camps. During the winter of 1944 and spring of 1945, 13,500 Jews were deported from Sered' to Auschwitz and Theresienstadt. The camp was liberated by the Red Army on 1 April 1945.

[80] Sachsenhausen-Oranienburg was a Nazi concentration camp inOranienburg, Germany, just 22 miles north of Berlin, used primarily for political prisoners from 1936 to the end of the Third Reich in May 1945.

A large task force of prisoners was used from the camp in nearby brickworks to meet Albert Speer's vision of rebuilding Berlin.

In November 1938, after Kristallnacht, about 6,000 Jewish prisoners arrived. In 1942 large numbers of Jewish prisoners were relocated to Auschwitz.

In the final months of the war, there were over 66,000 prisoners at the camp, their numbers increased with the evacuation of camps closer to the front [78].

As in other Nazi camps, Jewish prisoners were singled out for harsh treatment. In March 1943, gas chambers and ovens were built in order to facilitate the means of killing large numbers of inmates. In a room next to the crematorium, prisoners who believed they were having their height measured were shot in the nape of the neck through a hole in the wall. A gallows in the roll call area was used for hanging. Shootings were more common and often took place in a special pit in the industrial yard. The camp also provided unwilling subjects for often fatal medical experiments.

Disease, malnutrition, and exhaustion claimed the majority of lives lost at Sachsenhausen. As bad as conditions were, however, they did not become so dire as at many other camps until late in the war.

When the Red Army arrived at the main camp on April 2, 1945, only about 3,000 incapacitated prisoners remained there. The rest were marching to the northwest, where those who survived were gradually liberated over the next two weeks.

Between 40,000 and 50,000 prisoners died at the camp from 1936 through 1945. [81]

[81] Nahariya is the northernmost coastal city in Israel. It was settled by German Jewish immigrants who had escaped from Nazi persecution. Taking advantage of the natural surroundings and beaches, Nahariya was turned into a European-style resort town.

In 1948, the year of Israel's formation, Nahariya had a population of 1,700. In the 1950s it became a development town after a ma'abara established nearby was integrated. The town hence become a home to many Jewish refugees from North Africa, the Middle East and Europe. It had a population of 9,800 in 1955, which had increased to 23,800 in 1972. During the 1990s, the city absorbed a significant number of immigrants from the former Soviet Union and Ethiopia. In the late 1990s and early 2000s, Nahariya experienced a construction boom.

Due to its geographic location, 6.0 miles down the coast from Israel's border with Lebanon, Nahariya had been a frequent target of cross- border terrorist attacks by Palestinian militants, mortar attacks, and Katyusha rocket fire during the 1970s.

During the Lebanon War in July through August 2006, Nahariya sustained a barrage of several hundreds of Katyusha rockets launched by Hezbollah from southern Lebanon. As a result, the city suffered multiple civilian casualties and five fatalities. Significant damage was also inflicted on property and physical infrastructure. Nahariya's economy suffered a major blow, as two-thirds of the city's population had to evacuate, with the rest spending weeks in bomb shelters. By 2016, its population had grown to 54,903.

[82] Is the capital of the Republic of Slovakia. It is the largest city in Slovakia with an estimated population of about 430,000 although the greater metropolitan area population is nearing 650,000 inhabitants.

Bratislava is in southwestern Slovakia, occupying both banks of the River Danube and the left bank of the River Morava. Bordering Austria and Hungary, it is the only national capital that borders two sovereign states. It is only 11.2 miles from the border with Hungary and only 37.3 miles from the Austrian capital Vienna.

Bratislava is the political, cultural and economic center of Slovakia. It is the seat of the Slovak president, the parliament and the Slovak Executive. It has several universities, and many museums, theatres, galleries and other cultural and educational institutions. Many of Slovakia's large businesses and financial institutions have headquarters there.

In 2017, Bratislava was ranked as the third richest region of the European Union by GDP (PPP) per capita (after Hamburg and Luxembourg City). Bratislava has also benefited from tourism: around 1 million tourists visit the city every year.

In 1941–1942 and 1944–1945, the new Slovak government cooperated in deporting most of Bratislava's approximately 15,000 Jews; they were transported to concentration camps, where most were killed or died before the end of the war.

Bratislava was bombarded by the Allies, occupied by German troops in 1944, and eventually taken by troops of the Soviet 2nd Ukrainian Front on 4 April 1945. After the Communist Party seized power in Czechoslovakia in February 1948, the city became part of the Eastern Bloc. In 1968, after the unsuccessful Czechoslovak attempt to liberalize the Communist regime, the city was occupied by Warsaw Pact troops. Shortly thereafter, it became capital of the Slovak Socialist Republic, one of the two states of the federalized Czechoslovakia.

Bratislava's dissidents anticipated the fall of Communism with the Bratislava candle demonstration in 1988 against the one-party government of the Communist Party of Czechoslovakia. The city became one of the foremost centers of the anti-Communist nonviolent and bloodless demonstrations from November 17 to December 29, 1989 led by students and older dissidents which became known as the Velvet Revolution.

On January 1, 1993, after 41 years of one-party rule, Czechoslovakia split into two independent countries: the Czech Republic and the Slovak Republic with Bratislava as its capital.

[83] Kfar Masaryk is a kibbutz in northern Israel. The founders were immigrants from Czechoslovakia and Lithuania.

[84] Trigeminal neuralgia is a chronic inflammatory pain condition

that affects the trigeminal nerve, which carries sensation from the face to the brain. With trigeminal neuralgia, even mild stimulation of the face—such as from brushing teeth or putting on makeup—might trigger a jolt of excruciating pain.

Sufferers might initially experience short, mild attacks. But trigeminal neuralgiacan progress and cause longer, more-frequent bouts of searing pain.

Trigeminal neuralgia affects women more often than men, and it's more likely to occur in people who are older than 50. Because of the variety of treatment options available, having trigeminal neuralgia doesn't necessarily mean one is doomed to a life of pain. Doctors usually can effectively manage trigeminal neuralgia with medications, injections, or surgery.

[85] Tante Fini in Bratislava: Josephine Strelinger née Pikler [1903-1992] was Hansi's first cousin. Her father was Armin Pikler, Móric's brother. She had no children. We spent a lovely afternoon with her. A friend of her translated the conversations which mostly centered around the 'good old days' and the wonderful relationships all cousins had when the family lived close by.

Bibliography

1. Pikler, Endré A. *"Letter to My Dear Charliepikler."* Norwich, Connecticut, December 24, 1951.

2. Pratt, Michael. W. and Barbara Fiese, eds. *Family Stories and the Life Course: Across Time and Generations.* Mahwah, NJ: Lawrence Erlbaum Associates Publishers, 2004.

3. Duke, Marshall. P., Amber Lazarus, and Robyn Fivush. "Knowledge of Family History as a Clinically Useful Index of Psychological Well-Being and Prognosis: A Brief Report," 268-272. In *Psychotherapy Theory, Research, Practice, Training,* vol. 45, 2008.

4. Duke, Marshall P. "The Stories That Bind Us: What Are the Twenty Questions?" https://www.huffingtonpost.com/marshall-p-duke/the-stories-that-bind-us-_b_2918975.html.

5. Rottenberg, Dan. *Finding Our Fathers. A Guidebook to Jewish Genealogy.* New York: Random House, 1977.

6. Frankl, Peter and Pavel Frankl. *Židia v Žiline.* Bratislava: EDIS, 2008.

7. Cicaj, Viliam, Vladimir Seges, Julius Bartl, Dušan Skvarna. *Slovak History: Chronology and Lexicon.* Bolchazy-Carducci Publications, 2002.

8. Jelinek, Yesheyahu. "The Jews in Slovakia: 1945-1949" In *The Jews of Czechoslovakia. Historical Studies and Surveys. Vol III.* Philadelphia: The Jewish Publication Society of America, and New York: Society for The History of Czechoslovak Jews, 1984.

9. Klein-Pejšová, Rebekah. *"An Overview of the History of Jews in Slovakia." Slovak Jewish Heritage,* 2006. http://www.slovak-jewish-heritage.org/history-of-jews-in-slovakia html.

10. Schoenberg, Randol and Julius Mueller. "Getting Started With Czech- Jewish Genealogy." https://www.jewishgen.org/austriaczech/czechguide.html. Latest update August 19, 2013.

11. "Austria-Hungary." wikipedia.org/wiki/Austria-Hungary. Last edited June 3, 2020.

12. Subtelny, Orest. *Ukraine: A History.* 4th ed. Toronto, Ontario: University of Toronto Press, 2009.

13. Dimont, Max. *Jews, God and History.* New York: Penguin Books, 2003.

14. Stransky, H. "The Religious Life in Slovakia and Subcarpathian Ruthenia." In *The Jews of Czechoslovakia, Historical Studies and Surveys, vol. II.* Philadelphia: The Jewish Publication Society of America, and New York: Society for the History of Czechoslovak Jews, 1971.

15. "Eszterházy" Last edited May 31, 2020. https://en.wikipedia.org/wiki/Eszterházy.

16. "Familiants Laws" in *Jewish Virtual Library.* http://www.jewishvirtuallibrary.org/familiants-laws.

17. Cerman, Ivo. "Familiant Laws." http://yivoencyclopedia.org/printarticle.aspx?id=163.

18. Personal correspondence with Vladimir Lipscher, December 2017 and January 2018.

19. Rothkirchen, Livia. *"Slovakia: II."* In *The Jews of Czechoslovakia. Historical Studies and Surveys. Vol I.* Philadelphia: The Jewish

Publication Society of America, and New York: Society for the History of Czechoslovak Jews, 1968.

20. Schma, Simon. *The Story of the Jews. Belonging 1492-1900*. Vol. 2. 1ˢᵗ ed. Broadway, New York: HarperCollins Publishers, 2017.

21. *"Joseph II, Holy Roman Emperor." https://en.wikipedia.org/wiki/ Joseph II, Holy Roman Emperor. Date last modified: May 26, 2020.*

22. *"The Enlightened Despots, Joseph II of Austria."* https://www. biography.com/political-figure/joseph-ii.

23. Kohn, Hans. "Before 1918 in the Historic Lands." In *The Jews of Czechoslovakia. Historical Studies and Surveys. Vol I.* Philadelphia: The Jewish Publication Society of America, and New York: Society for the History of Czechoslovak Jews, 1968.

24. Teich, Mikuláš, Dušan Kováč, and Martin Brown, eds. *Slovakia in History*. Cambridge University Press, 2011.

25. Korbel, Joseph. *Twentieth-Century Czechoslovakia: The Meanings of Its History.* New York: Columbia University Press, 1977.

26. Rothkirchen, Livia. *"The Jews of Bohemia and Moravia:1938-1945."* In *The Jews of Czechoslovakia. Historical Studies and Surveys, Vol III.* New York: The Jewish Publication Society of America, Philadelphia and Society for the History of Czechoslovak Jews, 1984.

27. Miller, Michael L. *Rabbis and Revolution: The Jews of Moravia in the Age of Emancipation.* Stanford: Stanford University Press, 2010.

28. Gordon, Haim. *The Rise and Decline of the Jewish Community of Žilina: Memorial Booklet.* Jerusalem, Israel: Private ed. 2003.

29. Broadberry, Stephen and Mark Harrison. *The Economics of World War I*. Cambridge: Cambridge University Press, 2005.

30. Berenbaum, Michael and Fred Skolnik. *"The Events."* In *Encyclopedia Judaica*, 325-343. Vol.9. 2nd ed. Detroit: Macmillan Reference USA, 2007.

31. Spitzer, Leo. *Hotel Bolivia: The Culture of Memory in a Refuge From Nazism*. New York: Hill and Wang, ed. 1968.

32. Wischnitzer, Mark. *To Dwell in Safety: The Story of Jewish Migration Since 1800*. Jewish Publication Society of America, 1948.

33. Jelinek, Yeshayahu. *The Parish Republic: Hlinka's Slovak People's Party, 1939-1945*. New York and London: Columbia University Press, 1976.

34. Hayes, Kathleen. *The Journalism of Milena Jesenská. A Critical Voice in Interwar Central Europe*. Berghahn Books, 2003.

35. Lipscher, Ladislav. *Die Juden im slowakischen Staat, 1939–1945*. Munich: 1980.

36. Yahil, Leni. *The Holocaust: The Fate of European Jewry, 1932-1945*. New York: Oxford University Press, Inc, 1990.

37. Grossman, Kurt. R. *"Refugees to and from Czechoslovakia."* In *The Jews of Czechoslovakia. Historical Studies and Surveys. Vol II*. Philsdelphia: Jewish Publication Society of America, and New York: Society for the History of Czechoslovak Jews, 1971.

38. Lipscher, Ladislav. *"The Jews of Slovakia: 1939-1945."* In *The Jews of Czechoslovakia. Historical Studies and Surveys. Vol III*. Philadelphia: The Jewish Publication Society of America, and New York: Society for the History of Czechoslovak Jews, 1984.

39. Kreuter, Marie-Luise. *Wo leigt Ecuador?: Exil in einem unbekannten Land 1938 bis zum Ende der funfziger Jahre (Reihe Dokumente, Texte, Materialien).* German ed. Metropol, 1995.

40. Elkin, Judith L, and G, W. Merkx. *The Jewish Presence in Latin America.* Boston: Allen & Unwin, Inc., 1987.

41. Sobel, Louis. *"Jewish Community Life and Organization in Latin America." In The Jewish Social Service Quarterly*, 2-4, 20(4), June 1944.

42. Avni, Haim. *Argentina and the Jews: A History of Jewish Immigration.* The University of Alabama Press, 2002.

43. Lesser, Jeffrey. *Welcoming the Undesirables: Brazil and the Jewish Question. Berkeley, Los Angeles, Oxford.* University of California Press, 1995.

44. Tartakower, A and K, R. Grossmann. *The Jewish Refugee.* Institute of Jewish Affairs of the American Jewish Congress and World Jewish Congress, 1944.

45. zur Mühlen, P. von. *Fluchtziel Lateinamerika: Die deutsche Emigration 1933-1945: Politische Aktivitäten und Soziokulturelle Integration.* Bonn: Verlag Neue Gesellschaft, 1988.

46. Agar, Herbert. *The Saving Remnant: An Account of Jewish Survival Since 1914.* New York: Viking Press, 1960.

47. Linke, Lilo. *Andean Adventure: A Social and Political Study of Colombia, Ecuador and Bolivia.* London: Hutchinson & Co. LTD., 1945.

48. Kersffeld, Daniel. *La Migración Judía en Ecuador. Ciencia, Cultura y Exilio 1933-1945.* Quito, Ecuador: Academia Nacional de Historia, Artes Gráficas SILVA, 2018.

49. Strauss, Herbert. A. *Jewish Emigration from Germany: Nazi Policies and Jewish Responses*. Leo Baeck Institute, Year Book 26, no.1 (1981): no. 25 362.

50. Smith, Eugene W. *Passenger Ships of the World: Past and Present*. Boston: George H. Dean Co, 1963.

51. Marrus, Michael R and Robert R. Paxton. *Vichy France and the Jews*. Stanford: Stanford University Press, 1995.

52. Wischnitzer, Mark. *Visas to Freedom: The History of HIAS*. Cleveland: The World Publishing Company, 1956.

53. Jeanmougin, Yves and Robert Mencherini. *Memory of the Camp des Milles, 1939-1942*. Marseille: Métamorphoses, 2013.

54. Cesarani, David. *Final Solution. The Fate of the Jews 1933-1949*. New York: St. Martin's Press, 2016.

55. Linke, Lilo. *Ecuador: Country of Contrasts*. Third ed. London, New York, Toronto: Oxford University Press, 1960.

56. Acosta, Alberto. *Breve Historia Económica del Ecuador*. Corporación Editora Nacional, 3ra ed. 2012.

57. Eichler, Arturo. *Ecuador: Nieve y Selva: Snow Peaks and Jungles*. Edición del Autor. ed. Bilingüe Edition. Quito, Ecuador, 1970.

58. Lauderbaugh, George. *The History of Ecuador*. Santa Barbara, CA: Greenwood, 2012.

59. Cohen, J.X. *Jewish Life in South America: A Survey Study for The American Jewish Congress*. New York: Bloch Publishing Company, 1941.

60. Meneses, Marcelo and Jorge Vinueza. *Tren al Sol. Travesías A Bordo del Ferrocarril de Vapor Más Difícil del Mundo*. Ecuador: Trama, 2006.

61. Grubel Rosenthal, Manuel. *Ecuador: Destino de Migrantes. Una Biografía de la Comunidad Judía del Ecuador. Quito*, Ecuador: PPL Impresores, 2010.

62. Cohen, Martin. A. *The Jewish Experience in Latin America.* American Jewish Historical Society, Vol I. New York: KTAV Publishing House, Inc, 1971.

63. Ordóñez Chiriboga, R. *La Herencia Sefardita En La Provincia De Loja.* Quito, Ecuador: Casa de la Cultura Ecuatoriana, 2005.

64. Alexander, Gabriel. E. "*Casual Sanctuary or Permanent Settlement: Jewish Immigration to the Republic of Ecuador, 1933-1950." Personal correspondence,* 2001.

65. Roth, Cecil and Geoffrey Wigoder. "Ecuador." In *Encyclopedia Judaica*, Israel: Keter Publishing, December, 1944.

66. Hurtado, Osvaldo. *Las costumbres de los Ecuatorianos.* Editorial Planeta del Ecuador, 2007.

67. Beller, Jacob. *Jews in Latin America.* New York: Jonathan David Publishers, 1969.

68. Weiser-Varon, Benno. "Ecuador: Eight Years on Ararat. The Story of a South American Haven." *Commentary Magazine*, June 1, 1947.

69. Weiser-Varon, Benno. *Professions of a Lucky Jew.* New York, London, Toronto: Cornwall Books, 1992.

70. Hart, Peter: *The Great War. A Combat History of the First World War.* New York: Oxford University Press, 2015.

71. Palmer, R.R, Colton, J and Kramer L: *A History of Europe in the Modern World.* 11th ed. Vol 2. New York: McGraw Hill, 2014.

72. Hochschild, Adam. *To End All Wars. A Story of Loyalty and Rebellion, 1914-1918.* Boston, New York: Mariner Books. Houghton Mifflin Harcourt, 2012.

73. Davidson, Edward and Dale Manning. *Chronology of World War Two.* London: Cassell & Co., 1999.

74. Rothkirchen, Livia. *The Jews of Bohemia and Moravia: Facing the Holocaust. Lincoln:* University of Nebraska Press *and Jerusalem: Yad Vashem,* 2005.

75. Shirer, William. *The Rise and Fall of the Third Reich: A History of Nazi Germany.* New York: Simon & Schuster. 50 Anv. ed. 2011.

76. Dawidowicz, Lucy S. *The War Against the Jews: 1933-1945.* New York: Bantam Books, 1986.

77. Volavkova, Hana. *I Never Saw Another Butterfly: Children's Drawings and Poems from Terezín Concentration Camp, 1942-1944.* 2nd ed. McGraw-Hill Book Company, 1971.

78. Megargee, Geoffrey.P and Joseph R. White. eds. *The United States Holocaust Memorial Museum Encyclopedia of Camps and Ghettos, 1933-1945.* Indiana University Press, 2018.

79. Prečan, Vilém. "The Slovak National Uprising: The Most Dramatic Moment in the Nation's History." In *Slovakia in History.* Teich, Mikuláš, Dusan Kováč, and Martin Brown, eds. Cambridge: Cambridge University Press, 2011.

80. Feig, Konnilyn G. *Hitler's Death Camps: The Sanity of Madness.* New York, London: Holmes & Meier Publishers, 1981.

81. Lipscher, Ladislav. *"Jewish Participation in the Slovak Resistance Movement."* In *Soviet Jewish Affairs,* Vol. 7, Issue 2, July 1, 1977.

82. Tillion, Germaine. *Ravensbrück.* trans. by Gerald Satterwhite. Garden City, New York: Anchor Press/Doubleday,1975.

83. Buber-Neumann, Margarete. *Under Two Dictators. Prisoner of Stalin and Hitler. London: Pimlico and Random House, UK, 2008.*

84. Morrison, Jack G. *Ravensbrück: Everyday Life in a Women's Concentration Camp 1939-45. Princeton:* Markus Wiener Publishers, 2000.

85. Wachsmann, Nikolaus. *KL–A History of the Nazi Concentration Camps.* New York: Farrar, Straus and Giroux, 2015.

Concentration Camp Addendum

Terezín (Theresienstadt)

Terezín, located about 44 miles north-northwest of Prague, was built by the Austrian Emperor Joseph II between 1780 and 1790 and named it after his mother, the Empress Maria Theresa (who hated Jews). Its existence as a fortress town dominated its history. It consisted of the "Great Fortress" on the east side of the Ohre river and the "Small Fortress" on the left side of the river. The Small Fortress was a notorious Habsburg-era detention site.

After Germany invaded and occupied Czechoslovakia, on June 10, 1940, the Gestapo took control of Terezín and set up a prison in the Small Fortress. By November 24, 1941, the Nazis adapted the Great Fortress (the walled town of Theresienstadt), located on the west side of the river, as a ghetto.

After the Sarajevo assassination of Archduke Franz Ferdinand of Austria and his wife on June 28, 1914, it was at Terezín that the Austrian government jailed several of the murderers, including the ringleader, Gavrilo Princip, who died of tuberculosis in April 18, 1918. During World War I, Terezín became the largest Czech POW camp.

In 1940, Terezín hardly looked any different from the town of a hundred years earlier: it housed 3,700 people living in 219 homes, plus the barracks with a normal capacity of 3,500 soldiers. The camp was established on November 24, 1941. By June 1942, the SS forcibly expelled Czechoslovakia's non-Jewish inhabitants. It was this town that became the famous Terezín ghetto.

Originally intended for the Protectorate Jews, Terezín later held Jews from Germany, Austria, The Netherlands, Slovakia, Hungary and Denmark. In that "luxury camp," prisoners were not actually exterminated. They died instead of hunger, torture, beatings, and disease. At one point nearly 60,000 individuals were concentrated in a town with a "normal" living space for 7,000. Whenever the Nazis wished to reduce the congestion, they mercilessly dispatched large convoys to the gas chambers of Auschwitz and Majdanek. 200,000 people, most of them Jewish, passed through the three-camp complex: the ghetto, Small Fortress, and Litomerice/Richard. Only a third lived to see the end of the war. 34,000 Jews perished in from "natural causes." As the ghetto became a funnel to the killing centers, the Nazis sent 83,000 Jews, including small children, to the extermination camps in the east. [80]

Under the first Czechoslovak Republic that existed from 1918 to 1938 (composed of Bohemia, Moravia, Czech Silesia, Slovakia and Subcarpathian Ruthenia) the Small Fortress remained a military prison and a penitentiary for dangerous criminals. When the Nazis occupied Bohemia and Moravia on March 15, 1939, they arrested their opponents and jailed them in the Small Fortress. It took on the character of a transit prison whose inmates either died or were sent to German death camps [80].

During the war years the Nazis tortured thousands to death in the Small Fortress: members of the resistance movement, playwrights, composers, outstanding scientists, physicians, and politicians. Included in the prison after 1941 were Jews from the Great Fortress whom the SS wished to punish. After the number of inmates increased, the Small Fortress assumed the more formal features of a concentration camp. From June 1940 to May 1945, 35,000 prisoners passed through. Twenty-five hundred died in the bunkers [80]. In 1945 about 5,500 prisoners resided there.

By May 8, 1945, approximately 155,000 men, women and children had passed through Terezín. Some 35,000 of them died in the ghetto, another 83,000 perished after deportation to killing centers, ghettos, and labor camps in the east [80,85]. The SS commandants mistreated inmates both indirectly, through a system of orders and prohibitions, and directly, in the bunkers where inmates were interrogated and tortured.

As in other European ghettos, the Nazis required the Jews to select a Jewish Council, which nominally governed the ghetto. In Theresienstadt, this was known as the "Cultural Council"; later it was called the "Jewish self-government of Theresienstadt." The SS transmitted orders to the ghetto's inhabitants through the Council.

The community in Theresienstadt tried to ensure that all the children who passed through the camp continued with their education. The Nazis required all camp children over a certain age to work but accepted working on stage as employment. The prisoners achieved the children's education under the guise of work or cultural activity. Daily classes and sports activities were held. The community also published a magazine.

Many educated Jews were inmates of Theresienstadt including noted poets, composers, conductors and musicians, artists, architects, and members of almost every profession. The ghettos' diverse cultural activities included dramatic performances, lectures, and concerts, the adult chorus, drawing, story- and poem-writing classes for the children; they were the result of the active participation of these professionals, who shared their expertise with the inmates. In a propaganda effort designed to fool the western Allies, the Nazis publicized the camp for its rich cultural life.

The Germans promoted Theresienstadt as a spa for aged and privileged Jews. In fact, it was known in Germany as "Theresienbad." People over 65 years of age, and famous or privileged people, especially with foreign ties, were deported to this camp. This policy's ultimate purpose was to deflect international criticism of Nazi anti-Jewish policy. Because of its aura of safety and privilege, many Jews purchased the right to go there.

Within one year, 1942, almost 90,000 Jews were sent to Theresienstadt to occupy the normal living space of 7,000. By September 1942 the daily deaths averaged 131. In September 1942, 3,941 persons died.

A crematorium outside the town was completed in September 1942, capable of handling 190 corpses a day.

From January 1942 to October 1944, more than 87,000 persons were sent in 63 transports either to other ghettos or to the death camps; only 3,800 of them survived.

Succumbing to pressure from the Danish Red Cross and the International Red Cross (ICRC) to visit the camp following the deportation of Danish Jews to Theresienstadt, the German authorities sought to exploit the Terezín ghetto for propaganda, launching a "beautification" campaign which paid particular attention to the cosmetic improvement of houses and green space. Such measures included the planting of flowerbeds, the building of a musical pavilion for concerts on the square and erecting a children's pavilion and nearby playground. A former gym was turned into a "community center" with halls for cultural programs, a prayer room, a library, and a restaurant.

The Germans intensified deportations from the ghetto shortly before they permitted representatives from the Danish Red Cross and the International Red Cross (ICRC) to visit. The Nazis staged social and cultural events for the visiting dignitaries, who were taken on a tour following a predetermined path designated by a red line on a map. The representatives apparently did not attempt to divert from the tour route on which they were led by the Germans, who posed questions to the Jewish residents along the way. If the representatives asked residents questions directly, they were ignored, in accordance with the Germans' instructions to the residents prior to the tour. Despite this, the Red Cross apparently formed a positive impression of the town. It was all an elaborate hoax. Once the visit was over, the Germans resumed deportations from Theresienstadt, which did not end until October 1944.

In yet another propaganda tactic, the SS produced a film about Terezín in August and September 1944. It used as a backdrop the freshly renovated town, thereby creating the false impression of contentment within the "Jewish settlement area." [78]

Beginning in December 1944, new groups started to arrive at Terezín. Four transports holding 1,400 Slovakian Jews, including Klári and Shlomo, were sent from the forced labor camp at Sered.

Between 1942 and 1945, 15,000 children passed through Terezín. 100 survived. [77] Shlomo was one of them.

In April and May 1945, there was an influx of 15,000 prisoners brought from other camps by train and by foot. The population of the ghetto nearly doubled. The new arrivals were terribly emaciated. Many were dying, and dead bodies lay on the trains. The arriving transports were rife with contagious diseases, particularly louse-borne epidemic typhus. Typhus exacted a terrible death toll among ghetto inhabitants before and after liberation. Klári and Shlomo were quite fortunate to have escaped alive from this terrible curse and ordeal.

The fight against epidemics continued unabated in the days and weeks that followed. A group of doctors and nurses, named Czech Action for Help, arrived at the camp on May 4, 1945. Soon afterwards, the Red Army medical service furnished invaluable assistance. But the burden of combating epidemics still fell to Jewish medical personnel. More than 1,500 inmates died from disease during the last days of war and immediately thereafter. The death toll included 43 victims among the Jewish medical staff, four medics from Czech Action for Help, and some Soviet medical personnel.

After again visiting the camp on April 6 and April 21, 1945, the International Red Cross took over its administration on May 2, 1945.

Most of the SS fled on May 4, followed shortly thereafter by Terezín's commander and the rest of the SS on May 5 and 6. Scattered German military and SS units continued to fight Soviet forces in the vicinity of the camp-ghetto, which became part of the battlefront on May 8. The first Red Army units advancing to Prague passed through Terezín only in the late afternoon of May 8, 1945. Soviet troops entered the camp on May 9 and assumed responsibility for its prisoners the next day. They did not arrive soon enough to prevent a mass deportation effort. In eleven shipments to Auschwitz from September 28, 1944, to October 28, 1944—just one month—the SS transported 16,902 persons. Of that number, approximately 1,495 survived the war.

Just like at the Ravensbrück concentration camp, the Nazis at Terezín carried out their commandant's scheme to erase all traces of the German crime and remove the ashes of the dead. The group emptied 8,000 urns into a pit near Litomerice and 17,000 urns into the Ohre River. Twenty young prisoners were forced to dig up the remains of prisoners executed in 1942 and put them into coffins. Once the coffins were incinerated, the commandant killed the twenty prisoners [80].

Auschwitz-Birkenau

Auschwitz-Birkenau was a gigantic extermination center secluded on the edge of Oswiecim, a quiet, drab, small Galician town in Upper Silesia. It had 12,000 inhabitants about half of whom were

Jewish. The town was located 178 miles southwest of Warsaw, and 31 miles west of Cracow. It was one of the first Silesian towns in which Polish Jews settled during the middle ages. It was a spiritual center for Judaism.

The camp covered 15.4 square miles [80, 85], a vast complex of 39 camps divided into 3 main groups:

a) Auschwitz I, the main camp, lay outside Oswiecim's southeastern part. It included the central administration, the Gestapo, and various armament firms; it had 28 one- and two-story brick buildings including Block 11, which housed large holding cells, offices, and interrogation rooms, as well as a basement complex serving as a punishment block of torture rooms, darkened cells, and tiny standing cubicles, where prisoners would be crammed in and left to starve; it also had Crematorium I, which operated form August 15, 1940 until July 1943. 340 corpses could be burned every 24 hours after the installation of three other furnaces.

b) Auschwitz II, officially known as Birkenau, stood 1.86 miles from the main camp and was several times larger than Auschwitz I. It was dedicated to the killing of prisoners in the gas chambers; after the completion of its four crematoria with gas chambers, the burning of corpses in Crematorium I was halted; the crematoriums' ovens produced at night a thick black smoke and a high flame shooting out of the chimney. At times, the bodies of the people who had been murdered were also burned on pyres and in pits.

c) Auschwitz III, or Buna, was the labor camp for the construction of vast synthetic rubber and petrol works at Monowice.

Auschwitz opened for "business" on June 14, 1940 with the arrival of the first transport of 728 Polish political prisoners. The camp grew steadily. Prisoner transports with Jews from all over Europe arrived regularly. By the end of 1941 it could accommodate 18,000 prisoners, and by 1943, it held 30,000.

Gypsies, Soviet POWs, and Jews were considered the lowest-ranking inmates. They were the most frequent objects of SS and prisoner-functionary abuse and were routinely selected for systematic killing.

The Nazis began building Birkenau in 1941 and the largest of Hitler's camps was ready by October of that year. At its peak in 1943, Birkenau housed approximately 100,000 inmates. Planned to eventually hold a population of 250,000, in an area of almost one square miles, it required about an hour- and-a-half to walk around it. The Nazis continuously expanded Birkenau; by the end of the war they had completed Birkenau Section I, Birkenau Section II, and part of Birkenau III.

Birkenau I was the oldest, built in 1941, and it housed 20,000 inmates. It contained two camps: Birkenau I.a. and Birkenau I.b. After summer 1942, Birkenau I.a. became the camp for women.

Birkenau II was a men's camp for 60,000 prisoners. It also contained the hospital, experimental stations, and facilities for quarantine, Czech Jewish families, women criminals, and Gypsies.

Construction of Birkenau III intended for 60,000 prisoners started in 1944 but was never completed.

In practice, all inmates at Auschwitz had to work. Thousands of men and women perished during slave labor from hunger, dehydration, exposure, disease, and exhaustion. Others were beaten to death by Kapos, killed or maimed in accidents and bombing raids, or shot by SS guards for sport of for minor infractions, or while trying to escape. Still others were torn to pieces by SS guard dogs or, at the end of their strength, pulled from ranks by SS doctors and sent to the Auschwitz main camp or to Birkenau to be killed by toxic injection or gas.

In the Summer of 1941, under orders by Hitler to solve the Jewish question permanently, Himmler ordered Höss, the first Auschwitz commandant, to carry out the plans for the Final Solution. Eichmann visited Auschwitz and together with Höss discussed how to destroy millions of people and decided on gas [80,85]. On the Birkenau ramp the SS doctors, including Dr. Mengele ("the Angel of Death") and officers separated from the mass of arrivals those persons capable of working: young people, middle-aged men, and healthy women. They exempted them from extermination and sent them to the camp. Those deportees considered unfit for work were sent immediately to death in the gas chambers. [80,85].

Birkenau killed its inmates by starvation, inadequate diet, disease, injections of phenolic acid, beatings, torture, and execution. The inmates met death in unspeakably primitive, unsanitary conditions as medical guinea pigs, and as victims of sadists. They died of overwork, degradation, sadness, and despair. The SS gassed the majority of them. In fact, gassing in Auschwitz claimed more than 90% of the Jewish victims who perished there.

Usually, the Nazis did not allow children to be born at Birkenau. Pregnant Jewish women went to the gas chambers; any children were killed. The Soviets found only 156 children when they evacuated Birkenau in January 1945. Historians estimate the number of murdered young people below the age of eighteen at one million [80].

During the last phase of the war, Himmler asked that the selection and gassing of the Jews cease on November 2, 1944. On November 25 he ordered the gas chambers and crematoria destroyed to eliminate all evidence of the mass murders. The last transport arrived in Auschwitz on January 5, 1945. On January 18 the Nazis sent 58,000 freezing and starving inmates off on their death march. The Germans burned down twenty-nine of the thirty-five storerooms before they left. The survivors of the death march were dumped into other German camps. At least 80,000 inmates died in those camps in the last two months of the war. On January 27, the Soviet troops entered Auschwitz and saved the 5,000 sick prisoners left behind by the retreating Nazis [80,85].

We will never know exactly how many died in the complex. Accurate records were not kept and documents were destroyed. Historians estimate that between one and five million died at Auschwitz. Over 90% of the victims were European Jews. The official Auschwitz Museum figure is four million [80]. In connection with the operation intended to remove the evidence of their crimes, the SS blew up the building on January 26, 1945.

Ravensbrück

The Ravensbrück concentration camp during World War II was the only major camp in the Nazi system designed for women. It was located in northern Germany, across the Schwedt Lake from the town of Fürstenberg, about 55 miles north from Berlin. 30 miles away was the town of Oranienburg where the Sachsenhausen concentration camp was already in operation.

Construction of the Ravensbrück camp began in November 1938 when five hundred male prisoners from the Sachsenhausen camp and an advanced crew of women from the Lichtenburg concentration camp were brought by the Nazis to begin construction. They built 14 barracks, a kitchen, an infirmary, and a small camp for men which was totally isolated from the women's camp. The whole camp was surrounded by a high wall with electrified barbed wires on the top [78,85].

On May 18, 1939 the first transport, containing 867 female prisoners, was brought from Lichtenburg and the camp officially began its operations. A prisoner strength report of June 24, 1939 showed 127 Jews out of a total camp population of 1,048.

By the end of 1939 the camp housed 2,290 prisoners [80] and by the end of 1942, the female inmate population of Ravensbrück had grown to about 15,000. Another 70,000 prisoners were brought to Ravensbrück in 1944, most of whom were transferred to the 70 satellite sub-camps, although the main camp housed 26,700 female prisoners in that year. In November 1944 the total population of the camp was 80,000 representing 21 nationalities.

It is estimated that the ethnic structure of Ravensbrück inmates was the following: Poles 24.9%, Germans 19.9%, Jews 15.1% [82], Russians 15.0%, French 7.3%, Gypsies 5.4%, other 12.4%. Gestapo categorized the inmates as follows: political 83.54%, anti-social 12.35%, criminal 2.02%, Jehovah Witnesses 1.11%, racial defilement 0.78%, other 0.20%. The list is one of the most important documents that was preserved in the last moments of the camp's operation by courageous members of the Polish underground girl guides unitknown as "Mury" (The Walls).

One of the 70 satellite sub-camps, used for slave labor, was KZ Barth where Teri wound up after her ordeal at Auschwitz. These sub-camps, many of which were established adjacent to armaments factories, were located throughout the so-called Greater German Reich, from Austria in the south to the Baltic Sea in the north. Products that were manufactured by women in these sub-camps included aircraft components, weapons, munitions, and explosives.

Several sub-camps also provided prisoner labor for construction projects or clearing rubble in cities damaged by Allied air attacks. The SS also built several factories near Ravensbrück for the production of textiles and electrical components.

Ravensbrück was one of the Nazis' main depositories for confiscated clothing and furs. It had an SS-owned factory for remodeling leather and textiles. There was also a tailor shop that made the prisoners' striped uniforms and uniforms for the SS, and fur coats for the

Waffen-SS and the Wehrmacht. In another shop, the prisoners wove carpets from reeds. Women also did outside work, such as construction of buildings and roads. They were used like animals, with twelve to fourteen of them pulling a huge roller to pave the streets.

Some of the women worked in camp administration and some worked outside the camp, for example, in the nearby town of Fürstenberg. Those too old or disabled to perform other duties knitted for the army or cleaned the barracks and latrines. The women usually worked for twelve hours a day, under conditions of extreme exploitation.

The major private firm that used slave labor at Ravensbrück was the Siemens Electric Company. In a separate camp adjoining the main one, Siemens "employed" the women to make electrical components for V-1 and V-2 rockets. In addition to the Siemens Electric Company, other prestigious and well-known companies that employed slave labor in Ravensbrück's sub-camps included AEG and Daimler-Benz. (More than 55 years after the end of the war, Siemens and other companies finally began to agree to accept responsibility and pay some compensation to their former slave laborers from Ravensbrück.)

Beginning in May 1942, a section of Ravensbrück known as Jugendlager (camp for young persons) was established about one mile walking distance from the main camp [82], a kind of reform school for wayward girls, most of whom were teenagers who were considered criminal or just difficult. Those who reached the upper age limit were transferred to the Ravensbrück women's camp. In theory, they were sent to Jugendlager for re-education and rehabilitation. In practice, there was little emphasis on rehabilitation. The conditions were spartan, the discipline was draconic (any kind of chatting was forbidden, even in the evenings). The main purpose of the Jugendlager was to isolate them from decent society. A few were released to the custody of their parents, but of some 1,200 girls in the camp, only 80 (6%) were released. In the autumn of 1944, Himmler ordered the camp commander, Suhren, to kill 2,000 prisoners per month at Ravensbrück.

In January 1945, the camp administration began to make preparations for on-site mass killings. For this purpose, the juveniles' camp was closed and the infrastructure was subsequently used as an extermination camp. Women prisoners from the main camp were "selected" if considered ill, elderly, or unable to work, and were transferred to the Jugendlager which quickly developed into a "death zone" because conditions there were even worse than in the main camp. The inmates were housed in barracks without beds, latrines, or water. They were set on half rations, without coats, blankets, or medical attention. Roll calls lasted longer than at the main camp. They were subsequently placed on transports to eastern concentration camps or sent to the gas chamber or the crematorium. Up to mid-April 1945, over 8,000 women, including Elsa, were transferred to the Jugendlager camp [82].

There were children in the camp as well. Of the nearly 900 children registered at Ravensbrück from 1939 to April 1945, perhaps 2-3% survived the experience. The rest all perished, most of them dying or being killed in the last months of the war. With a few exceptions all of these children died of starvation [80].

The SS at Ravensbrück systematically destroyed potentially incriminating documents and virtually the entire holdings of official records in the closing stages of the war. As the Soviet Army approached the camp in the spring of 1945 the rest of the camp documents were burned by escaping SS hierarchy, guards and SS overseers in pits or in the crematorium. This is most likely the reason why I could get no information about Elsa Pikler from the ITS (International Tracing Service).

One of the most significant components of the processing of new prisoners was their placement into one of several distinct categories: prisoners were required to wear a color-coded triangle (a "Winkel") with a letter sewn within the triangle indicating their nationality: red for political prisoners (resistance fighters, those who helped Jews, members of the Soviet Army, Communists); Jewish women wore yellow triangles, but sometimes, unlike the other prisoners, they wore a second triangle for the other categories (yellow and red, arranged as a Star of David for political Jews or yellow and black if guilty of "racial offenses"); common criminals wore green triangles. Members of the Jehovah's Witnesses were labeled with lavender triangles. Classified separately with black triangles were "asocials": prostitutes, Gypsies, lesbians, or women who refused to marry. Homosexuals wore pink triangles. The prisoners were also assigned a number (order of arrival) that went directly above the badge and both were sewn on the upper left sleeve of a striped jacket [82, 83, 84]. At Ravensbrück, prisoners were never tattooed.

Some transports had their hair shaved, such as from Czechoslovakia and Poland, but "Aryan" transports did not. For instance, in 1943 a group of Norwegian women came to the camp. Norwegians/ Scandinavians were ranked by the Nazis as the purest of all Aryans. None had their hair shaved.

Ravensbrück was essentially run through the efforts of two overlapping hierarchies, a prisoner hierarchy and an SS hierarchy. To a surprising extent, the actual day-to-day running of the camp was in the hands of the prisoners themselves, and some of the prisoner officials wielded considerable influence. The ultimate authority and real decision-making power was, however, in the hands of the SS [84,85].

The office of Camp Doctor was headed by the Garrison Doctor (*Standortartzt*) who supervised the functioning of the infirmary and its staff. Beginning in 1942, he also played a major role in the medical experiments performed on Ravensbrück prisoners and directed the "selections," determining which prisoners were "work-capable" and which were not. A few of the doctors and many of the nurses were inmates. They were part of an elite group within the camp and were *de facto* under the authority of the camp doctor rather than the overseers.

Without exception, the overseers at Ravensbrück were women. They were called *Aufseherinnen* (female overseers). Prisoners were instructed to address them as *Frau Aufseherin* ("Madame Overseer"). There were about 150 of them by 1944, not counting trainees. Each block or barracks was headed by an overseer called a Block Leader (*Blockleiter*), and the prisoners had their closest contact with her, for the supervised roll calls, meals, and other activities taking place in and around the barracks. But by far the greatest number of overseers were employed to supervise the work crews. Several dozen Block Overseers (*Blockfuehrerin*), accompanied by dogs, SS men and whips oversaw the prisoners in their living quarters in Ravensbrück, at roll call, and during food distribution. These women were usually described as inhumane and sadistic.

The only workplace that seems to have been relatively free of supervision by overseers was the infirmary; prisoner doctors and nurses were directed more by SS doctors than overseers. Infirmary workers were automatically classified as prisoner officials, they wore yellow armbands, giving them unrestricted movement anywhere inside the camp. Most lived in Block 3, one of the elite, less crowded blocks, and because of the nature of their work, they never had to stand roll call.[83]

By far, the most dreaded experience for the prisoners were the daily roll calls as described by Leika in her Survivors of the Shoah interview and in Morrison's "*Ravensbrück: Everyday Life in a Women's Concentration Camp 1939-45*" [84]: every morning, long before dawn, there were two roll calls in quick succession: the first and longest at 4:00 a.m. when the first sirens sounded, unleashing a torrent of activity in the barracks and on the camp streets lasting several hours. Inmates had to get up, some went to the washroom and got in line; others made their beds in the military precise manner required. Others had to go to the kitchen for that day's bread ration and a "dark liquid resembling coffee." These would be distributed, but most inmates saved their bread for later. The second siren sounded at about 5:00AM. Now the block seniors marshaled their troops out into the roll call grounds. The prisoners lined up in rows of ten in front of their respective blocks, each prisoner knew her place in the formation, and the block seniors would count and recount them interminably since the total for all blocks had to correspond to the official aggregate list for the camp. If there was a discrepancy of even one number, all inmates had to remain in place until an explanation was found. Even for the dying there was no question of being excused from that roll call. It was usually at least an hour before all numbers checked out and the overseers appeared. The block senior, standing on the right flank of her block, would call the block to attention when the overseer approached, then would make her report. Occasionally the overseer would walk between the rows, and if she noticed any breach of regulations, she would stop to discipline the offender, even striking her. Roll calls generally went more quickly in the morning than at night in order to get the prisoner laborers off to their workplaces. Once all prisoners had been accounted for, another siren sounded, indicating dismissal.

The morning roll call could last anywhere from about twenty minutes to several hours. If it went smoothly there might be time for the women to go back to the barracks before they would have to report to their work crews. Those who had no regular work assignments, but were classified as "Availables," could be made to take the place of an absent worker in a regular crew. But, for the most part, they were used in outside work, heavy menial labor that took no skills or training. The Availables not chosen for work in the morning could return to the barracks. They were expected to clean the washrooms and the sleeping areas, and they joined other, mostly older women, in a kind of knitting detail.

At noon, the women who worked inside the camp returned to their blocks for lunch. The Availables brought the heavy soup kettles from the kitchens to the separate blocks. Lunch time progressively became shorter, about thirty to forty minutes by 1941. Then it was back to work for the remainder of the day. The workday also gradually was expanded from the original eight hours, and by 1942, it was eleven hours for many prisoners. There was no time for a free hour when the day shift ended at 7:00 p.m. and "lights out" occurred at 9:00 p.m. As soon as the prisoners returned to their barracks, they sat down for their evening meal. Eventually the siren would sound and the women would have to assemble for the evening roll call. Talking was forbidden. Punishment would be instituted if the rules were bent. Roll call sometimes lasted hours, while overseers and block seniors checked and rechecked their head counts. It was painful for all the inmates, but for the old and the sick, it could be life threatening. It was against regulations to support anyone or help her up, so if an inmate fell over, she had to be left on the ground until roll call was over. In winter months, merely standing for hours was an agony in the cold, and scores of women suffered from frostbite. The doctors were unable to keep pace with the innumerable amputation cases, and many women died of gangrene [83]. At 9:00 p.m. the lights were turned out and prisoners were in bed. If they were lucky, they could sleep until 4:00 a.m. But their sleep was sometimes interrupted by the night watch, whose responsibility it was to see that prisoners did not wear unauthorized clothing, such as stockings or trousers, to bed. In cold weather, most prisoners took the risk and wore all their clothes to bed, then slept lightly to detect a visit by the overseers. Even worse, there were occasional "special roll calls" in the middle of the night, carried out purely for harassment purposes [82,84].

The conditions of life in Ravensbrück were as shameful and difficult as in all other concentration camps: death by starvation, beating, torture, gassing, hanging, and shooting, as well as illness [84]. Lice infestation as described by Leika was rampant, and many prisoners died when the overcrowding, aggravated by abominable sanitary conditions, resulted in a typhus epidemic that spread throughout the camp [78]. Punishments were handed out, often indiscriminately, and frequently for the most minor of "offenses" like "unsatisfactory bed-building," failing to pass an inspection more than once, talking during roll-call, etc. The prisoner was then liable to get a "report." A 'report' was the constant threat which hovered over each prisoner's head. It was invariably followed by punishment: the first stage was "punishment standing without food," which entailed up to eight days' loss of either morning or evening meal, and standing at attention for hours on the camp square facing the Bunker; the second was "solitary confinement at the Bunker in a dark cell," and the third, most terrible of all, was "25 stick lashes" but sometimes 50 or up to 75, and in the two latter cases, generally meted out in two or three installments, but not always [83].

The "Bunker," a building of cellblocks completed in 1939, served as the camp prison, where solitary confinement in dark and airless cells became the usual punishment for acts of sabotage or resistance [84] often accompanied by severe beatings or other torture methods including attacks by SS dogs [83]. In addition to the "Bunker," there was a barrack separated from the camp by a fence, which served as a punishment block where inmates were whipped beginning in April 1942. A prisoner categorized as a criminal carried out the orders and received extra rations. The camp doctor was required to be present at each punishment, to confirm it had been carried out [84].

Starting in the summer of 1942, medical experiments were conducted without consent on 86 women; 74 of them were Polish inmates. There were two types of the experiments done on the Polish political prisoners. The first type tested the efficacy of sulfonamide drugs. These experiments involved deliberate cutting into and infecting leg bones and muscles with virulent bacteria, cutting nerves, introducing substances like pieces of wood or glass into tissues, and fracturing bones. The second set of experiments studied bone, muscle and nerve regeneration, and the possibility of transplanting bones from one person to another. Out of the 74 Polish victims, called "Rabbits" by the experimenters, five died as a result of the experiments, six with unhealed wounds were executed and the rest survived, with permanent physical damage, due to the help of other inmates in the camp. [80] Four of them testified against Nazi doctors at the Doctors' Trial in 1946.

"The forced sterilization of Gypsy girls must rank as one of the most insidious of Nazi programs. These women were offered their freedom if they would "volunteer" to be sterilized. None of them were ever released, as promised. Between 120 and 140 Gypsy women were sterilized, almost all in January 1945. The procedure was done in one of several ways: by spraying a chemical solution into the uterus, by using a high-powered X-ray machine, or by the use of a "high tension apparatus" in which one electrode was placed inside the vagina and the other over the abdominal wall by the ovaries. It was experimental medicine, to say the least. Several of the women sterilized with the X-ray technique got very ill, and some died." [83]

Until 1942-1943, Jews had their own block, always presided by a non-Jewish block overseer. It was one of the first blocks to experience significant overcrowding. As the number of Jewish women in the camp rose to over 400 in 1941, and over 600 in 1942, the inhabitants of one Jewish block had to make room for the newcomers, however uncomfortably. In those years, Jews were mostly assigned hard physical labor. The road-building crew, which pushed the monster concrete rollers, was almost exclusively Jewish, as was the crew that loaded stones and gravel for construction.

The camp conditions became clearly worse for Jewish women late in the summer of 1944. Work-capable Jews from camps and ghettos in the east were dispatched to camps in the west, in advance of approaching Soviet armies. In August 1944, as the inmate population began to get out of hand, the authorities procured a huge tent and erected it in an open area between Blocks 24 and 26, calling it Block 25. There were no toilets; inmates had to use latrines dug just outside the tent. Because it was to be temporary, it had no electricity nor plumbing at first, the only heat generated by the multitude of bodies huddled closely together.

Women assigned to the tent did not work. They were not permitted to leave the tent except for morning and evening roll calls. Conditions at the tent were appalling, particularly once cold weather set in. Prisoners who were sick and weak had almost no chance of survival. In the Fall of 1944, a large transport of two to three thousand mostly Hungarian Jewish women evacuated from Auschwitz were dumped into the tent. Many did not have blankets, let alone warm clothes. The women lay in their own dirt in the freezing cold. If they did not starve, they would freeze. Almost the whole transport of inmates died. [84,85]

When Elsa and Leika arrived in Ravensbrück in December 1944, the camp had taken on the character of a human distribution center as thousands of newcomers were brought into a camp already overcrowded beyond belief. Luckily they were assigned to block 23 and not dumped in the tent. Later they were assigned to block 12 (built for a maximum of 250 women but housing as many as 2,000 by then). Inmates shared bunks, up to three to four to a bunk. Thousands of women did not even have part of a bunk but lay on the floor without even a blanket. [84]

Most of those who were sent to a regular block at this time were not given work assignments. This was because there were simply not enough jobs for all the new arrivals, but it did cause animosity between them and the other prisoners who had to work every day. Leika, as we learned, volunteered for survival purposes to push the "corpse-cart" three days after her internment.

In the summer of 1943, Himmler issued a directive to create brothels in concentration camps. Eighteen to twenty women "volunteers" branded "asocials" by the Nazis were recruited at Ravensbrück and taken to ten other camps with the promise to set them free after six months. None were ever released. [84] Historians used testimonies by former Ravensbrück prisoners, excerpts from Nazi SS files, and accounts by camp guards to put this information together.

Under Fritz Suhren's leadership, a new commandant assigned in 1942, the operating principle of extermination through work was: feed the women as little as possible, work them as much as possible, and when they can no longer work, push them aside and let them die. Every two to three weeks, he and the SS doctors subjected prisoners in the camp to "selections": women had to lift their skirts over their hips and run in front of the SS guards and doctors. Those with swollen feet, injuries, or scars, or those simply too ill or too weak to run were immediately selected for a "recovery" period in the Jugendlager (before 1942, "selected" prisoners were shot). They were handed a red card and placed on a list for the "transport to Mittweida." That is how Elsa was separated from Leika in early February 1945 (according to her 1945 testimony, Elsa was able and eager to continue working). This "recovery" period consisted in fact of being jailed in sealed barracks without medical care and food until death. But most of the selected women were only briefly at the Jugendlager before being sent to the Auschwitz-Birkenau extermination camp or gassed in special vans transformed to mobile gas chambers, and, during the camp's last months, in the camp gas chamber. [84,85] "Mittweida" was an imaginary place, just a synonym for "gas chamber." The SS staff also murdered some prisoners in the camp infirmary by lethal injections. Milena Jesenská, a Czech political journalist assigned to the infirmary, saved the lives of countless of women from these injections (Evipan to the heart).[83] She also deliberately falsified "medical reports" and so doing prevented inmates from being used for medical experiments or taken by the "sick transports," starting in early 1942, to be gassed. [83]

Women who were sentenced to death for acts such as espionage or sabotage were shot, at times, in a special corridor between buildings, and other women were killed by lethal injections. [80]

In the last half of 1944, the number of transports bringing in prisoners was simply phenomenal. Transport lists that somehow survived in Polish archives give evidence that in November 1944 more than fifty transports arrived at Ravensbrück, adding over 7,000 new inmates in that month alone.

During the final Winter of 1944-1945 and in the absence of solid data, which the SS destroyed, only estimates are possible about the numbers of prisoners. One document that did survive, a letter to the SS-Business Administration Main Office (WVHA) of January 15, 1945, reported the presence of 46,070 female prisoners and 7,848 male prisoners in Ravensbrück and its subcamps. [78]

Until 1943, the town crematorium in Fürstenberg was easily able to handle all the bodies brought to them from the camp. When the deaths began to mount in that year, the SS authorities built a crematorium with two ovens at a site near the camp prison. In the autumn of 1944, a gas chamber was built near the crematorium at Ravensbrück. In 1944, a second oven was built at Fürstenberg.

By early 1944, these ovens were operating full time, burning two or three bodies at once. In that year, too, the SS ordered the town crematorium to burn five or six bodies at the time. By the end of 1944, the ovens could not keep up with the arrival of corpses, and many of the bodies were buried in mass graves on the far side of the camp. A daily scene throughout the camp: a two-wheeled "corpse cart" loaded down with several layers of corpses, was pushed and pulled by two prisoners, rattled out of the camp gate since the entrance to the crematorium ovens were outside the camp. A haze of the ashes created by the burning of flesh hung over the camp. When the number of women dying increased, the corpse crew to which Leika was assigned, was expanded, and went through the camp twice each day picking up bodies (an average of 70-80 bodies a day). There were times when numbers of corpses would be stacked outside, next to the door. It was a ghastly sight. Many were nothing but skin and bones.

The existence and operation of a gas chamber at Ravenbrück are not in doubt. It was used until nearly the end of the war. It was closed down in early April 1945 and destroyed by the SS who wanted to remove the evidence that might be used against them. It is estimated that approximately 4,500 to 6,000 women were gassed at Ravensbrück.

In the closing days of April 1945, as the Russian Army was moving close to the camp, Himmler gave the order to the SS to exterminate as many prisoners as they could, in order to avoid leaving anyone to testify as to what had happened in the camp. With the Russians only hours away, on April 24 and 26, the male prisoners were force-marched in several columns in a northwesterly direction. On April 27 and 28, the SS ordered the women still physically well enough to walk to leave the camp, forcing over 20,000 of them on a brutal death march toward northern Mecklenburg. Shortly before the evacuation, the Germans had handed over another 7,000 female prisoners, most of them from Scandinavia, the Benelux countries,

France, and Poland to officials of the Swedish and Danish Red Cross. [78]

We now know that there was a cover-up at the end: the camp files were burned as the Allies drew near. Later, Soviet tanks bulldozed the buildings. [85] The camp's history soon became divided, like Europe. East Germany had its own, selective version, stressing the heroism of the Communists among the inmates; the West, without ready access to the site and with evidence from war crimes trials on the camp classified as "secret," largely ignored it.

By the time the vanguard of the Russian army arrived at the camp on the afternoon of April 30, 1945, less than 3,500 malnourished, exhausted, and sickly women and 300 men remained in the camp. [85] These numbers increased on a daily basis, as some prisoners who had fled in the early part of the death march now filtered back into Ravensbrück. Advancing Soviet forces intersected the route of the death march survivors and liberated the prisoners. [85] On May 1, the regular units of the Red Army appeared and liberated the last of the Ravensbrück prisoners. [78] But this rescue was not by any means entirely benign: upon entering the camp, many drunken Russian soldiers raped the survivors.

Soviet officials took prompt action to prevent the further spread of disease and to slow the death rate. Squads of townspeople were dragooned into working at the camp, cleaning barracks and burying the bodies that had been stacking up for some days. The entire camp was organized into a hospital, its barracks again arranged by nationality. Medicines and food were quickly brought in. Within days, electrical power and running water were restored. In June the remaining sick prisoners were moved elsewhere, while others, like Leika, were interviewed by doctors at the camp before being released. Soon after all the prisoners had been evacuated, the former women's concentration camp was transformed into a Soviet military post until they left in 1993.

All in all, between 1939 and 1945, over 132,000 women and children passed through this camp system (of which some twenty percent were Jewish) [84], though only as many as 123,000 prisoners were noted in the camp register [82]; it is estimated that 92,000 of them died in the camp by starvation, disease, executions, or weakness. 40,000 survived.

Appendix

The "Do You Know" Scale (DYK) [4]

Developed by psychologists Marshall Duke and Robyn Fivush to determine how well children know their family history.

Please answer the following questions by circling "Y" for "yes" or "N" for "no." Even if you know the information we are asking about, you don't need to write it down. We just wish to know if you know the information.

1. Do you know how your parents met? Y N

2. Do you know where your mother grew up? Y N

3. Do you know where your father grew up? Y N

4. Do you know where some of your grandparents grew up? Y N

5. Do you know where some of your grandparents met? Y N

6. Do you know where your parents were married? Y N

7. Do you know what went on when you were being born? Y N

8. Do you know the source of your name? Y N

9. Do you know some things about what happened when your brothers or sisters were being born? Y N

10. Do you know which person in your family you look most like? Y N

11. Do you know which person in the family you act most like? Y N

12. Do you know some of the illnesses and injuries that your parents experienced when they were younger? Y N

13. Do you know some of the lessons that your parents learned from good or bad experiences? Y N

14. Do you know some things that happened to your mom or dad when they were in school? Y N

15. Do you know the national background of your family (such as English, German, Russian, etc)? Y N

16. Do you know some of the jobs that your parents had when they were young? Y N

17. Do you know some awards that your parents received when they were young? Y N

18. Do you know the names of the schools that your mom went to? Y N

19. Do you know the names of the schools that your dad went to? Y N

20. Do you know about a relative whose face "froze" in a grumpy position because he or she did not smile enough? Y N

Score: Total number answered Y.

Important Note: About that last question! Fifteen percent of our sample actually answered "Yes!" This is because the stories that families tell are not always "true." More often than not they are told in order to teach a lesson or help with a physical or emotional hurt.

As such, they may be modified as needed. The accuracy of the stories is not really critical. In fact, there are often disagreements among family members about what really happened! These disagreements then become part of the family narrative. Not to worry!

The authors stated that these are only a representative sample of the kinds of questions children should be able to answer. Families can make up others. The main criterion is that the questions should be about things the children could not have learned on their own or experienced directly. "Each family will have different stories and different key moments and memories that are shared." [4]

Julius Müller: Archival Research References

Primary sources:

National Archives in Prague

Familiant book Prachen region (Volyne) HBF 127

Familiant book Caslav region (Schtitens) HBF 44

Jewish Census Prachen region 1793 (Volyne)

Bzenec birth records 1784-1846, HBMa 189

Bzenec marriage records 1784-1846, HBMa 190

Bzenec death records 1784-1846, HBMa 191

Dolni Kounice, birth records 1799-1848, HBMa 316

Holesov incl. Bystrice pod Hostynem, birth records 1784-1841, HBMa 437

Jevicko birth records 1784-1846, HBMa 675

Kojetín birth records 1784-1844, HBMa 808

Kyjov birth records 1846-1874, HBM 965

Napajedla (under Uhersky Brod, HBMa 2252 and Kromeriz HBMa 907)

Rousinov birth records 1784-1815, HBMa 1810

Rousinov birth records 1814-1839, HBMa 1811

Slavkov birth records 1800-1848, HBMa 1867

Uhersky Brod birth records 1784-1822, HBMa 2252

Uhersky Brod death records 1784-1848, HBMa 2250

Usobi birth records 1814-1850, HBM 845

Brno regional archives

Bzenec estate records F 287

Bzenec register of Jewish house owners 1771-1829

Bzenec *Familiant* book Uhersky Brod estate files F 281

Uhersky Brod register of Jewish house owners 1731-1879

Uhersky Brod registers of synagogue seats' owners 1811-1873

Mikulov birth records 1762-1850; Archives of Prague's Jewish Museum

Rajec Census: 1781, 1788, 1795, 1811, 1837, 1847; Bytca District archives

Rajec vital records: 1778-1885

Rajec Census: 1827 and town records: 1476-1871; Žilina District archives

Trencin Census: 1771-1848; Trencin District archives

Secondary sources:

Augustin M. "A Brief History of Jews in Slovakia" *Judaica Slovaca*, 1993

Barkany E., Dojc L. *Jewish communities in Slovakia*. Vesna, Bratislava, 1991.

Büchler R. *Encyclopedia of Jewish Communities in Slovakia*, volumes 1-4, Museum of Jewish Culture, Bratislava, 2015.

Gold H. *Die Juden und Judengemeinden Mährens in Vergangenheit und Gegenwart,* Jüdische Buch-und Kunsteverlug, 1929.

Miller, Michael L. *Rabbis and Revolution: The Jews of Moravia in the Age of Emancipation*. Stanford: Stanford University Press, 2010.

Maygar Zsidó Oklevéltár/Monumenta Hungariae Judaica, *Magyar Izraeliták Országos,* 1903-1980 (last volume published in 1980).

www.ingramcontent.com/pod-product-compliance
Lightning Source LLC
Chambersburg PA
CBHW072006270326
41928CB00009B/1560